Technical Report 24

Prehistoric Settlement Patterns and Cultures in Susiana, Southwestern Iran

The Analysis of the F.G.L. Gremliza Survey Collection

by

Abbas Alizadeh

With a foreword by
Henry T. Wright

Ann Arbor
1992

Printed in the
United States of America

ISBN 0-915703-29-7

The paper used in this publication meets the requirements of the
ANSI Standard Z39.48-1984 (Permanence of Paper)

TABLE OF CONTENTS

LIST OF TABLES

LIST OF ILLUSTRATIONS

LIST OF PLATES

FOREWORD

by Henry T. Wright

The publication of this Technical Report continues the Museum of Anthropology's tradition of making available the detailed evidence of archaeological surveys relevant to the world's earliest civilizations. Archaeological survey provides us with evidence of broad region-wide changes in population, land use, and social organization. Evidence of ancient landscapes all over our planet is being rapidly destroyed by agro-industrial expension, and only comprehensive publication of site and artifact characteristics provide an enduring record for future reanalyses using different assumptions and methods.

The Susiana Plain is the largest and richest agricultural area of lowland Southwestern Iran, one of the key geographical elements in the mosaic of greater Mesopotamia. It lies near the limits of the rainfall needed for crops of wheat and barley, and was thus important in the development of both the earlier dry-farming villages and the later irrigation-based urban systems. It has been the object of systematic archaeological survey since the work of the Mission Archéologique Française between the two World Wars (LeBreton 1947; Adams 1972; Johnson 1973; Wenke 1976; Miroschedji 1981; Dollfus 1985; Hole 1985).

The particular survey reported here was undertaken by a remarkable researcher. All archaeologists who have studied the ancient peoples of southwestern Iran owe this scholar a number of debts. It is well kown that Dr. F.G.L. Gremliza made contributions to the epidemiology of endemic diseases which have affected the lives of people in southwest Asia for millennia (Gremliza 1962). The same publication presents evidence of settlement demography which helps us to estimate the populations of long-abandoned ancient settlements. However, until Dr. Abbas Alizadeh undertook this study of Gremliza's carefully documented archaeological collections, his contributions to archaeology wee unrecognized.

Alizadeh has presented Gremliza's survey data in the terms in which he collected it. There has been no effort to force Gremliza's site designations into other exiting survey designations. Alizadeh has also tried to render the spellings of site names in a standardized manner which closely approximates how they are pronounced locally. This should not inconvenience users of this study, since the spellings used by other scholars are indicated in the bibliography.

Another contribution of this study is to show the advantages of the system of designating prehistoric Susiana ceramic assemblages developed by the Chogha Mish project under Helene J. Kantor and P.P. Delougaz. This system of phase designations will be defined precisely when the first volume on the Chogha Mish excavations is made available as *Oriental Institute Publication 101*, but this technical report serves to illustrate its value pending that important forthcoming publication. It also amends the Chogha Mish phase system, adding a new unit termed "Late Susiana 1." For those who use other systems, the detailed illustration of all ceramic variants present in the collection give future readers the means for re-dating and reanalyzing these site collections in the future.

Alizadeh also provides an analysis of the developmental implication sof the Gremliza data. It is notable that his analysis broadly reinforces those based on other survey collections and using other phase criteria.

In the future, the Museum of Anthropology hopes to publish other monographs fo this type on southwest Asia. Almost completed is one on the surveys of James A. Neely of the Deh Luran Plain. We hope that detailed reports on other Susiana surveys will be prepared in the future.

REFERENCES

Dollfus, Geneviève

1985 Le peuplement de la Susiane au cours du Ve millénaire, in *Paléorient 11/2*:11-20.

Hole, Frank

1985 The organization of Susiana Society. Periodization of Site Distributions, in *Paléorient 11/2*: 21-24.

Miroschedji, Pierre de

1981 Prospections archéologiques au Khuzistan en 1977, in *Cahiers de la Délégation Archéologique Française in Iran 12*:169-192.

PREFACE

Dr. F. G. L. Gremliza is well known to the older generation of archaeologists who worked in southwestern Iran in the 1950s and the early 1960s. Others who did not have the opportunity to meet him personally may know him through his invaluable ethnomedical publications. But perhaps the best way to introduce Dr. Gremliza is to use David Lilenthal's description in his daily journal.

"Dr. F. G. L. Gremliza, our boyish-looking German doctor, grows on you. He and his wife had spent seven years in the saddest spot I know, the Susangerd area almost on the Iraq border. These abjectly poor Arabs (Arabic-speaking people) had been given no attention for--well, never. He ministered to them, they (Gremliza and his wife) adopted a little Arab (ic-speaking) girl, learned how confidence and respect and love are won, among desperately poor--or anyone.

"Then we brought him into the Khuzistan program. The American high-powered experts on public health didn't think much of him and his methods; too much emphasis on field work, not enough on research, I gather. But he turned out to be right. Bilharzia is not the major problem the experts asserted it might be. It is manageable and only one of the environmental difficulties of the people of the Gelbi area... He has personally visited every one of the more than fifty villages, and been in every house, usually for an overnight stay. As a doctor, and one they trust, Dr. Gremliza can ask questions no census taker could ask and get a genuine answer: How many shoes do you have? How many sugar [sic] do you use a day, a week? When you have a chicken or some eggs, do you eat them, and if not, where do you take them to sell?

"He has become, as he puts it, 'a doctor who is part of a team of nondoctors'; the way he functions is explained by his concept of the development of this pilot area: to understand the facts about how people live, and on what they live, so 'impressions can give way to facts'" (Lilenthal 1963:261).

In his studies, Gremliza described and explained regional disease patterns. Moreover, the wide range of information he collected in his work, such as village and population size, village settlement patterns, age and sex ratios, and living standards, is invaluable for the social scientist who wishes to study various socioeconomic and demographic trends in the region (see, for example, Gremliza 1953, 1959, 1960, 1962, 1965).

The survey material presented here was collected by Gremliza in the course of his medical work in Khuzestan. He was interested and educated in art, and the painted potsherds scattered over the ancient sites in Khuzestan immediately attracted his attention. He was also fascinated by, as he puts it, the "continuation of life" in Khuzestan, where many villages are either next to or in close proximity to ancient settlements. His medical practice in Khuzestan also brought him into close contact with French and, later, American archaeologists. This association familiarized him with basic ideas about recovering archaeological artifacts through excavations and surveys. Thus, as a member of the Khuzestan Development Service, he started surveying and collecting archaeological material as best as he could.

My acquaintance with Dr. Gremliza began in 1987. At that time, I was preparing for a trip to Berlin to study some archaeological materials, when Helene J. Kantor suggested that I stop over in Munich to meet him and to see his collection. Dr. Gremliza was then exploring the possibilities of publishing his survey material. After some correspondence, we arranged a visit to Munich for a short study. There, Dr. Gremliza introduced to me his collection which was, indeed, vast. It soon became apparent that a detailed analysis of the collection was impossible during my short stay in Munich. However, Dr. Gremliza was so eager to see a comprehensive presentation of his collection that he donated and shipped the collection to the Oriental Institute of The University of Chicago, thus enabling me to study the material in detail and to prepare this monograph.

ACKNOWLEDGMENTS

I would like to take the opportunity to express my gratitude to Professor Helene J. Kantor for her constant encouragement and for the time she devoted to going over the material with me in Chicago. I have always profited her invaluable insight.

The cost of preparing the illustrations was in part supported by a generous gift from Albert and Cissy Haas; I would like to express my gratitude to them. I would also like to thank the office of the Provost of The University of Chicago for granting me a travel fellowship to visit the survey collection in Munich.

To

Helene J. Kantor

1

INTRODUCTION

The millennium before the emergence of complex societies in the ancient Near East (ca. 3400 B.C.) is crucial to our understanding of the processes which led to the formation of the first states in that area. Though much of our knowledge about specific aspects of the early civilizations is based on the data from excavated sites, these data are not sufficient for understanding important regional and interregional transformations, such as population changes, societal conflicts, development of various regional polities, settlement hierarchies and their spatial relations, and systems of settlement integration.

Information gathered by archaeological surface surveys has been crucial in understanding such transformations. Scholars have used and incorporated survey data in reconstructing historical developments in Susiana, and in making propositions concerning profound theoretical issues such as the emergence of urban centers and the formation of early states (Hole 1987; Johnson 1987; Wright 1987). The analysis of various sets of archaeological data from Susiana has led to conclusions about demographic changes there and to building a theoretical framework within which the formation of complex societies and early states is understood.

Archaeological excavations and surveys in southwestern Iran entered a new age about three decades ago. Both foreign and domestic teams intensified archaeological activities and much was learned about historical developments in the region. The knowledge thus acquired also has helped scholars to reach the degree of sophistication required to discuss refined chronological subdivisions, so crucial to the reconstruction of successive stages of socioeconomic and political development in Susiana. Developments in the study of surface survey has taken us to a point where even slight chronological differences lead to propositions regarding socioeconomic and political life of ancient communities. A good example is the refined, albeit tenuous, subdivision of the Uruk period into Early, Middle, and Late, each representing a developmental stage in the formation of complex societies in southwestern Iran (Johnson 1973, 1987; Wright & Johnson 1975, 1985:25-29).

With few notable exceptions, most of the scholars who worked in southwestern Iran have not had the opportunity to publish or fully publish excavated and survey materials. The accumulation of the unpublished materials and data has resulted in a situation where no one scholar may effectively undertake a synthetic approach to various socioeconomic and political issues pertaining to ancient Susiana society without access to such materials. A great deal of cooperation is needed to put together all the pieces of the puzzle. A good example of the results of such an effort is the recent publication The Archaeology of Western Iran (Hole 1987), which deals with various methodological and theoretical issues concerning historical developments in western Iran. Emphasizing the urgency of publishing the results of the unpublished excavations and surface surveys, Hole states that "Restudy of this material [excavated and surveyed], as in the case of the Susiana burial ceramic...or Le Brun's (n.d.) contextual analysis at Susa may be more productive than conducting further excavations, particularly when these data are unusually important and cannot be duplicated" (Hole 1987:27).

From the start of the present project, it has been my hope that the publication of the Gremliza collection will contribute to the studies of Susiana prehistoric societies. The present study is intended to be a self-contained, detailed analysis of the early sherds which form the bulk of the Gremliza survey collection. The sources of the material and data presented here may have long been destroyed by agricultural activities and construction programs, as well as a decade of military operations in the region. (Sites G25 I and II, Sham'un, and G26, Deylameh Sofla, for example, have already been raised to the ground by road and canal construction.) Comprehensive treatment of the data and issues would require detailed publications of survey results as a point of departure. With subsequent cooperation of the authors, a framework could be provided which would make possible a deeper understanding of socioeconomic and political developments in Susiana.

Background of Archaeological Surveys in Khuzestan

In the late 1950s, the Iranian government embarked on a series of ambitious large-scale plans to develop the province of Khuzestan. In the spring of 1956, David E. Lilenthal, then the chairman of the Development and Resources Corporation, and his colleague, Gordon R. Clapp, were invited to visit Khuzestan, in order to assess the feasibility of redeveloping the region. The Corporation was engaged under contract with the Khuzestan Water and Power Authority of Iran to provide management and technical services in connection with the Khuzestan regional development program. The main objectives of this program included the building of dams, power lines, canals, the development of modern irrigation and farming practices, and the introduction of modern seeds and fertilizers. These projects ushered in the systematic collection by David Lilenthal's team of many kinds of data, most of which are crucial for a deeper historical understanding of climatic, environmental, demographic, and ultimately cultural development of southwestern Iran.

Few regions in the world have been so intensively and extensively investigated. The availability of information gathered by the Khuzestan Water and Power Authority, such as soil surveys, hydrographic reports, demographic surveys, and aerial photographs, presented a fertile ground for social, scientific, and environmental investigations. Moreover, the encouragement of the government, its eagerness and receptive policy, augmented by its hospitable attitudes, made Khuzestan the object of numerous archaeological surveys and excavations.

From 1960 to the late 1970s, major problem-oriented archaeological investigations were carried on in Khuzestan (for example, Adams 1962, Hole 1969, Wright et al. 1972; Johnson 1973; Wright and Johnson 1975). The pioneering work of Robert McC. Adams (1962) in Khuzestan was part of his systematic projects to understand historical developments in Iran and Mesopotamia. Adams was specifically interested in changes in the size of settled population and its spatial and temporal distribution, as well as in changes in subsistence technology and their long range impacts on the settlement patterns of the region. The detailed data from his Susiana survey remain unpublished, although they were used by Adams to propose models on the socioeconomic and cultural development of Susiana (Adams 1962).

Subsequent surveys focused on more specific problems. Hole was primarily interested in refining the prehistoric sequence and its settlement patterns. Henry Wright conducted three surveys in Susiana and its immediate environs. Wright's first survey was intended to expand that of Adams's to the east (Wright n.d.). His second survey was concentrated in the heartland of Susiana. Some of the results of this campaign were published by G. Johnson as part of his doctoral dissertation (Johnson 1973). Wright's survey in 1975-76 was conducted in northeastern Susiana to investigate patterns of seasonal migration of mobile pastoralists in marginal zones (Wright et al. 1979). E. Carter used her survey material to study Susiana societies in the second millennium B.C. in southwestern Iran (Carter 1971). Among all these surveys, the most extensively published is that of Wenke on the settlement patterns in Susiana during the Parthian and Sasanian periods. Wenke was primarily interested in empirically testing hypotheses derived from the works of J. Steward (1949), K. Wittfogel (1957), and R. McC. Adams (1966) concerning economic and political changes in ancient empires (Wenke 1976). The political upheaval of 1979 in Iran brought an abrupt end to many projects in progress, and prevented future research. The inability to continue field work has given some scholars the opportunity to publish the results of their archaeological investigations (for example, Wright 1981; Dollfus 1983a,b; Voigt 1983; Beale et al. 1986). These publications provide a solid framework for future research in Iran when it becomes possible.

Methods and Circumstances of the Gremliza Survey

In archaeological surveys, the circumstances and conditions of the investigation influence its scope and methodology. Much of Gremliza's research was conducted during his routine visits to villages in Khuzestan, between 1959 and 1966. Gremliza regularly visited villages with a mobile clinic, provided by the Iranian government. During these visits, he and his crew surveyed every ancient mound he sighted on his way to the target village.

Dr. Gremliza described to me his method of surveying as follows. When a mound was sighted, the convoy would stop and the crew would walk to the mound. Gremliza himself marked the location of the site on his mosaic maps. The crew climbed up the mound and, starting from the top, collected all the painted pottery evident on the way down. Gremliza marked the name of the mound on the sacks of potsherd collected. If the site was located near a village, the local children would also help collect the pottery. The pottery was then taken to Gremliza's home to be processed. His wife, the late Frau Maria Gremliza, who also participated in the survey on weekends, did the unpacking, washing, and marking of sherds in their home in Ahwaz.

Several important points should be made in connection with the limitations of the collection. Needless to say, the survey was not conducted according to the scientific methods and measures common today. Moreover, Gremliza was interested only in prehistoric painted potsherds and so tended to ignore the unpainted ones. Nevertheless, he did collect some objects such as spindle whorls, clay figurines, mace heads, and occasionally some plain wares of the Protoliterate and Middle Elamite periods. Except for the spindle whorls and some figurines which could be dated with some certainty on stylistic and typological grounds, the other objects are excluded from this monograph. The pottery of the Middle Elamite period is also excluded because it was not collected systematically and because its presentation here could not add much to our present knowledge of Middle Elamite archaeology and history. However, because of the importance of the Protoliterate period in the development of complex societies in southwestern Iran, its materials, though scanty, are included here for future reference. Finally, since the sites were not systematically measured, rather than rely on Gremliza's recollections, I have chosen to exclude such information. An idea of the relative size of some of the sites is given by the photographs on Plates 1-5.

The Recording of the Sites

The numbers and names of the sites are taken from a catalogue Gremliza prepared for his own reference. Thirty-five sites are listed with names and arabic numbers. In addition, ten sites are listed with only Roman numerals, raising the total number of sites to 45. In order to distinguish the sites surveyed by Gremliza from those reported by others, site numbers in the catalogue are preceded by "G" (i.e., Gremliza). Gremliza gave to some clusters of sites one arabic number and subdivided them by Roman numerals. To avoid confusion in an already complex literature of survey materials from Khuzestan, I have retained Gremliza's numbering system instead of introducing a single sequential list of numbers for his sites.

The Survey Maps

I have prepared the maps from a series of aerial mosaic photographs Gremliza put at my disposal. All the villages he recorded and all the sites represented by pottery are included (Fig. 2). Important sites such as Susa and Chogha Mish are also marked, but other known sites and features that could also be located on the aerial photographs are excluded in order to simplify the maps. Comprehensive maps of all the known Susiana sites with a common numbering system will have to wait until detailed reports of all the surveys are published. For future surveys and attempts to locate individual sites, a map locating villages and their proximity to the neighboring sites is also given (Fig. 3). The same villages are listed in Table 1. Although most of the sites are named after their nearest village, the numbers assigned to the villages are not necessarily the same as those assigned to the sites. A separate column in Table 1 helps to identify the site names and numbers that are different from those of the villages.

The Transliteration of Local Names

Save for Susa, all local names used in this monograph are transliterated according to their Persian and local phonetic. Moreover, the silent 'h', as in Boneh, is written unless such names are in genitive case. In this case, the 'h' is omitted and the genitive ending is indicated by 'ye' following a '-' (e.g., Qal'e-ye Sefid); the same rule is applied to names ending in a long vowel as in Pa-ye Kotal. In cases where names end with a consonant, the genitive ending is indicated by an 'e' following a '-' (e.g., Tall-e Bakun). This system, however, was not applied to the maps, because these maps were reproduced before I started writing the manuscript.

TABLE 1. LIST OF MODERN VILLAGES IN KHUZESTAN

Village Number	Village Name	Site Number	Village Number	Village Name	Site Number
1	Qaleh Qotb	—	49	Dehbar	—
2	Qaleh Allah	—	50	Boneh Sharafabad	—
3	Cham Golak	—	51	Anjirak	—
4	Boneh Ali	—	52	Sharafabad-e Mostofi	—
5	Chichali Shahrokni	—	53	Sharafabad-e Sofla	38
6	Chichali Sanjar	—	54	Qaleh No-ye Bishe Ney	—
7	Chichali Sagvand	—	55	Ali Koli	—
8	Chichali Hermushi	—	56	Qalvand	—
9	Anbarieh	—	57	Qaleh Aqa Hasan	—
10	Beyzeh	—	58	Abbasabad-e Ashrafi	—
11	Jari-ye Seyd Karim	—	59	Abbasabad-e Fakhraii	—
12	Boneh Seyd Musa	—	60	Jeibar	—
13	Qaleh Babu	—	61	Boneh Chiti	—
14	Qaleh Nasiabad	—	62	Qaleh No-e Askar	—
15	Hasanabad	—	63	Hajiabad	—
16	Hasanabad	—	64	Farrash	—
17	Radadeh	—	65	Qaleh Rob-e Jeibar	—
18	Davudabad	157	66	Qaleh Rob-e Kuyekh	—
19	Amaleh Seyf	145	67	Kuyekh	—
20	Kheirabad	—	68	Qaleh Abbas	—
21	Kharkub	—	69	Balenjan	—
22	Boneh Morad	—	70	Huseinieh Balenjan	—
23	Qaleh Shahrukhi	—	71	Boneh Tileh	—
24	Bonvar-e Nazer	—	72	Dacheh	—
25	Siheh	—	73	Boneh Latan	—
26	Sanjar	—	74	Davudabad	—
27	Qaleh Toq	—	75	Mirza Ali Khan	—
28	Jateh	—	76	Huseinabad (Hamidabad)	115
29	Ganjeh	—	77	Boneh Neis	—
30	De-ye Iji	—	78	Abbasieh	—
31	Mian Choghan	—	79	Boneh Seyd Mohammad	—
32	Dobandar	—	80	Boneh Seyd Reza	—
33	Bonvar-e Hosein	—	81	Boneh Hasan	—
34	Khanabad-e Qotb	—	82	Sovidieh	—
35	Qaleh No-e Moezzi	—	83	Amaleh Teymur	—
36	Khanabad-e Moezzi	—	84	Boneh Morad Hadi	—
37	Qaleh Shohan	—	85	Talebabad	161
38	Ali Bol Hosein	—	86	Khalaf Heydar	—
39	Aliabad	—	87	Boneh Muezza	—
40	Zavieh Moradi	—	88	Aliabad	—
41	Zavieh Hajian	—	89	Boneh Mahmud	—
42	Zavieh Hamudi	—	90	Boneh Lusi	—
43	Zavieh Mashali	—	91	Haft Tappeh	—
44	Zavieh Sultan	—	92	Sheikh Sakhi	—
45	Bandebal	—	93	Sheikh Moayyad	—
46	Qaleh Sheikh	—	94	Mehibes	—
47	Kermalak Tahmasbi	—	95	Boneh Hamzeh	—
48	Kermalak Aliabad	—	96	Zabeh	—

TABLE 1. LIST OF MODERN VILLAGES IN KHUZESTAN (*cont.*)

Village Number	*Village Name*	*Site Number*
97	Abul Bashir (Sheikh Darchal)	97
97a	Sheikh Hojjat	97a
98	Sheikh Hosein	—
99	Boneh Jawi	—
100	Sheikh Duwih	—
101	Sheikh Ahmad Molla	—
102	Sheikh Khashan	—
103	Kutiyan	—
104	Najafabad	—
105	Khosroabad	—
106	Boneh Rahimeh	33
107	Salarabad	—
108	Boneh Yaghub	—
109	Qalehabad-e Shah	—
110	Amirabad	—
111	Sardarabad	—
112	Qaleh No-ye Saradarabad	—
113	Deylameh Olia	—
114	Boneh Haji Ali Sharif	—
115	Sham'un	25
116	Deylameh Sofla	26
117	Boneh Seyd Taher	31
117a	Boneh Yunes	56
118	Boneh Benhan	—
119	Boneh 'Alvan	27
120	Boneh Khepel	—
121	Hosein Kalvali	—
122	Qaleh Rob-e Bandebal	—
123	Bonvar-e Shami	—
124	Siah Mansur	—
125	Ab Kenar	—
126	Qaleh No-ye Shamsabad	—
127	Ab Kuweit	—
128	Boneh Abdul Mohammad	—
129	Qaleh Seyyed	—
130	Shamsabad	—
131	Khalteh	50
132a	Shamsabad (east)	—
132b	Shamsabad (west)	—
133	Chogha Sorkh	—
134	Qaleh No-ye Sardar	—
135	Qaleh Qazi	—
136	Chogha Sabz	—
137	Kheirabad	—
138	Dolati	—
139	Boneh Fazili	—
140	Shalgahi Olia	—
141	Shalgahi Sofla	—
142	Qaleh Khalil	—
143	Bayation-e Raf'at	—
144	Bayation-e Arshad	—
145	Banut-e Moezzi	—
146	Banut-e 'Enayeh (Seydom)	—
147	Banut-e Morteza Khan	—
148	Seyfabad	64
149	Beladieh	62
150	Shahdera	—
151	Shangar-e Olia	61
152	Shangar-e Sofla	60
153	Boneh Mazban	—
154	Boneh Javaz	—
155	Farrashabad	—
156	Deilam	—
157	Chogha Cheshmeh	86
158	Boneh Seyd Nur	87
159	Boneh Hatam	—
160	Boneh Zobeidi	—
161	Boneh 'Obeid	—
162	Boneh Lazem	—
163	Boneh Ya'ghub	—
164	Deh No (Khalaf Halak)	93
165	Gomar	—
166	Jali'eh	—
167	Badili	79
168	Abdullah Shahin	—
169	Shahvali (Samandi)	81
170	Khoveyyes (Tahef)	176
171	'Alvan-e Karkheh	171
172	Chenaneh	172

Figure 1. Map of Iran, showing the survey area.

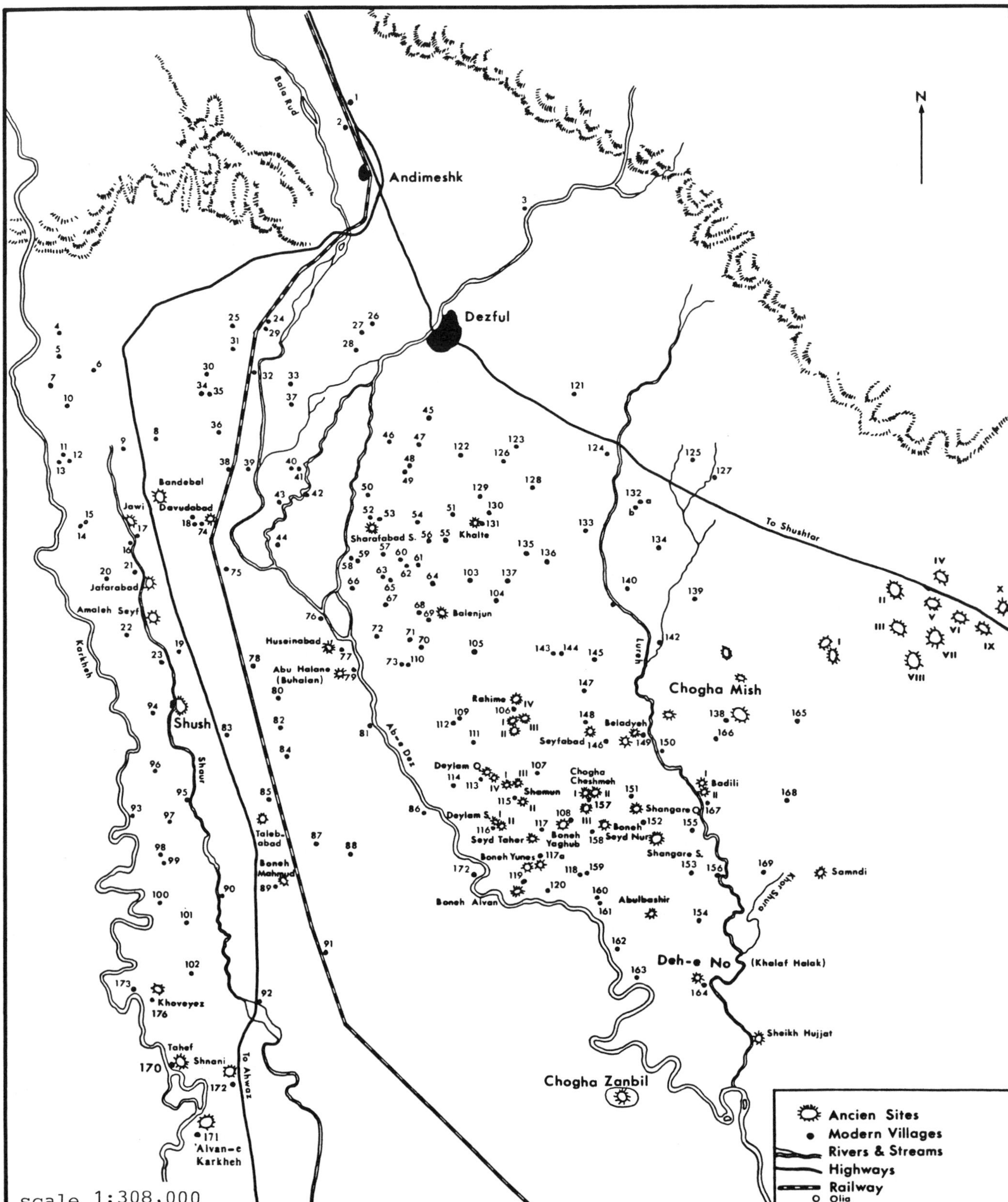

Figure 2. Map of Upper Khuzestan, showing villages and ancient sites.

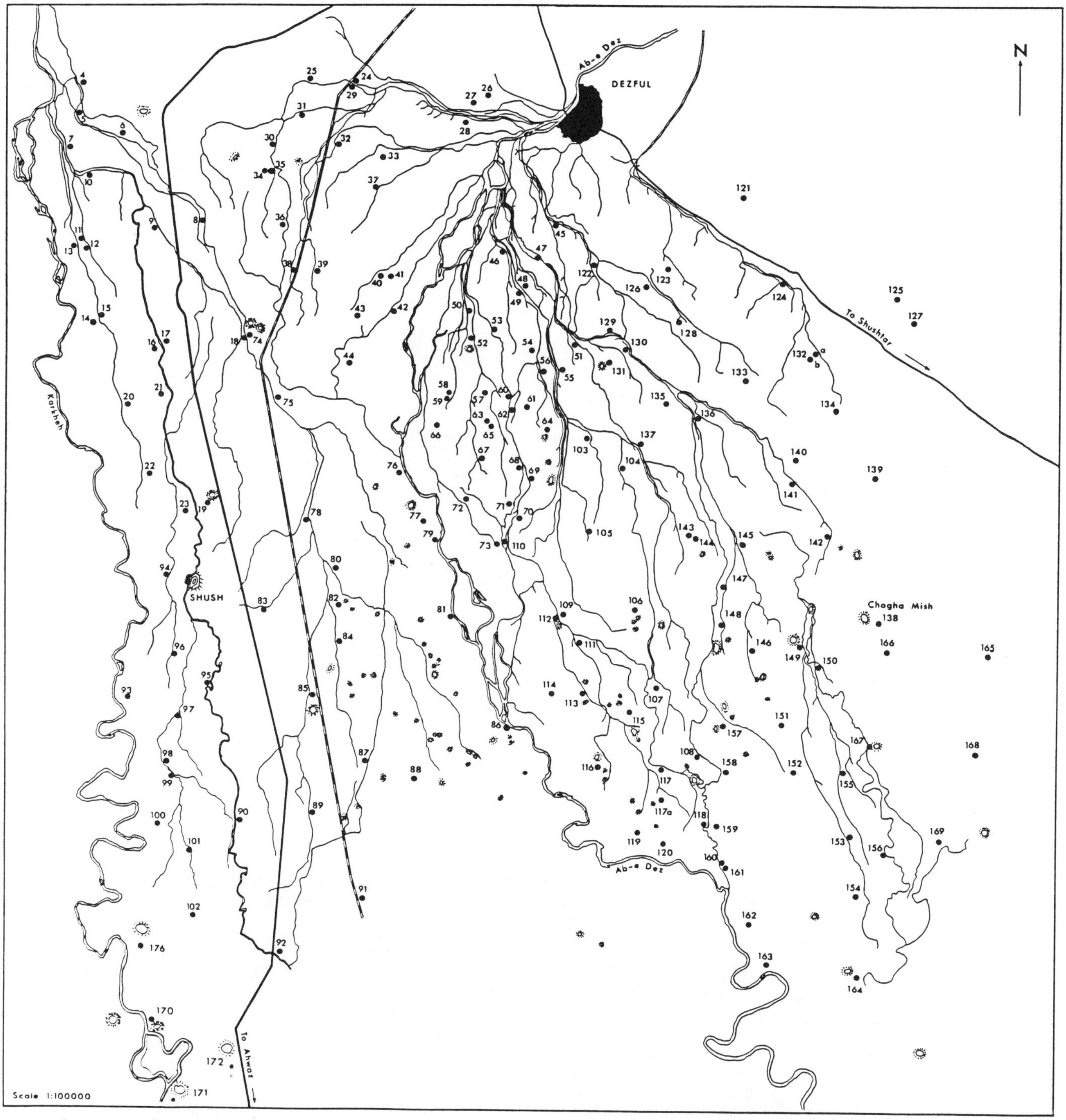

scale 1:250,000

Figure 3. Map of Upper Khuzestan, indicating villages (numbered) and major water courses.

Pl. 1A,B. Tappeh Deh-e No

Pl. 2A. Tappeh Rahimeh I

Pl. 2B. Tappeh Rahimeh II

Pl. 3A. Tappeh Sheikh Hujjat

Pl. 3B. Tappeh Deilameh Sofla

Pl. 4A. Tappeh Sham'un II

Pl. 4B. Tappeh Sham'un III

Pl. 5A. Chogha Cheshmeh

Pl. 5B. Tappeh Beladieh

2

KHUZESTAN ENVIRONMENT

Introduction

The use of geographic and environmental data by archaeologists studying historical developments has become commonplace. This comprehensive approach is particularly important and fruitful in the study of prehistoric societies. The geography of Khuzestan was a major factor in the development and shaping of its prehistoric and even historic cultures and civilizations. Several detailed studies of the geology and geography of the region have been carried out and published (Schroeder 1953; Bakker et al. 1956; Pabot 1961; Fisher 1968; Helbaek 1969; Kirkby 1977). Here, it suffices to give only an overview of the Khuzestan environment, based on such studies.

The alluvium plain of Khuzestan lies in southwestern Iran (Fig. 1). It is surrounded by the Zagros range to the north and east, the Persian Gulf to the south, and the Iraqi border to the west. Khuzestan can be divided into three climatically different zones. Pabot (1961:9-14) has summarized the pattern of environmental zones as follows:

1. Arid, less than 200 mm rainfall and an area of ca. 20,000 km^2.
2. Semi-arid, rainfall of 200-300 mm and an area of ca. 15,000 km^2.
3. Dry, rainfall of 300-900 mm covering an area ca. 25,000 km^2.

Table 2

Average monthly precipitation in mm at Abadan, Ahwaz, & Dezful*

Month	Abadan	Ahwaz	Dezful
Oct.	2.7	2.5	0
Nov.	25.0	31.24	55.6
Dec.	34.6	51.5	78.5
Jan.	37.1	54.7	82.2
Feb.	33.8	47.0	52.1
Mar.	16.2	18.0	52.0
April	14.5	17.7	33.1
May	6.1	1.8	22.4
June	0	0	2.3
Annual average	ca. 155	ca. 230	ca. 378

*Source:Bakker et al. 1956, Tables 10, 11.

The Arid Zone

This region covers the alluvial plain south and southwest of Ahwaz. It consists of fine silt with no hard rocks or sand dunes. Large areas of this zone are covered with saline marshes, which partially dry up in summer. The soil is mostly saline, especially in the southeastern part, with severely limited agricultural possibilities. The arable lands are constantly reduced by active erosion. Outside the marshes, the land is like desert with very poor flora (Pabot 1961:19).

The Semi-arid Zone

The southwestern limit of this zone is the region of Susangerd and Ahwaz; its northern limit lies some 10-15 km south of Dezful and Shushtar and at the foot of Agha Jari hills (ibid.:20). This area is much less homogeneous than the arid zone. It is mostly silty, with large saline areas and some marshes. It also contains all the sandy areas and dunes of Khuzestan, as well as low sandstone or marl-gypseous hills (ibid.). Erosion is very active in the region east of Ahwaz and south of Shushtar. Although this region is the thoroughfare of major rivers, loaded with silt from the Zagros range, the degradation of ancient irrigation systems and lack of drainage have brought so much salt to the surface that extensive stretches of once cultivated land have been deserted. The flora in this region is much richer than in the arid zone (ibid.). Because of the high content of minerals, such as salt, gypsum, and calcium carbonate, especially in the semi-arid area, due to intense evaporation and poor drainage, over-irrigation can cause irreversible salinization (Kirkby 1977:253).

The Dry Zone

Extending from the middle of the Karkheh River valley up to the east of Gachsaran, this zone contains some conglomerate and sandstone, but gypseous marls are predominant. Erosion is prevalent throughout this zone, especially in the southeast where the rains are more violent and irregular. The dry zone has relatively few silty areas with somewhat stony ground. The natural flora, of at least five hundred species, is much richer than in the other zones (Pabot 1961:24). In general, there is no precipitation in the summer, and the winter precipitation comes in the form of torrential rains which saturate the soil quickly. Thus much of the water is lost as run-off (Bakker et al. 1956:52).

The Rivers

The Karkheh, Dez, and Karun, the three major rivers and smaller streams, which irrigate Khuzestan, drain ca. 100,000 km^2 of the Zagros mountains (Kirkby 1977:251). These streams, created by high precipitation in the mountains (400-800 mm), are vital since dry farming is marginal even in the rainy winter season (ibid.:253).

The rivers follow the lines of three major northwest-southeast geological ridges resulting from vertical tectonic movements that had considerable impact on the hydrology and drainage of the plain (Lees and Falcon 1952:24ff.). The areas between these ridges form a series of independent plains. Immediately below a ridge, the soil is less saline and has coarser sediments with, accordingly, better drainage (Schroeder 1953:12). According to statistics, the flow of water in the three major upper Susiana rivers is out of phase with the agricultural regime, that is, the maximum river discharge occurs in mid-spring, when the crops are ready to be harvested and are thus often in danger of flooding. Minimum discharge occurs in late fall/early winter and late summer when water is most needed (Oberlander 1968:267). Unlike the major rivers, the Shaur, a small river flowing west of Shush and originating from a perennial spring and seepage of the Karkheh (Hansman 1967:28), has its maximum and minimum discharge respectively in November and in April-May. Because the Shaur has its maximum discharge in the dry seasons, it is very heavily tapped, especially for summer crops.

Among the rivers that irrigate Khuzestan, the least saline is the Dez and the most saline are the lower Khuzestan rivers of Jarrahi and Hendijan. The major alluvial fan, which is neither too saline nor too silty for irrigation, lies in the region between Dezful and Susa, or between the rivers of Karkheh and Dez (Pabot 1961:263-266). This region is mainly irrigated by the low salinity waters of the Dez. Its relative high summer flow also allows summer irrigation (ibid.:266). Although the Karun has similar advantages, most of its waters are used in the south in the region of Ahwaz, with large areas of flat lands (ibid.). The Karkheh is more saline and has less summer flow; thus, it suffices for the summer irrigation of only small areas (ibid.). River fans experience minor floods annually, but major ones also occur. The sediments deposited by these floods cover existing saline surfaces, creating nonsaline ones. Such conditions encourage winter cultivation, which probably influenced the choosing of settlements above the plain level on the already existing mounds in antiquity, an important environmental factor in the formation of many high mounds with long history of occupation in Khuzestan (ibid.).

3

THE POTTERY OF THE GREMLIZA SURVEY

In archaeological surface surveys, the method of using ceramics from sites with established stratigraphic position to date surface collections, which would then represent site occupation, is widely applied (Adams 1962; Carter 1971; Johnson 1973; Wright et al. 1979). This method has been employed here to date the survey material, with parallels for each sherd cited in the Appendix.[1] In cases where no stratified parallel was available, the pottery is dated on stylistic grounds.

The Chronological System Adopted

The sequence of Susiana cultures as proposed by L. Le Breton (1957) has been corroborated in general by several stratigraphically controlled excavations in Khuzestan. Nevertheless, the evidence from these excavations suggests that some of Le Breton's phases can be grouped as subphases of a major period or they can be divided into individual phases. This division will affect the broad conclusions about the historical development of Susiana, based on surface materials.

Throughout this study, I have followed, with one modification, the terminology proposed by Helene Kantor for the Susiana sequence because it is neutral, simple, and inclusive. It also indicates the underlying unity in the cultural development of prehistoric Susiana without implying absence or presence of socioeconomic differentiations in various prehistoric periods. Furthermore, it avoids site names as identifications of cultural periods and thereby reduces further confusion in an array of chronological charts already filled with site names.

Kantor's Susiana sequence is based both on the stratigraphic position and various styles and techniques of pottery found at Chogha Mish, Chogha Banut, and Boneh Fazili (Kantor 1976). These sites have provided evidence of earlier cultures and their distinctive ceramic traditions preceding the Early Susiana period, the earliest in Le Breton's sequence. Excavations at Chogha Banut (Kantor 1977) have also suggested the presence of an even earlier, aceramic phase there. Kantor has divided Susiana prehistoric cultural sequence into five major periods: Formative, Archaic, Early, Middle, and Late Susiana. The Archaic and Middle Susiana periods are further subdivided into three phases: Archaic 1-3, and Middle Susiana 1-3. Because there is still uncertainty about the stratigraphic position and definition of the Middle Susiana 2 phase, only certain bowls with their interior bases decorated with filled ovals are tentatively dated to this phase.[2]

Pottery of the Early Periods

Archaic Susiana (AS). The evidence for the AS period is scanty and comes from only three sites (G25-II, G26-II, and G33-IV). Except for one sherd which seems to be a local variation of the Matt-painted ware (Fig. 36V), the sherds exhibit characteristics of the Close-line ware (Figs. 32D, 33U). However, none of these pieces can be comfortably dated to the AS 3 phase, because some of the painted motifs, particularly the **X** motif, continued into the following ES period. Because of this problem, these sites are excluded from the tabulation tables.

Early Susiana (ES). The evidence for the ES period is more numerous and more certain. The ware typically has a high proportion of grit and sand tempering, with occasional denser and finer ware. Typical ES flanges are not represented because Gremliza ignored unpainted pottery. Among the painted vessels, open bowls with either horizontal or diagonal reserved wavy lines separating broad bands are the most frequent (see, for example, Figs. 32E-D, 36H). Painted pedestaled bowls (Figs. 31K, 50P) and open bowls with a sharp carination and broad painted bands below the lip (Figs. 32G, 38A,E), all characteristics of the Early Susiana period, also occur.[3] Figure 64G is an open bowl with at least two rows of crosshatched lozenges on the interior and with large festoons on the exterior. This piece may represent a transitional phase from ES to MS, because of the combination of the interior design with the unmistakably MS exterior design. A similar design is reported from ES levels at Jafarabad (Dollfus 1975, Fig. 17:11). Figure 67P is a lipsherd of an open form. The decoration consists of a row of zigzags, bordered presumably by triangles. Although the painted motif and its execution are more akin to the AS 2 Red-line ware tradition, I have tentatively dated it to the ES period because of its buff color ware and dark painted design.

Pottery of the Middle Susiana (MS) Period

Middle Susiana 1. This phase is better represented in the collection. Notable are bell-shaped bowls decorated on the interior with dense cross-hatching; the exterior is either covered with paint or decorated with opposed diagonal bands (Figs. 29F, 44E). Also common are "tortoise" vessels (Figs. 30L, 56F) and bowls with outflaring walls and flat or slightly concave bases. The interior of the base is usually painted with "rosettes" or "sunbursts"; interlocking "butterflies" or rows of superimposed solid triangles are also common (Figs. 30P, 45N, 55G). Pedestaled bowls with painted interior bases are also represented (Fig. 44F). Figure 34O is an example of the rather common ladle with a handle rising from the lip. This specimen has a short handle and as such may belong to the earlier part of this phase (Hole et al. 1969:141). Also represented is the characteristic design of wide horizontal bands dividing the exterior surface into registers filled with large solid dots (Fig. 30K). Bowls ornamented with a row of "butterflies" separated by areas of crosshatching also occur (Fig. 55D).

Middle Susiana 2. As pointed out before, only open bowls with certain painted decorations on the interior base are dated to this phase. The most prominent of these motifs are circles with their interior area divided into four ovals. The blank space in these ovals is usually decorated with naturalistic and stylized fish (Figs. 30N, 71K) or simple geometric elements. These motifs are absent from both Jafarabad and Jawi, but occur at Chogha Mish.

Middle Susiana 3: This phase is well represented in the collection. "Tortoise" vessels continued from the MS 1 phase (Fig. 5D).[4] Common are tall beakers decorated with vertical lines on the exterior and scallops on the interior lip (Figs. 6C, 33O), and bowls with large festoons bordered with broad bands on the exterior and interior (Figs. 29E, 37E). A curious, and so far unique, example is Figure 5E (see also Fig. 56E). In this example the blank areas inside the festoons are filled with an animal that resembles a hedgehog. Jars with short everted rims and pronounced interior ledges with simple decoration on the upper shoulders consisting of horizontal lines and series of **X**'s (Fig. 28B), and jars with flaring plain high necks also occur. These jars are usually decorated with a horizontal band on the base of the neck under which a large floating dot is framed by a scalloped circle (Fig. 46A). Other characteristic pieces are open bowls decorated with vertical lines that divide the exterior surface into panels, each containing a solid circle surrounded by small dots (Fig. 27E), large cups decorated with numerous scattered solid triangles randomly placed on the exterior surface (Fig. 51H), decorated stands with a central perforation (Fig. 71E), and large basins with pronounced inner ledges and painted decoration consisting of a series of hatched lozenges superimposed on a row of "ladder motif" (Fig. 27K).

Pottery of the Late Susiana Period (LS)

Introduction: The LS period is well represented in the collection. The pottery of this period constitutes the bulk of Gremliza's collection. This portion of the survey material consists of two classes of pottery. The distinction is made based on both vessel shapes and painted designs. One class contains various forms and decorations primarily known from Susa (Susa A, [Le Breton 1957]; Acropole I, levels 27-25 [Le Brun 1971]), but also found at many other sites. The other class is characterized by a well and evenly fired fine ware with little sand or, in most cases, no visible inclusion. The ware has a typical creamy buff appearance, resembling a slip. The repertoire of the painted motifs is large and varied. Naturalistic, stylized, and geometric motifs occur. The most characteristic examples of this class are bowls with a sharp carination near the base and numerous dots as a subsidiary design element.

Recent excavations in Khuzestan demonstrated that the vessel types and painted designs Le Breton attributed to "stage d" of his Susiana sequence can be divided into two distinct classes of pottery, representing two chronologically sequential phases. The characteristic shapes and decorative motifs that comprise the earlier phase are now attributed to the MS 3 phase. This class is known from Chogha Mish, Jafarabad (levels 3m-n), Jawi (period II), Bandebal (period II, Levels 27-16) in Khuzestan, and Farrukhabad and Chogha Sabz (Bayat phase) in Deh Luran.

The ceramic of the later phase is discovered on many sites by surface surveys. But only three sites provide stratigraphically controlled evidence of this ceramic. In Khuzestan, comparative material comes from Bandebal and Qabr-e Sheikhein. In Deh Luran, Farrukhabad is the only site that has produced stratified materials for this later phase. Materials from Bandebal and Farrukhabad are published, but those from Qabr-e Sheikhein await publication.

There is an obvious danger with assigning surface survey collections to various chronological phases and periods in the absence of comparative stratified materials. To avoid a stylistic selection in order to isolate a chronological phase, I have relied mostly on the excavated materials from Bandebal, Farrukhabad, and occasionally Qabr-e Sheikhein. However, this methodology of searching for parallels and diagnostics only among stratified materials is serviceable up to the point of establishing a chronological niche for the survey materials. The number of the published examples from Bandebal and, particularly, Farrukhabad is limited. Even with a greater number of examples, the strong possibility remains that not all characteristics are represented at any given site. Therefore, pieces that are not represented in the excavated materials are included in the pottery repertoire of this later phase on stylistic grounds and on the basis of their absence from sites with known stratigraphic hiatus between the MS 3 phase and Susa A (e.g., Chogha Mish and Jafarabad). Admittedly, this supplementary method of relying on "negative evidence" is not an ideal way to date unrepresented pieces. It is, nevertheless, warranted and practical because of the rather well-known pottery sequence of Susiana and our knowledge of its relative chronology.

In Susiana, this distinctive phase is considered as part of Dollfus's long period II of the Bandebal sequence. Period II includes levels 27-11. Only levels 12-11, and possibly level 13, are dated to this phase.[5] More specifically, this phase corresponds in part with Dollfus's Period 12 (Bandebal levels 13-11) and is considered by her to be terminal MS of short duration (Dollfus 1983b:166). In Deh Luran, this phase is known as "Farukh Phase" from excavations at Farrukhabad (Wright 1981). No stratigraphic "break" between this phase and those which precede it is reported from these two sites and Qabr-e Sheikhein. Moreover, there is evidence of continuity from one phase to another, and the appearance of new ceramic types appear to be gradual.

The change in the ceramic tradition seems to coincide with, or was the result of, changes in settlement pattern and some regional developments. Chogha Mish was abandoned after the conflagration of its "Burnt Building," marking the end of the MS period.[6] It was reoccupied sometime during the Late Susiana period, probably when Susa had already been founded as a fullfledged town. Evidence from archaeological surface surveys indicates that during the period between the desertion of Chogha Mish and the founding of Susa, no one site attained, as far as size is concerned, a central position, as did Chogha Mish before and Susa later. Moreover, there was a slight decrease in the size of the regional population and a general tendency for the settlements to move to the west of the plain (Hole 1987:85-86).

To underline the individuality of this phase in the Susiana sequence and to be consistent with the chronological system adopted here, based on the preceding and following observations, I am introducing "Late Susiana 1" for this phase and "Late Susiana 2" for Susa Acropole levels 27-25, and other related assemblages.

Since there is continuity from the MS 3 phase to the following LS 1, one might choose the term "Middle Susiana 4" to underline such continuity. I have opted for the term "Late Susiana 1" for this phase and its pottery repertoire, taking into account the following observations:

(1) There seems to be more continuity from this phase to the LS 2 (Susa A) than there is between this and the preceding MS 3;
(2) a number of important constituents of MS 3 pottery disappeared in the following phase, while a number of new shapes and painted motifs appeared;
(3) the change in the pottery repertoire coincided with or was the result of some regional and inter-regional developments such as:
  a) the abandonment of Chogha Mish as the largest site in Susiana,
  b) the gradual shift of the Susiana settled community from the east to the west,
  c) the appearance of isolated cemeteries in highland Iran, suggesting the existence of developed and organized mobile pastoralist groups,
  d) the subsequent prominence of Tall-e Bakun A in Fars and the spread of its ceramic style in the highland (Alizadeh 1988a, 1988b).

These observations suggest that the end of the MS period cannot be considered as simply due to stylistic change in the ceramic tradition. Rather, the new forms and painted motifs seem to be symptomatic of far greater socioeconomic and political changes that were paving the way to urbanization and formation of state organizations. These transformations occurred at an historical juncture when there were signs in southwestern Iran and southern Mesopotamia of increasing socioeconomic complexity.

Stratigraphic Evidence for LS 1 Phase. As mentioned before, the LS 1 assemblage is stratigraphically above that of the MS 3. This assemblage is absent from Chogha Mish and Jafarabad, indicating a gap at Jafarabad between levels 3m-n and 3d-1, and between the MS 3 and the LS periods at Chogha Mish.

Farrukhabad and Bandebal help to establish a stratigraphic niche for that distinctive portion of the Gremliza survey material for which I have proposed the term LS 1. Bandebal's levels 28-10 have been divided into three periods, Bandebal I-III. Level 28 is assigned to Bandebal I; levels 27-11 to Bandebal II, and level 10 to Bandebal III. Period II is in turn divided into three phases. The earliest, levels 27-19, correspond to the MS 3 phase; levels 18-13 to "terminal" MS 3, and levels 12-11 to the period between MS 3 and LS/Susa A, i.e., LS 1 in the proposed terminology (Dollfus 1983b).

Bandebal level 16 seems to be basically MS 3, but with some presumptive LS 1 pottery mixed in. Among them, large bowls decorated with sets of concentric rectangles separated by solid bands are noteworthy (Fig. 46B; ibid., Fig. 74:5). Another characteristic motif is found on some decorated bowls. The exterior is covered with paint, with opposed hatched diagonal bands in reserve (Fig. 8H; ibid., Fig. 71:8). These bowls do not occur at Farrukhabad, but are found at Qabr-e Sheikhein (Weiss 1976, Fig. 18:92). Simple bowls decorated with multiple broad horizontal bands first appeared in level 17 and 16 and continued into level 11; this motif was later accompanied by dots (Dollfus 1983b, Figs. 65:1, 74:1-2, 83:9). At Farrukhabad this type is found in Layers B44-37 and A30-24, indicating that the multiple band motif appeared a little later than some other characteristic motifs (Wright 1981, Table 8). These bowls are absent from Tappeh Sabz, "Bayat phase," Chogha Mish MS 3, and Jawi, but common at Bandebal and

Qabr-e Sheikhein (Weiss 1976, Fig. 29:3-4).

The pottery from level 15 is not illustrated. Level 14 still has some MS 3 pottery, but the prominent LS 1 bowls with sharp carination near the base appeared in this level (Dollfus 1983b: Fig. 85:15, 17). It is interesting to note that these bowls, along with another LS 1 characteristic as indicated below, appeared first in level 19 and became frequent in levels 17-11 (ibid., Fig. 65:8-9, Table 27).

An important constituent of the LS 1 painted designs, bold motifs combined with dots (dot motif),[7] appeared for the first time in level 14 at Bandebal (ibid., Fig 82:2). Another characteristic of the LS 1 ceramic motifs in level 14 is the combination of opposed hatched bars linked by chevrons whose apices touch the upper and lower framing bands (ibid., Fig. 82:8). This motif and its variants occur at Qabr-e Sheikhein (Weiss 1976, Fig. 18:92-94) but are absent from Farrukhabad. In addition, some painted designs more common in eastern Iran also appeared in level 14 (see, Stein 1936, Pls. 21:41, 28:27; Langsdorff and McCown 1942, Pl. 61:2; Egami and Sono 1962, Fig. 20:12; Caldwell 1967, Fig. 4-5; Lamberg-Karlovsky 1970, Fig. 37M; Beale et al. 1986, Fig. 4.21C) One example is found on a bulbous jar. The design consists of a row of crosshatched lozenges, probably an abstraction of a "lizard," linked by chevrons (Dollfus 1983b, Fig. 81:14). This design is absent from Chogha Mish, Jafarabad, and Qabr-e Sheikhein, but common in Kerman and, especially, in Fars (for references see Fig. 57G) Another example decorates an elegant ring-based bowl. The decoration consists of one file of crosshatched rectangles which are attached to one another and to the framing elements with small solid squares at their corners (ibid., Fig. 82:1). One example of this type was found at Chogha Mish and, therefore, may not necessarily date to the LS 1 phase.

LS 1 motifs and shapes became dominant in levels 13, 12, and, especially, 11. They include: bowls with sharp carination near the base (ibid., Fig. 81:15,17), opposed crosshatched bars (ibid., Figs. 81:15, 82:8), and bowls decorated with dot motifs (ibid., Fig. 82:2). None of these shapes and motifs occur either at Chogha Mish or Jafarabad.

At Farrukhabad the LS 1 pottery was found in two excavation areas A and B. Levels 31-23 in area A and levels 47-37 in area B are dated to "Farukh phase" (Wright 1981:8, 57-60). Whereas the LS 1 was the earliest phase reached in area B, in area A LS 1 depositional layers were found above the deposits of the MS 3 phase ("Bayat phase" in Deh Luran) with no apparent gap. The site seems to have been abandoned sometime during the LS 1 phase and was reoccupied during the Protoliterate period.

At Farrukhabad the LS 1 ceramics were also found with the pottery of the earlier MS 3 phase, but the published examples do not show the variety in shape and decoration found at Bandebal and Qabr-e Sheikhein. Tall beakers with narrow and pointed bases occur. In many cases, the base is scraped and rounded, but examples with shaved bases also occur (Wright 1981, Figs. 13-14, 24-26). The two examples that are reported from Bandebal (Dollfus 1983b, Fig. 83:2) and Qabr-e Sheikhein (Weiss 1976, Fig. 29:11) are plain. At Farrukhabad both the plain and painted types occur. The latter has a simple design that consists of lip and base bands which border a wavy line framed by four vertical lines (Wright 1981, Fig. 14a-b). These large version beakers are reported to be restricted to "Farukh phase" (ibid.:26). Again, they are absent from Chogha Mish and Jafarabad.

Simple bowls with multiple band motifs (ibid., Fig. 15h) and dot motifs also occur. The dot motifs typically occur on bowls with concave or flaring walls (ibid., Fig. 17a-g). A specific bold decorative element termed "step motif" is attributed by Wright to this phase (ibid., Fig. 19a-f). This motif is absent from Bandebal and Qabr-e Sheikhein.

Certain shapes and decorations of LS 1 ceramics seem to be absent from Farrukhabad. They include flat base cylindrical jars (Fig. 7I), bowls with a sharp carination near the base which is decorated with simple bands (Fig. 8C-F), open bowls ornamented with a series of concentric circles, inscribing an "hour glass" or a "sun disc" (Fig. 9A), the combination of various stylized animals and dots (Fig. 7G), and bowls decorated with opposed hatched diagonal bands. Most of these shapes and motifs occur at Bandebal and Qabr-e Sheikhein (Weiss 1976, Figs. 18, 20, 22). The absence at Farrukhabad of these types might be viewed as representing temporal differences.[8] However, the fact that several typical MS 3 pottery types continue into the Farrukh phase assemblage, as well as the absence of any stratigraphic gap between layers A 33 (MS 3) and A 31 (LS 1), render such assumptions unlikely.

Characteristics of Late Susiana 1 Pottery. The preceding discussion of the characteristic LS 1 vessel types and painted motifs and elements with stratigraphic position can now be used to date the survey materials. The most prominent among the painted designs is the decorative element consisting of series of small dots usually arranged in horizontal rows accompanying solid elements, termed the dot motif. These dots appear with simple geometric designs (Fig. 8A, C-D, 33H) and stylized animal motifs (Fig. 7G, 39T).[9] Various combinations of these elements usually appear on bowls with a sharp carination above the base and slightly incurved walls (Fig. 8C-D). They also appear on cylindrical vessels with flat bases (Fig. 7I). Bowls decorated with multiple painted bands without the dots also occur (Fig. 8E-F). Another typical and new form is a deep, conical goblet with a shaved, pointed base and simple painted geometric decoration (Fig. 7B-C). In the examples illustrated in Fig. 7B-C, not much of the body was preserved to see whether it was decorated. Figure 7A and J are also characteristic. They are bowls with a horizontal band painted on the lip; the inside decoration usually consists of three sets of broad bands radiating diagonally from the lip. The interstices are usually filled with dashes or wavy lines; but blank ones also occur (Figs. 42B, 45I). Similar pieces appeared in the MS 3 phase. One example of this type comes from level 3m at Jafarabad (Dollfus 1975, Fig. 49:9).

Bowls decorated with a series of concentric circles inscribing an "hour glass" or a "sun disc" also appear in this phase (Fig. 9A). These bowls are absent from Farrukhabad and Bandebal, but common at Qabr-e Sheikhein (Weiss 1976, Fig. 20:110-11). Another prominent type, apparently absent in the Deh Luran plain but present in the Susiana plain and in the Zagros mountains (see, Contenau and Ghirshman 1935, Giyan Vc, Pl. 48:22; Vanden Berghe 1975, Fig. p. 56) consists of bowls with either concave or flaring walls (Weiss 1976, Fig. 18; Dollfus 1983b, Figs. 71:8, 81:15). The latter usually have a sharp carination close to the base. Two narrow bands in reserve separate the central motif from the lip and base bands (Fig. 8C). The area between these bands is covered with paint, leaving opposed diagonal bands and equilateral triangles in reserve. The bands are ornamented with hatching. In a variant of this type, the middle frieze is executed in the positive (Fig. 9C). This type is also absent from Chogha Mish and Jafarabad; but since it appeared in Bandebal levels 17 and 16, it must have started in late MS 3 phase and subsequently became popular and common during the LS 1 phase. Exact parallels and many other variants of this type occur at Tall-e Bakun B (Egami and Masuda 1962, Figs. 15:13, 17:8) Tall-e Gap (Egami and Sono 1962, Figs. 14:7, 17:10, Pl. 21:1), Tappeh Siyalk (Ghirshman 1938, Pl. 81:14), and Tappeh Giyan (Contenau and Ghirshman 1935, Pl. 48).

There are also some singletons that may or may not date to the LS 1 phase. Figure 5A is a shoulder fragment that belonged to a closed form, as indicated by the stance of the regular striations on the inside. The decoration consists of a stylized shaggy "goat," one of the characteristic motifs of the LS 2 pottery. Figure 56C is a very fine and almost complete beaker with straight sides. The shape resembles some beakers from Tall-e Bakun A, (Langsdorff and McCown 1942, Pl. 16:1; Alizadeh 1988b, Fig. 6C) but the painted pattern is an evolved form of the Susiana long-lived painted composition that started in the ES period and continued into the LS period (De Mecquenem 1943, Buhalan, Fig. 112:24-25; Dollfus 1975, Jafarabad, level 4, Fig. 22:2; Dollfus 1978, Jawi I, Fig. 14:2). Figure 7H is most interesting; it is a body sherd of an open form. The decoration consists of what appears to be a canine shown in solid black and an ungulate, probably a sheep/goat, shown in reserve. This motif and its variants seem to be common in Fars,[10] but so far it is the only example from the Susiana plain. Except for the evidence from Tall-e Gap, there is no stratigraphic basis for dating these pieces to the LS 1 phase. However, since this phase seems artistically to be an experimental period of new shapes, motifs, and compositions, I have tentatively dated them to the LS 1 period.

There is also evidence of continuity from the earlier Middle Susiana pottery tradition. Prominent among carry-overs are: large basins decorated with a lip band and usually three sets of festoons hanging from the interior lip (Fig. 48E); simple, shallow lids decorated with intersecting double lines (Figs. 6B;

and 50L); bowls decorated with one or two rows of solid lozenges, bordered with multiple horizontal bands (Figs. 31E, 62N, 64A), small hemispherical jars (Fig. 28C-D, F), bowls decorated with a frieze of crosshatched triangles and sigma motif (Fig. 31C; Wright 1981, Fig. 18a-c), and jars with completely painted necks (Fig. 35G; ibid., Fig. 24a, Table 8). Other prominent MS 3 ceramic types are bowls and hemispherical jars with a decorative design that has evolved throughout the Susiana sequence. The decoration usually consists of a frieze of large and bold zigzags. Large triangles fill the interstices of the zigzags. These triangles are broken up into three crosshatched smaller triangles (Figs. 8G, 9D). A simpler version of this design appeared first in the ES period, and evolved as it continued into the LS 2 phase (see Fig. 28D for various references).

Presence of LS 1 at Susa. Susa A is known to be chronologically later than Bandebal 12-11, Qabr-e Sheikhein 5-2, Farrukhabad B37-47/A23-31, and contemporary with Jafarabad 3-1, Chogha Mish Late Susiana, Bandebal III 10, and Qabr-e Sheikhein 1. However, the following observations indicate that Susa may have been occupied earlier than usually considered.

As mentioned before, the dot motifs are distinctive painted patterns and rank high in the LS 1 pottery repertoire, providing a reliable diagnostic for the LS 1 phase. These motifs are absent from Late Susiana Chogha Mish, Jafarabad 3-1, and Bandebal III, level 10, all contemporary with Susa A. They are present at Bandebal II, levels 14-11, Qabr-e Sheikhein 4-2, Farrukhabad B 37-47/A 23-31, all earlier than Susa A. The presence of these and other LS 1 motifs (see below) at Susa, therefore, argues for an earlier date for Susa A than traditionally thought, making Susa partly contemporaneous with the LS 1 sites mentioned above.

The presence of LS 1 dot motifs at Susa is indicated by various examples published from the site, namely Le Breton 1947, Figures 47:26-30, 32-33, and Steve and Gasche 1971, Plates 40:17-18, 41:35. Other early motifs at Susa include bowls decorated with pendent scallops on the interior lip (Le Breton 1947, Fig. 47:8), concentric bold circles framing a central element (Figs. 55C, 65A; Le Breton 1947, Fig. 48:12-15; Steve and Gasche 1971, Pl. 39:17) and bowls decorated with a multiple band motif (Steve and Gasche 1971, Pl. 34:23; here, Figs. 40F, 42F).

It can be argued, however, that, as with the MS 3 carry-overs in the LS 1 phase, the typical LS 1 motifs at Susa are also survivors which do not necessarily indicate a chronological presence of the LS 1 phase. This argument would be strong and convincing if other contemporary sites such as Chogha Mish, Jafarabad 3-1, and Bandebal III, level 10 had similar assemblages. But they do not. The presence at Susa of the above motifs and shapes, characteristic of the LS 1 phase, and their absence at Chogha Mish, Jafarabad 3-1, and Bandebal III indicate that Susa A partly overlaps with the LS 1 phase and, therefore, may have been founded some time before the end of the LS 1 phase. If further investigation and detailed analysis of the unpublished materials from Susa, or future investigation at the site, provide solid stratigraphic evidence for the above observations, then that evidence will be theoretically significant in the study of socioeconomic and political development in Susiana.

If we are justified in stretching the initial settlement of Susa earlier than usually accepted, then it is reasonable to suggest that when Chogha Mish was deserted following a regional upheaval, its inhabitants sought to resettle in a less volatile region away from the troubled area, and so founded Susa on the western part of the plain, if not immediately, soon after they left Chogha Mish.[11] This suggestion also helps to explain the initial large size of Susa and its associated socioeconomic eminence from the onset, a development that must have started prior to the founding of Susa, whether at Chogha Mish or at some as yet undiscovered site.

Late Susiana 1 and the Highland Connection. Late Susiana 1 was a period of increasing contact between the lowland and the highland. This contact is indicated by the similarities between the ceramics of these regions. There is also evidence, though admittedly weak, that suggests some of the new types in the LS 1 phase were introduced from the highland, especially from Fars. The use of dots in specific motifs and arrangements, prominent in the LS 1 assemblage, started in the Bakun B II period (Egami and Masuda 1962, Figs. 14:3-4; 15:9) when the pottery assemblage was primarily close in character to that of MS 3 (see, Egami and Masuda 1962, Fig. 14:6-8, 14). Dot motifs continued into the Gap phase and Bakun A, (see, Langsdorff and McCown 1942, Pls. 54:15; 62:6-7; 64:5; 65:5; 70:3, 5-6, 15; and 71:3, 10; Egami and Sono 1962, Fig. 17:6-11) suggesting that these motifs started earlier and survived perhaps longer in the highland than they did in Susiana, although this observation cannot be substantiated by the present archaeological data from Fars. These motifs also occur in Behbahan, (Dittmann 1984, Fig. 24:8-21; 25:1, 6, 9) Ram Hurmoz (Tall-e Qasir) (Caldwell 1968, Fig. 1), and Lurestan (Tappeh Giyan) (Contenau and Ghirshman 1935, Giyan Vc, Pls. 49-51), indicating their wide geographic distribution.

One of the most interesting painted motifs is Figure 7H. As mentioned before, this is the only example found in Susiana so far. The same motif and its variants occur in Fars, suggesting that this is a highland painted motif.[12] Very close parallels between the Gap phase and Bandebal II are pots usually with three vertical bands issuing from the lip,[13] and bowls decorated with broad zigzags whose interstices are filled with solid triangles and the background filled with dots.[14] Double and single zigzag bands with their triangular interstices divided into three crosshatched triangles are also common to the highland and the lowland (Fig. 9D).[15] This motif started in the MS 3 phase but became common in the LS 1 phase. Other common lowland/highland motifs are: slash motif, decorating the reserved areas between solid rectangles,[16] multiple band motif,[17] and rows of solid lozenges with elongated horizontal ovals in reserve. This last motif, usually used to decorate bowls, first appeared in the MS 1 phase in Susiana (Jawi I, L 16, Dollfus 1983a, Fig. 15:9-10) and became popular during the LS 1 phase in both the highland and lowland.[18]

These and other examples (see references cited in the Appendix) suggest increasing contact between the lowland and the highland at the end of the MS period. This unprecedented contact between the lowland and the highland has been attributed to the development of mobile pastoralism in southwestern and southern Iran (Alizadeh 1988a, 1988b), a factor that may also have contributed to the gradual desertion and shifting of sites from the eastern part of the Susiana plain, traditionally the winter pasture of the mobile pastoralist groups, to the western sector of the plain.

Late Susiana 2. The LS 2 pottery assemblage is well known and discussed in detail by various scholars (Le Breton 1957; Le Brun 1971; Dollfus 1971). It suffices to mention only some prominent characteristics represented in the survey collections, which are used for dating. Characteristics of this phase are the well-known tall beakers (Figs. 27A, 39G, 43D, and 54C), shallow open bowls with complex interior painted designs (Figs. 39H,J, 49K), hemispherical open bowls decorated with "eagles" with wide-spread wings (Fig. 30A), and miniature stylized clay birds (Fig. 54J).

Pottery of the Protoliterate Period

Prominent among the ceramics of this period are straight and drooping spouts (Fig. 10A-B), incised decorated four-lugged jars (Fig. 10D), and clay and marble cones (Fig. 10C). Since this type of cones was usually used in public/monumental buildings during the Protoliterate period, the location and size of the sites where these cones were found provide additional information for future studies of the settlement patterns during this period.

NOTES

1. I am well aware of the problem of using diagnostics to date surface materials, and of the problem of the size and nature of the samples from which diagnostics are drawn. However, until all archaeological excavations adopt statistical methods, such as discriminant and cluster analyses (see Weiss 1976), to retrieve and analyze pottery, this seems to be an adequate methodology in this study.

2. The phase "Middle Susiana 3c" (MS 3c) appeared in Dollfus 1983a:166, followed by Dittmann 1984 does not exist. It stems from a misunderstanding of a notation in the plate catalogue of Chogha Mish I (OIP 101, forthcoming) that was made available by Helene Kantor to some of her colleagues.

3. A good example of this type of bowl occurred in an early Middle Susiana context at Jawi and therefore appears to have survived the ES period (see Dollfus 1983a, Fig. 15:1). The shape, however, seems to have lasted even longer (ibid., Fig. 23:1-2, 5).

4. Figure 57P possibly belongs to this, though it is not reconstructed as such.

5. In her chronological chart, Dollfus separates levels 12-11 from level 13 and 10 by dashes. But in the text, level 13 is added to levels 12-11 to represent her "Periode 12" (Dollfus 1983b:166-67, Table 41).

6. There is probably a Late Susiana 1 occupation at Chogha Mish on the High mound, as a few sherds recovered there indicate. (Helene Kantor, personal communication). Although the question of a general conflagration resulting in the total abandonment of the site by the end of the Middle Susiana period should remain open, there is no question that Chogha Mish lost its status as the largest site in the Susiana plain after the Middle Susiana 3 period.

7. Although in the majority of cases, dots are used as filling or subsidiary motifs, following Henry Wright (1981), I use the terms "dot motifs," "multiple band motif," and "step motif" because they are simple and graphic.

8. This situation seems to be limited to Farrukhabad. At the Louvre storage area, there are several drawers full of typical LS 1 types from Tappeh Khazineh.

9. Sources for the LS 1 pottery types are given in the Appendix.

10. It occurs at Tall-e Gap (Egami and Sono, 1962, Fig. 21:5), at Tall-e Saku (Stein 1936, Pl. 24:14), and at the site 5K2 in the Kur River Basin surveyed by W. Sumner.

11. This does not mean that in such an early stage of historical development only one site (Chogha Mish) dominated the whole plain of Susiana. There may have been other major MS sites there, as yet unexcavated, which were probably centers of local polities.

12. It occurs at Tall-e Gap (Egami and Sono 1962, Fig. 21:5), Tall-e Saku (Stein 1936, Pl. 24:14) and at Site 5K2 in the plain of Marv Dasht (Sumner unpublished survey).

13. Tall-e Gap, Egami and Sono 1962, Fig. 17:3-4; Bandebal, Dollfus 1983b, Pl. 19:4.

14. Tall-e Gap, Egami and Sono 1962, Fig. 17:10; Bandebal, Dollfus 1983, Fig. 82:2.

15. They occur at Tall-e Bakun A (Langsdorff and McCown 1942, Pls. 53:14; 54:1-2; 55:4), Giyan Vc (Contenau and Ghirshman 1935, Pls. 53, 55), in Behbahan (Dittmann 1984, Fig. 60:21), at Farrukhabad (Wright 1981, Fig. 20b), and at Bandebal II (Dollfus 1983b, Pl. 16:12, Fig. 73:2).

16. At Farrukhabad (Wright 1981, Fig. 18f), Gap (Egami and Sono 1962, Fig. 13:5, 7-8), Bakun A (Egami and Masuda 1962, Fig. 8:7), and Tall-e Qasir (Caldwell 1968, Fig. 3).

17. At Farrukhabad (Wright 1981, Fig. 15h), Bakun A (Egami and Masuda 1962, Fig. 8:2), Tall-e Qasir (Caldwell 1968:349), and Bandebal II (Dollfus 1983b, Figs. 74:2, 85:2, 86:4).

18. At Farrukhabad (Wright 1981, Fig. 20d), Bakun A (Langsdorff and McCown 1942, Pl. 48:12-13), and Giyan Vc (Contenau and Ghirshman 1935, Pl. 46).

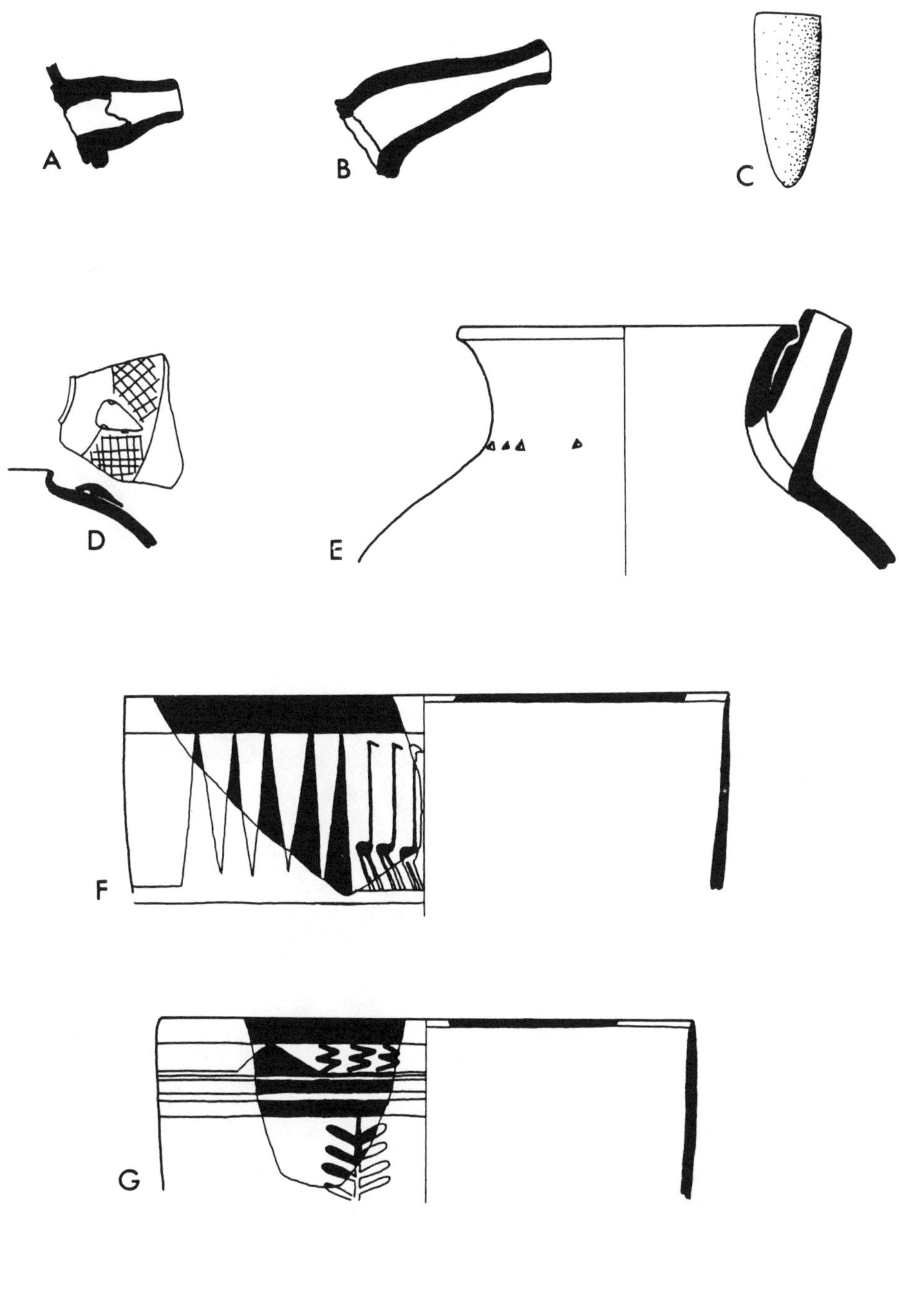

Figure 4. Selected pottery from various periods and sites.

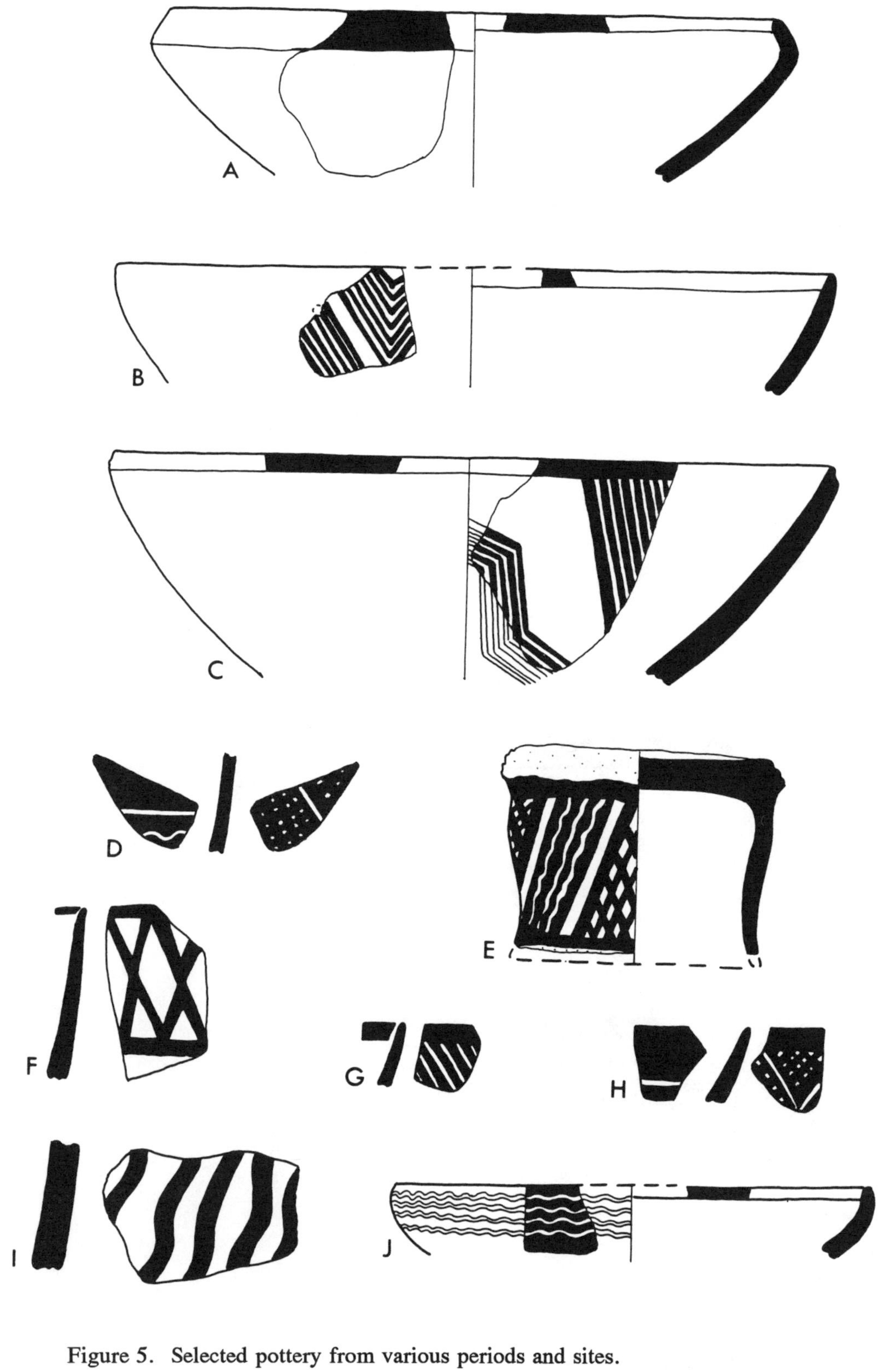

Figure 5. Selected pottery from various periods and sites.

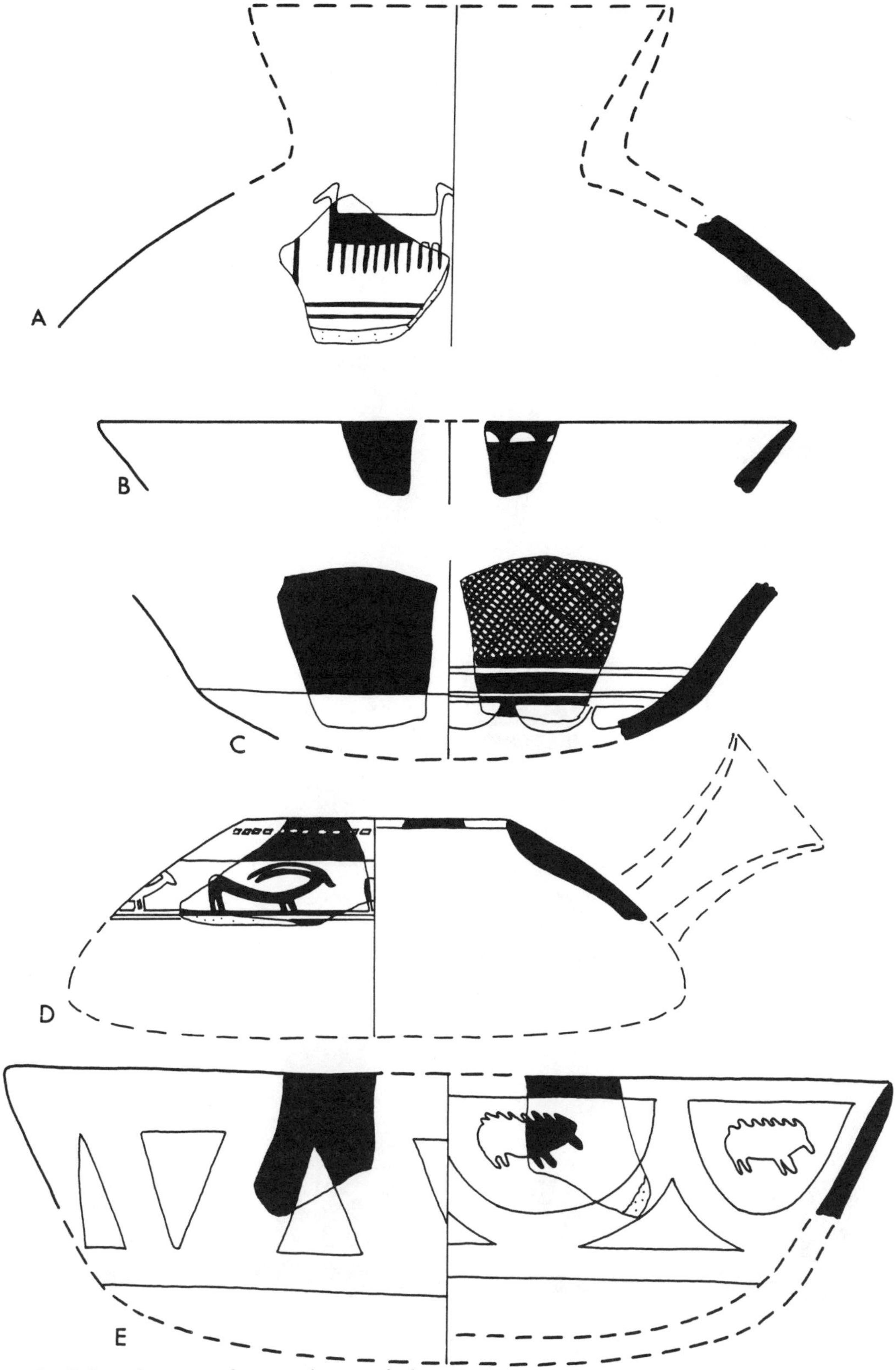

Figure 6. Selected pottery from various periods and sites.

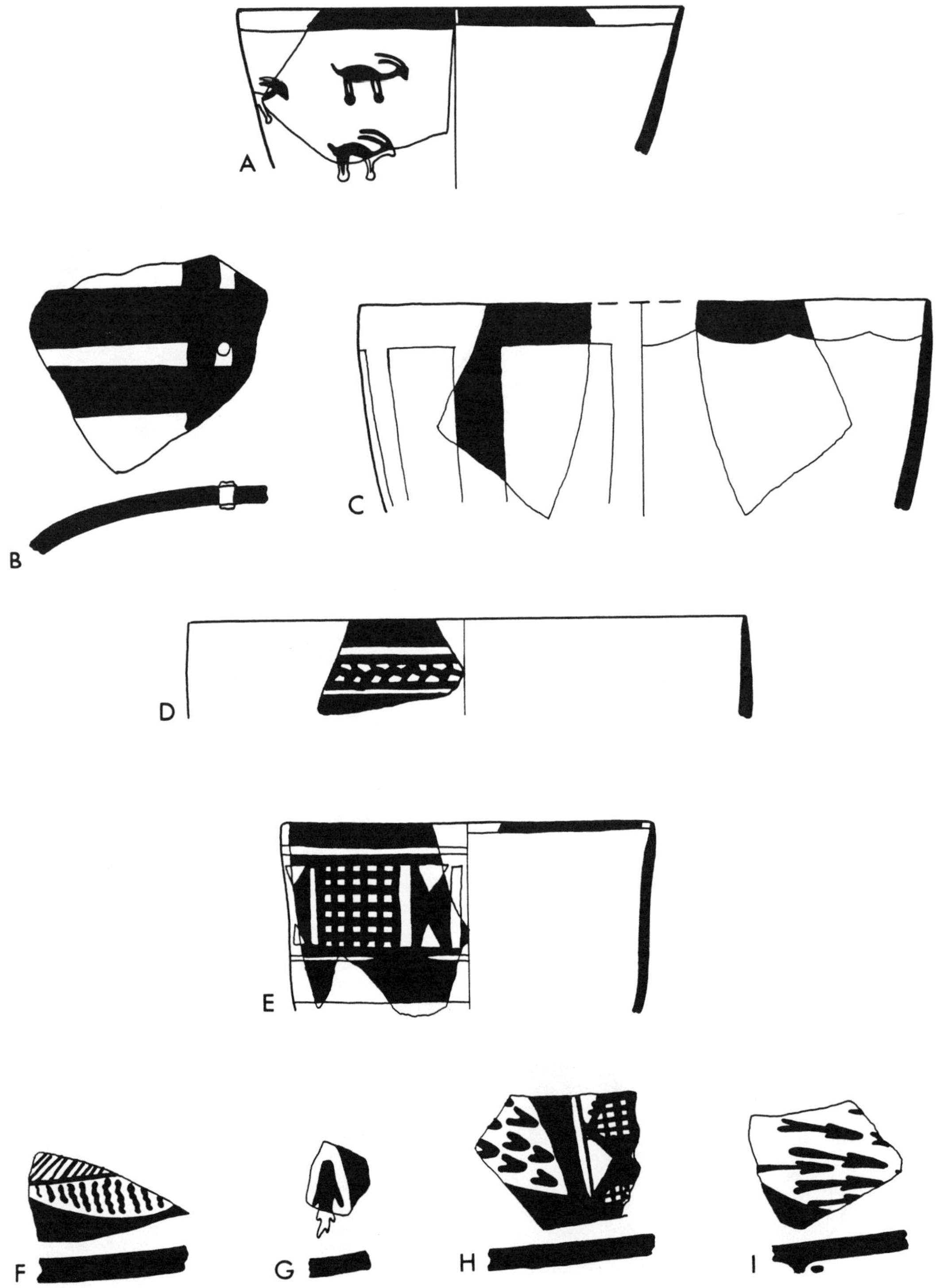

Figure 7. Selected pottery from various periods and sites.

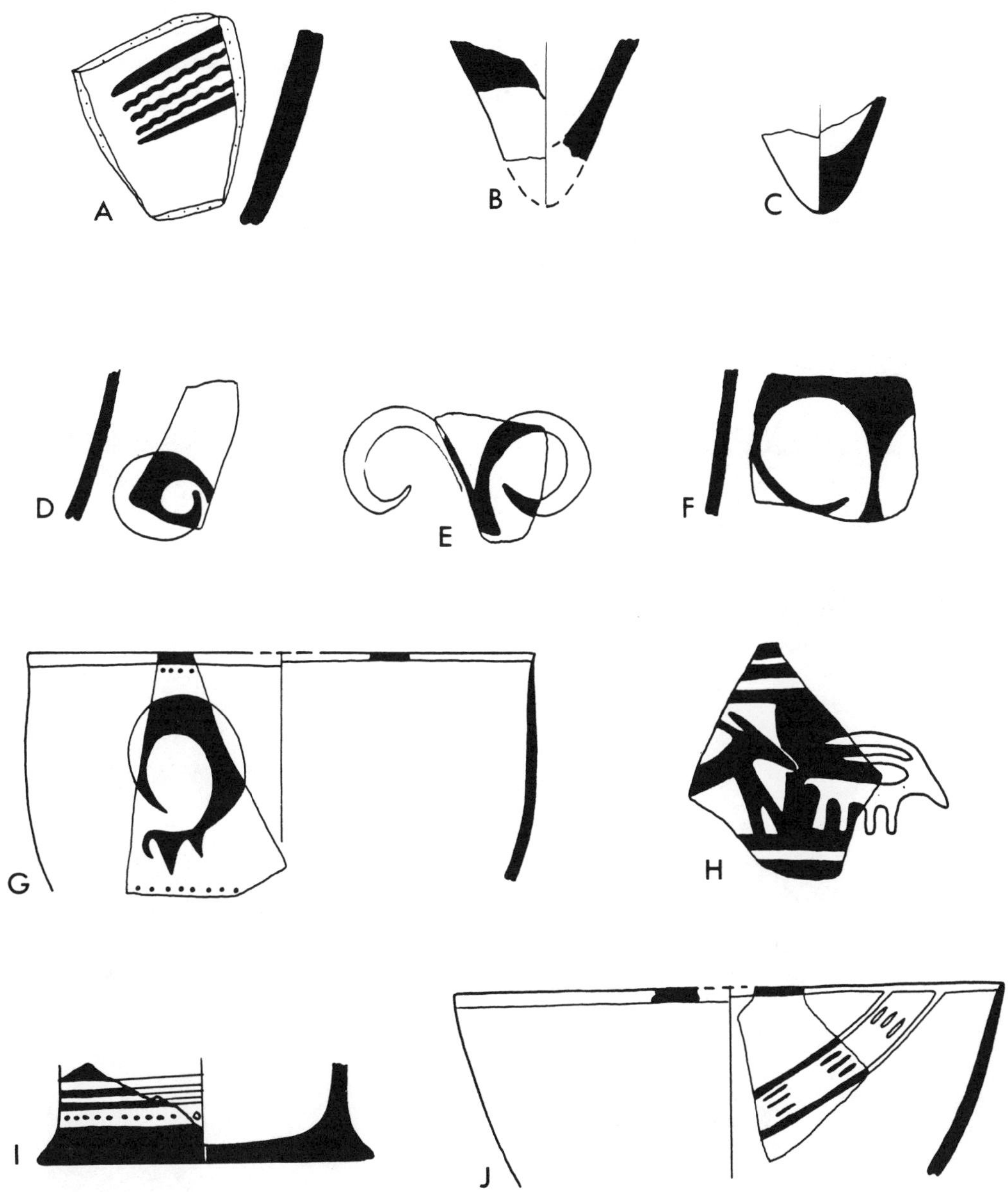

Figure 8. Selected pottery from various periods and sites.

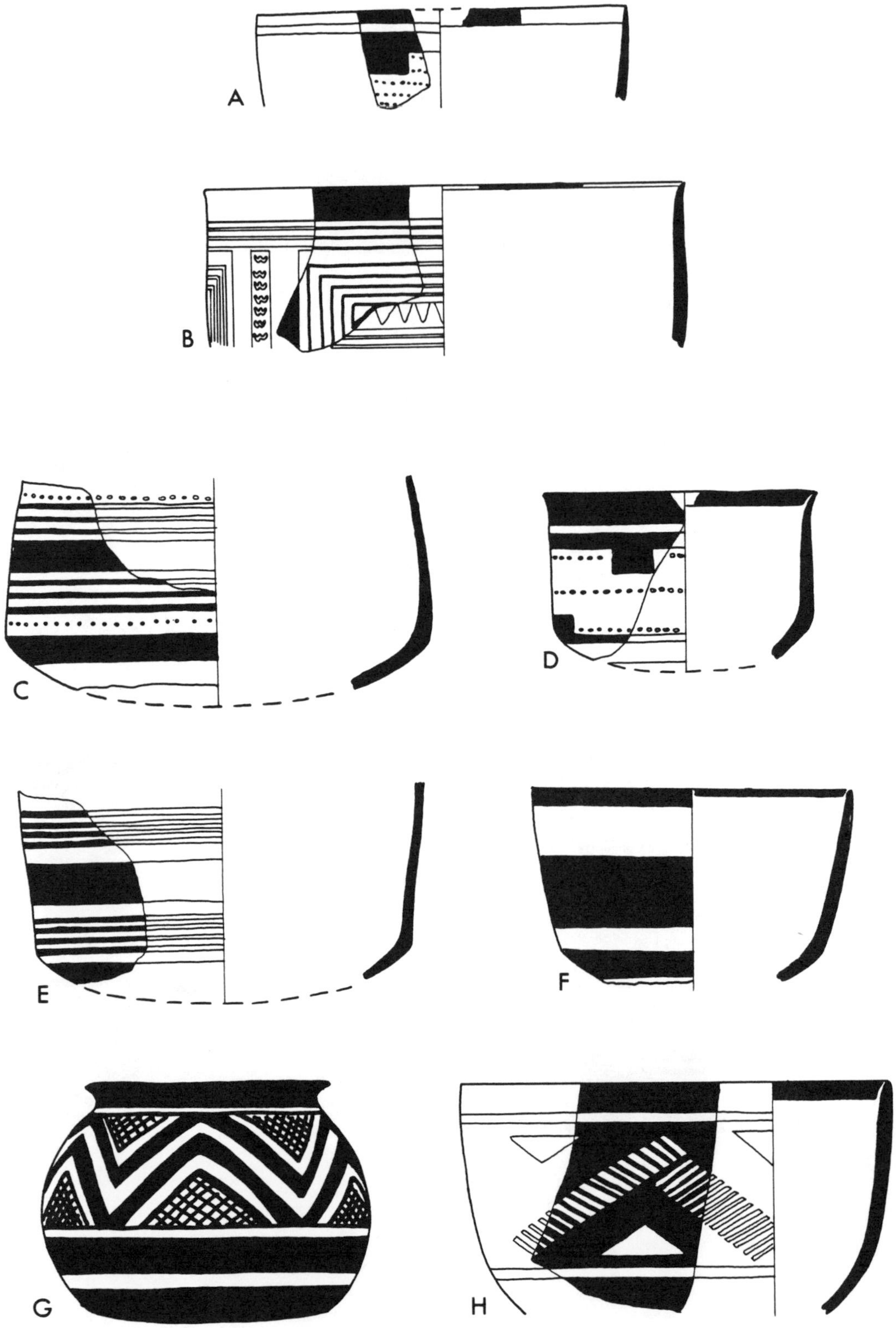

Figure 9. Selected pottery from various periods and sites.

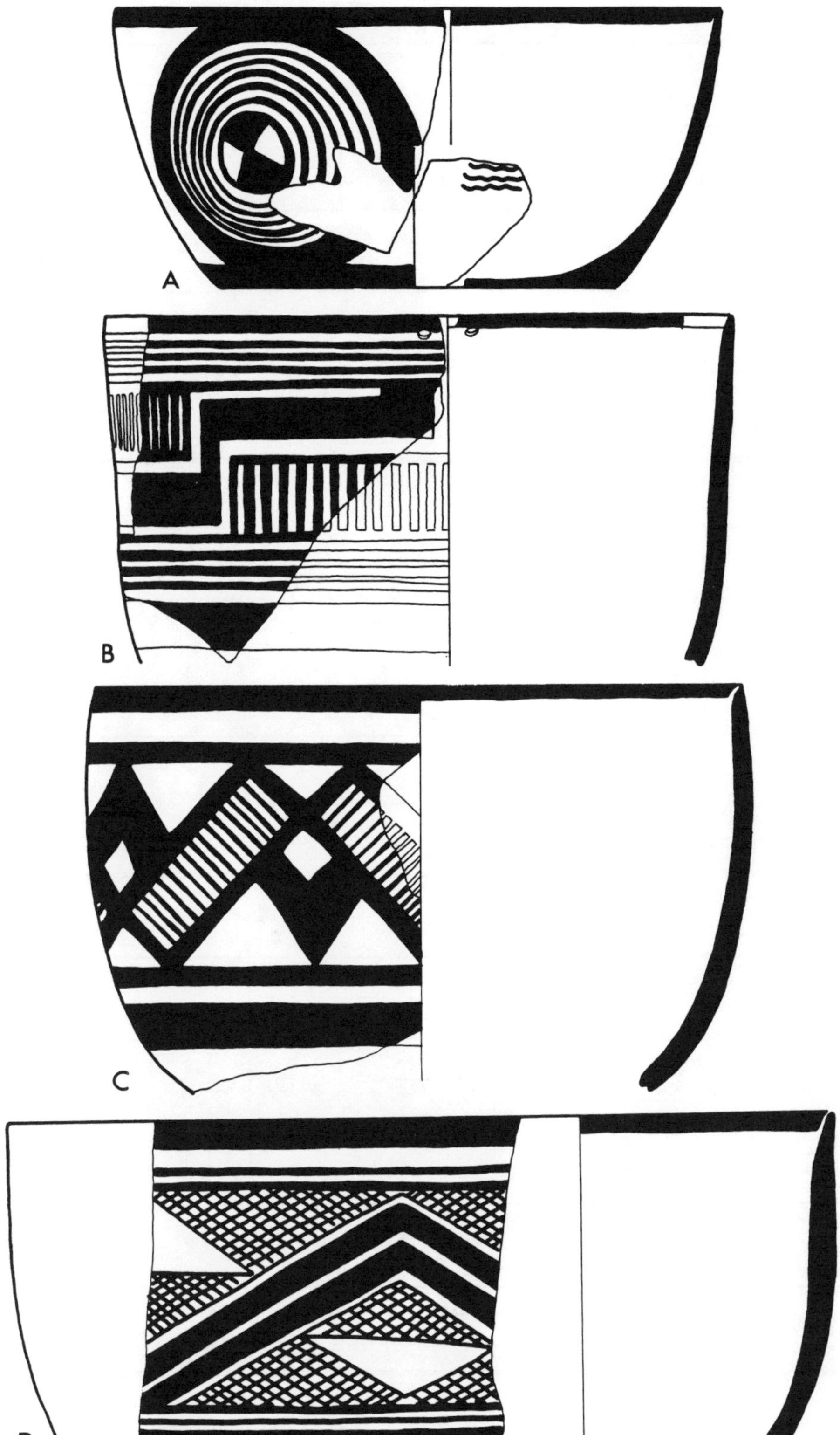

Figure 10. Selected pottery from various peridos and sites.

TABLE 3. RELATIVE CHRONOLOGY OF PREHISTORIC SITES IN SOUTHWESTERN AND SOUTHERN IRAN.

SOUTHERN MESOPOTAMIA	SUSIANA Periods	SUSIANA Sites: Chogha Mish	Jafarabad	Bandebal III	Jawi	Susa *acropole*	DEH LURAN Sites: Farrukhabad	Tappeh Sabz	Chogha Sefid	FARS Periods	FARS Sites: Tall-e Bakun A	Tall-e Gap	Tall-e Bakun B	Tall-e Jari A	Tall-e Mushki
'OBAID 4	LATE SUSIANA 2	LS	1–3	Level 10		25 27	*gap*			LATE FARS	4				
	LATE SUSIANA 1	*gap*	*gap*	II Levels 11, 12, 13, 14, 15, 16, 17	*gap*	?	Levels A 23–31 B 37–47	*gap* Zone A			1	*gap* II	*gap*	*gap* Levels	*gap*
'OBAID 3	MIDDLE SUSIANA 3	MS 3	3m-n	18–27	II Ls.		A 33–36	Zone B		MIDDLE FARS		I	II *gap*	1 *gap*	
	MIDDLE SUSIANA 2	MS 2 ?	*gap*		4–10 I 11										
'OBAID 2	MIDDLE SUSIANA 1	MS 1		I 28	17			Zone C		EARLY FARS			I	2	
'OBAID 1	EARLY SUSIANA	ES	6–4	?			?	Zone D	Zones J–I					3	Upper
'OBAID 0	ARCHAIC SUSIANA 3	AS 3							Zones H–G (CMT)	ARCHAIC FARS				?	Lower ?
?	ARCHAIC SUSIANA 2	AS 2							Zones F–C2						
	ARCHAIC SUSIANA 1	AS 1													

A. Alizadeh

4

ANALYSIS OF THE SURVEY MATERIAL

Introduction

Gremliza divided his survey area into five sections: (1) Upper Shaur; (2) Lower Shaur; (3) Pilot Area; (4) Greater Dez; and (5) Greater Dez east. Based on the original division made by the Khuzestan Development Project to facilitate research in the area, Gremliza conducted both his archaeological and ethnomedical surveys within these boundaries, which are also suggested by the Khuzestan topography and agricultural practices. I have retained this division to avoid confusion in future research and references. Each area is represented by one or more mosaic maps. These maps, as noted, are reproduced from the aerial photographs Gremliza put at my disposal. Each map illustrates villages, Gremliza's surveyed sites, and major natural and artificial waterways.

The following observations pertaining to population size, settlement density, and so forth are based solely on the results of this survey. In the following chapter, however, a more detailed description of the Susiana prehistoric phases is presented, based on the results of various archaeological surveys and excavations.

The Survey Areas

<u>Upper Shaur Area (Table 4, Mosaic maps B and E, Figs. 11,13,16).</u> This appears to be the least populated area of the survey; only three sites are listed. The actual situation is different because Gremliza excluded all the sites in this area which the French Mission had investigated. The earliest reported sites date to the MS 3 phase. The number of sites increased slightly in the following LS period. This increase contrasts with the situation in other areas where the MS period had the highest number of settlements. The anomaly may be accidental, and closer observation may reveal more sites of the MS 3 phase. No sites of the Protoliterate period were reported. The settlement pattern is one of gradual increase and total desertion of settlements by the end of the LS period.

Table 4
Number of Sites, by Period, in the Upper Shaur Region (Mosaics B,E)

PERIOD	No. of sites	% of total	New sites	Sites continued	Sites abandoned
PL	-	-	-	-	3
LS2	3	100	0	3	0
LS1	3	100	1	2	0
MS3	2	66	2	0	0
MS	-	-	-	-	-
ES	-	-	-	-	-
AS	-	-	-	-	-

Lower Shaur Area(Table 5, Mosaic map H, Fig. 19). With a total of only four sites, this area was sparsely settled. It was occupied in the beginning of the MS period, a period of general population increase in the Susiana plain. As in the Pilot Area (see below), the population apogee was reached during the MS 3 phase. The size of the population decreased slightly in the following LS period. As in the Upper Shaur area, no Protoliterate site is reported and the area was subsequently totally deserted by the end of the LS period.

Table 5
Number of Sites, by Period in the Lower Shaur Region (Mosaic H)

PERIOD	No. of sites	% of total	New sites	Sites continued	Sites abandoned
PL	-	-	-	-	3
LS2	3	75	0	3	1
LS1	3	75	0	3	0
MS3	4	100	2	2	0
MS1	2	50	2	0	0
ES	-	-	-	-	-
AS	-	-	-	-	-

The Pilot Area (Table 6, Mosaic maps C,F,I, Figs. 14,17,20).The majority of the sites are located in this area. Fifteen sites were found altogether. ES, represented by four sites, is the earliest period attested. If all fourteen of the MS sites were simultaneously occupied, then the maximum population would have been reached during the MS 3 phase. After the MS 3 phase, a gradual, then subsequent sharp drop in the number of sites occurred. In the following LS 1 phase no new sites were founded, and some of the settlements of the previous period were abandoned. A dramatic abandonment, however, occurred at the end of the LS 2 phase when 8 sites were deserted. Whereas the ES sites are scattered on the plain,[1] later settlements, especially in the southern part of this area, tended to be in clusters within sight of one another.

Table 6
Number of Sites, by Period, in the Pilot Area (Mosaics C,F,I)

PERIOD	No. of sites	% of total	New sites	Sites continued	Sites abandoned
PL	3	20	0	3	8
LS2	10	66	0	10	5
LS1	12	80	1	11	3
MS3	14	93	6	8	0
MS1	5	33	4	1	2
ES	4	26	4	4	0
AS	-	-	-	-	-

<u>Greater Dez (Table 7, Mosaic maps G and J, Figs. 18,21)</u>.The general settlement pattern is similar to that of the Pilot Area. This area was first settled in the ES period with three sites (see map for their proximity). These early sites continued to be occupied in the following MS 1 phase, when three more sites were founded and the population doubled. Later, during the MS 3 phase, seven more sites were occupied and the area reached its peak population with 13 sites. The population and settlement pattern remained unchanged in the following LS 1 phase. In the LS 2 phase, one site was abandoned. The sharp drop in the population occurred with the advent of the Protoliterate period when the number of sites dropped from 12 to 2. It is interesting to note that no new sites were founded during this period, and that the two Protoliterate sites had been occupied since the MS period.

Table 7
Number of Sites, by Period, in the Greater Dez Area (Mosaics G, J)

PERIOD	No. of sites	% of total	New sites	Sites continued	Sites abandoned
PL	2	15	0	2	10
LS2	12	92	0	12	1
LS1	13	100	0	13	0
MS3	13	100	7	6	0
MS1	6	46	3	3	0
ES	3	23	3	0	0
AS	-	-	-	-	-

<u>Greater Dez East Area (Table 8, Mosaic map D, Fig. 15)</u>.This region was not occupied until the MS period. One site marks the initial settlement of the area. A dramatic change in the area took place later in the period when the number of sites rose precipitously with seven new settlements. This situation remained unchanged until the end of the LS 2 phase when all the sites were abandoned.

Table 8
Number of Sites, by Period, in the Greater Dez East Area (Mosaic D)

PERIOD	No. of sites	% of total	New sites	Sites continued	Sites abandoned
PL	-	-	-	-	7
LS2	7	87	0	7	1
LS1	8	100	0	8	0
MS3	8	100	7	1	0
MS1	1	12	1	0	0
ES	-	-	-	-	-
AS	-	-	-	-	-

1. Since Early Susiana layers may have been buried under massive deposits of later periods, this situation may be artificial.

TABLE 9. VARIOUS PERIODS ATTESTED AT EACH SITE.

SITE NUMBER	PL	LS 2	LS 1	MS 3	MS 1	ES	AS
G II	—	X	X	X	X	—	—
G III	—	X	X	X	—	—	—
G IV	—	X	X	X	—	—	—
G V	—	—	X	X	—	—	—
G VI	—	X	X	X	—	—	—
G VII	—	X	X	X	—	—	—
G VIII	—	X	X	X	—	—	—
G IX	—	X	X	X	—	—	—
G 25-I	—	X	X	X	X	—	—
G 25-II	—	X	X	X	X	X?	—
G 25-III	—	?	X	X	X	—	—
G 25-IV	—	—	X	X	—	—	—
G 26-I	—	X	X	—	—	—	—
G 26-II	—	X	X	X	—	—	X?
G 27	—	X	X	X	—	—	—
G 31	—	X?	—	X	—	—	—
G 33-I	—	X	X	X	X?	X	—
G 33-II	—	—	X	X	—	X	X?
G 33-III	X	—	—	X	—	—	—
G 33-IV	—	X	—	X	—	—	X?
G 38	X	X	X	X	X	—	—
G 56	—	—	X	X	—	X?	—
G 60	—	X	X	X	X	—	—
G 61	—	X	X	X	—	—	—
G 62	—	X	X	X	—	X	—
G 64	—	X	X	X	X	X	—
G 79-I	—	X	X	X	—	—	—
G 79-II	—	X	X	X	—	—	—
G 81	—	X	X	X	—	—	—
G 86-I	—	X	X	X	X	—	—
G 86-II	—	X	X	X	X	X	—
G 87	—	—	X	X	X	—	—
G 93	X	X?	X	X	—	—	—
G 97	—	X	X	X	—	—	—
G 97A	X	X	X	X	X	X	—
G 115	—	X	X	X	—	—	—
G 131	X	X	X	X	—	X?	—
G 145	—	X	—	X	—	—	—
G 157	—	X	X	—	—	—	—
G 161	—	X	X	X	X	—	—
G 171	—	X	—	X	X?	—	—
G 172	—	—	X	X	—	—	—
G 176	—	X	X	X	—	—	—
TOTAL	5	35	38	41	14	9	3

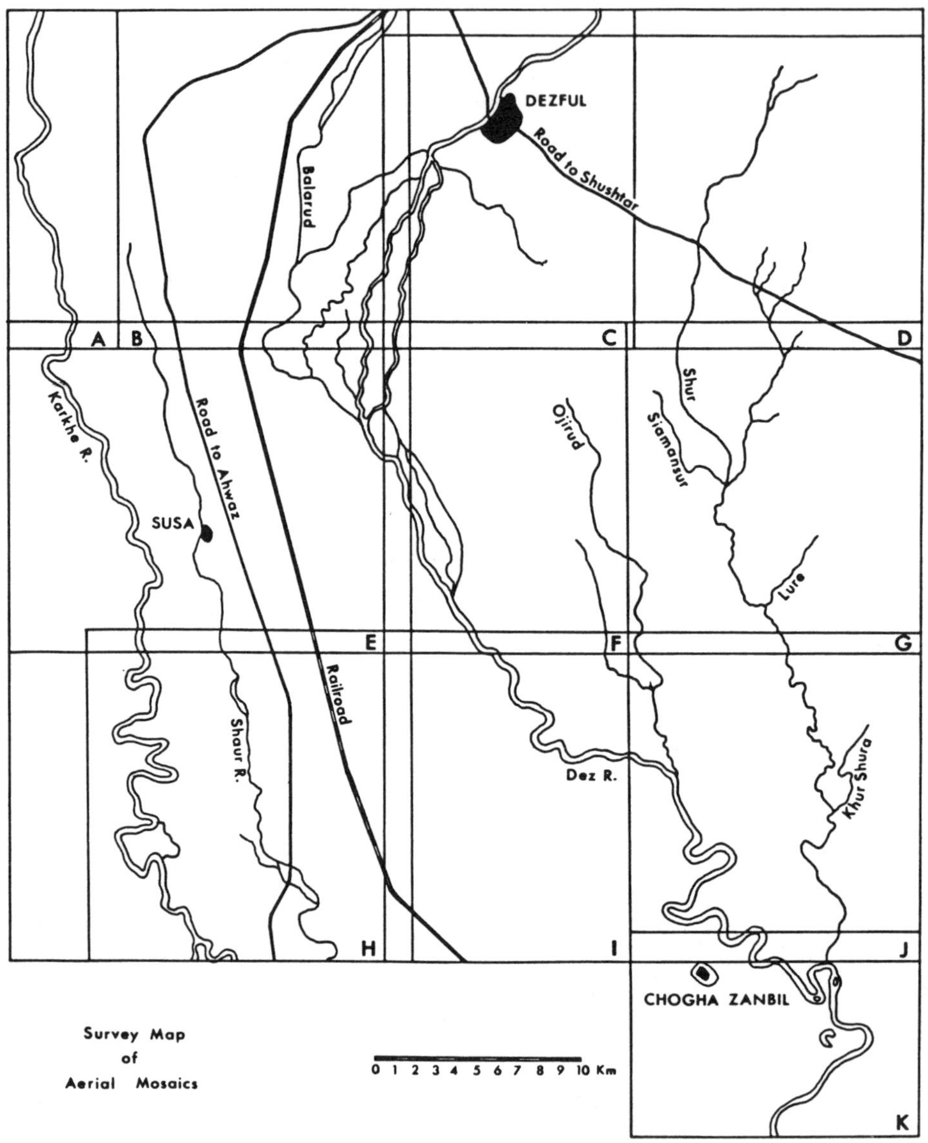

Figure 11. Survey map of aerial mosaics of Upper Khuzestan.

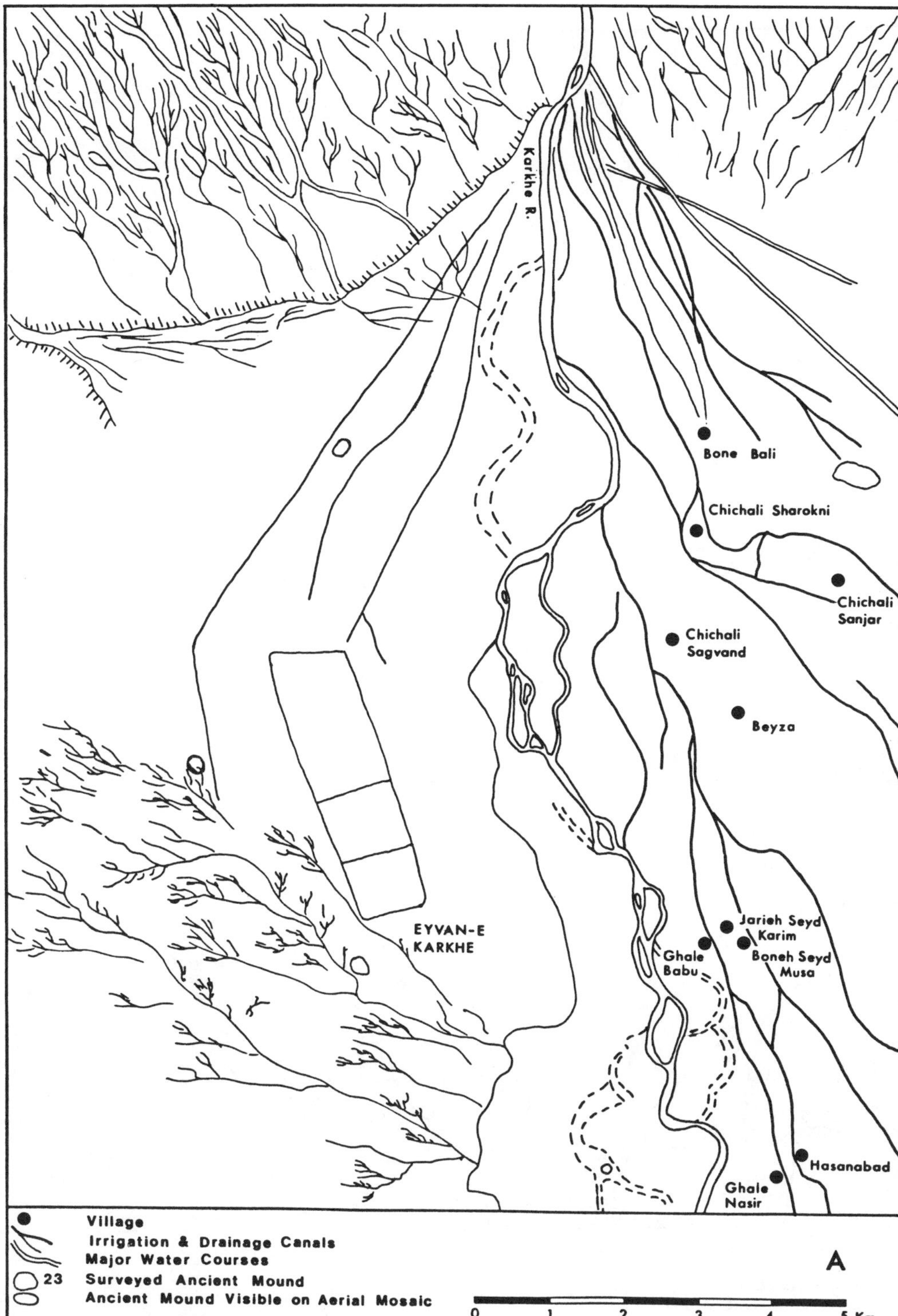

Figure 12. Detailed map of villages, ancient sites, and irrigation canals in Mosaic A.

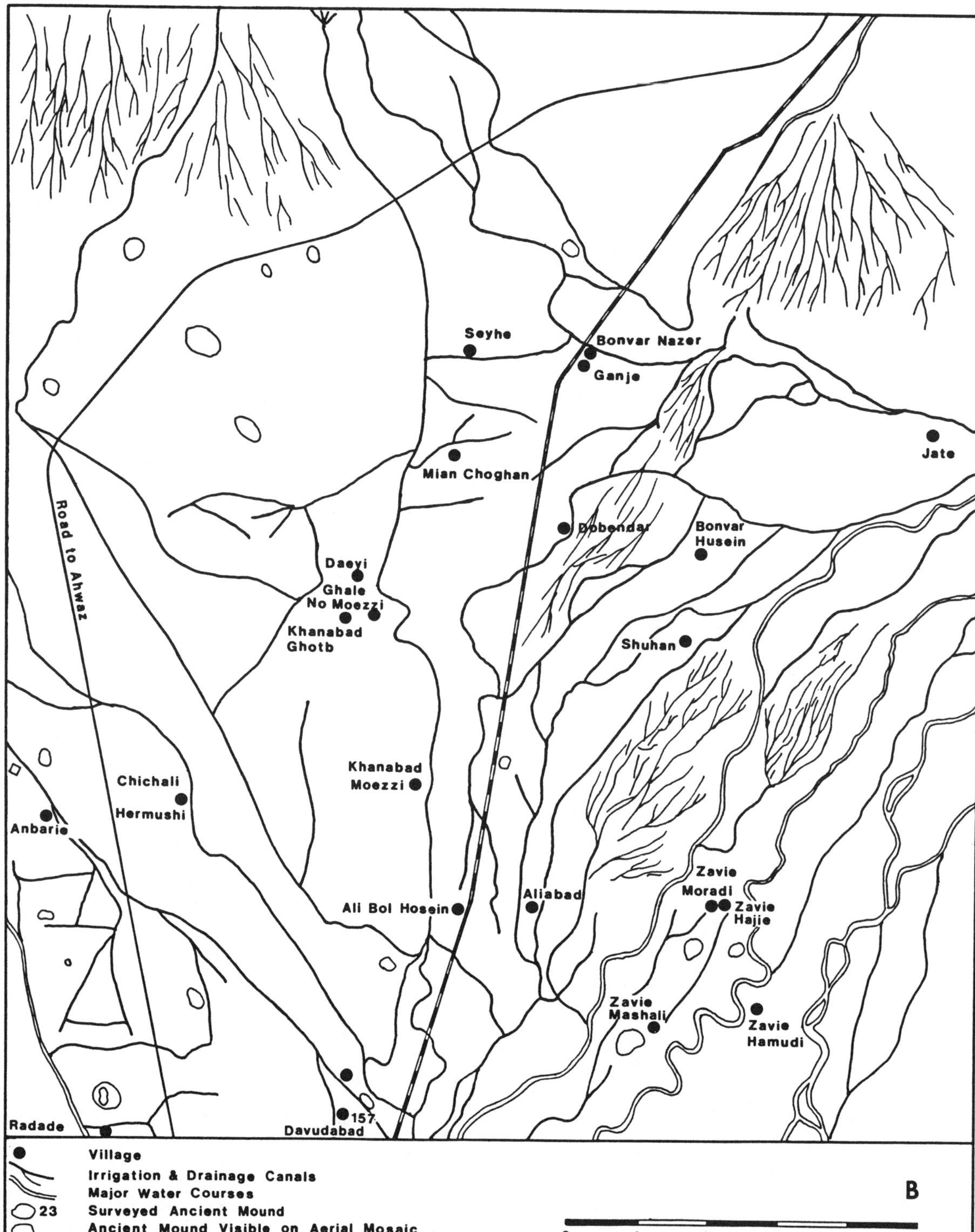

Figure 13. Detailed map of villages, ancient sites, and irrigation canals in Mosaic B.

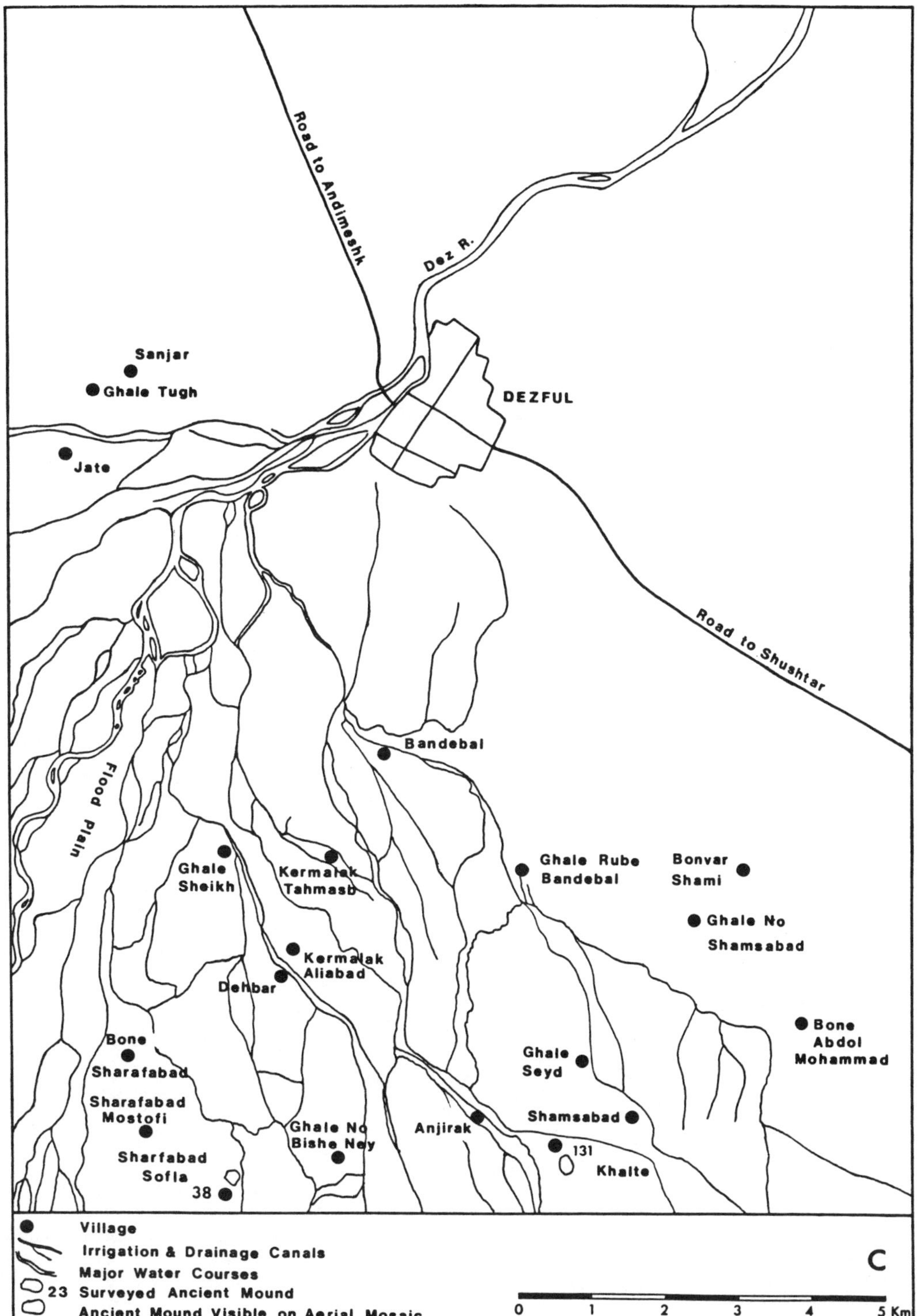

Figure 14. Detailed map of villages, ancient sites, and irrigation canals in Mosaic C.

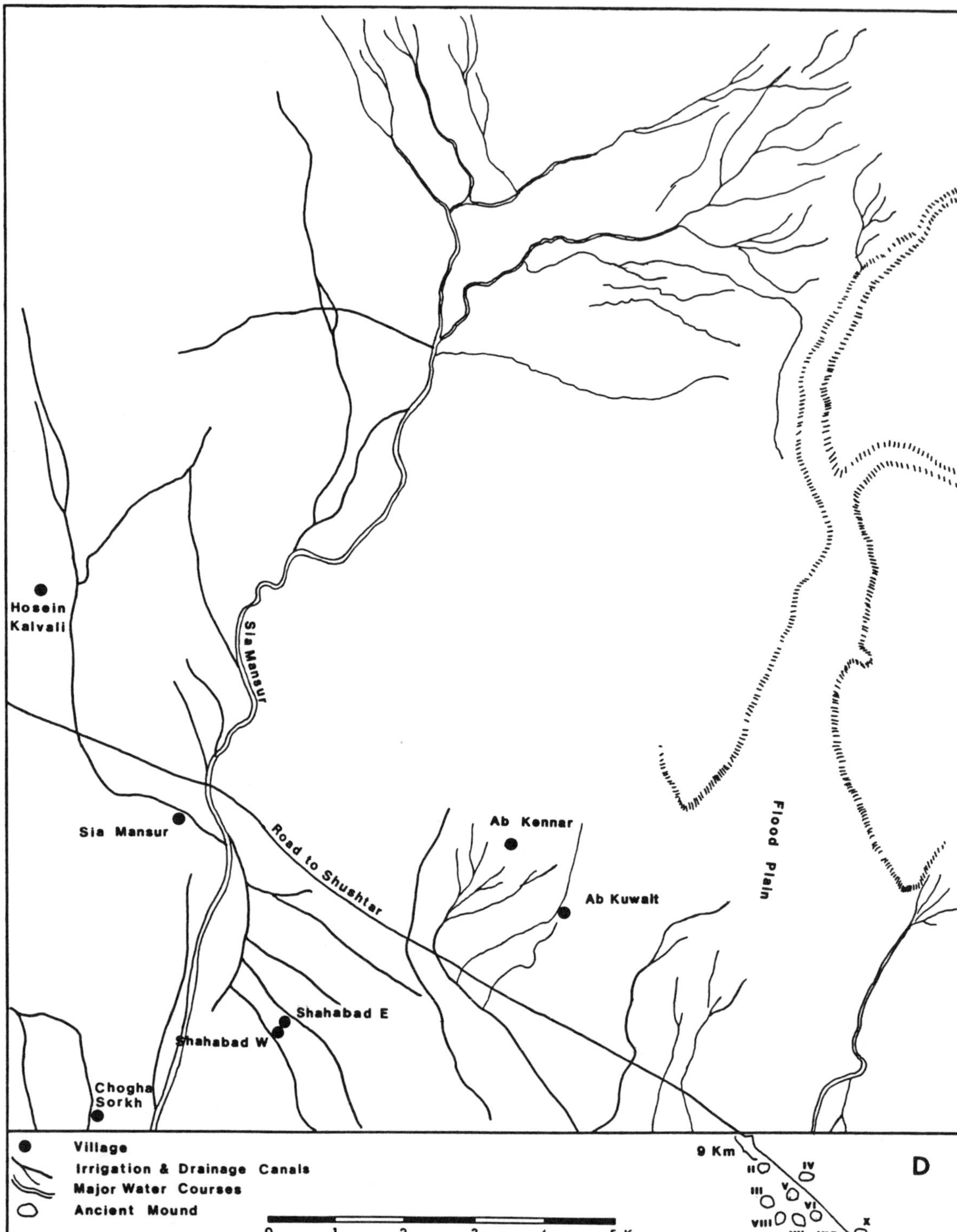

Figure 15. Detailed map of villages, ancient sites, and irrigation canals in Mosaic D.

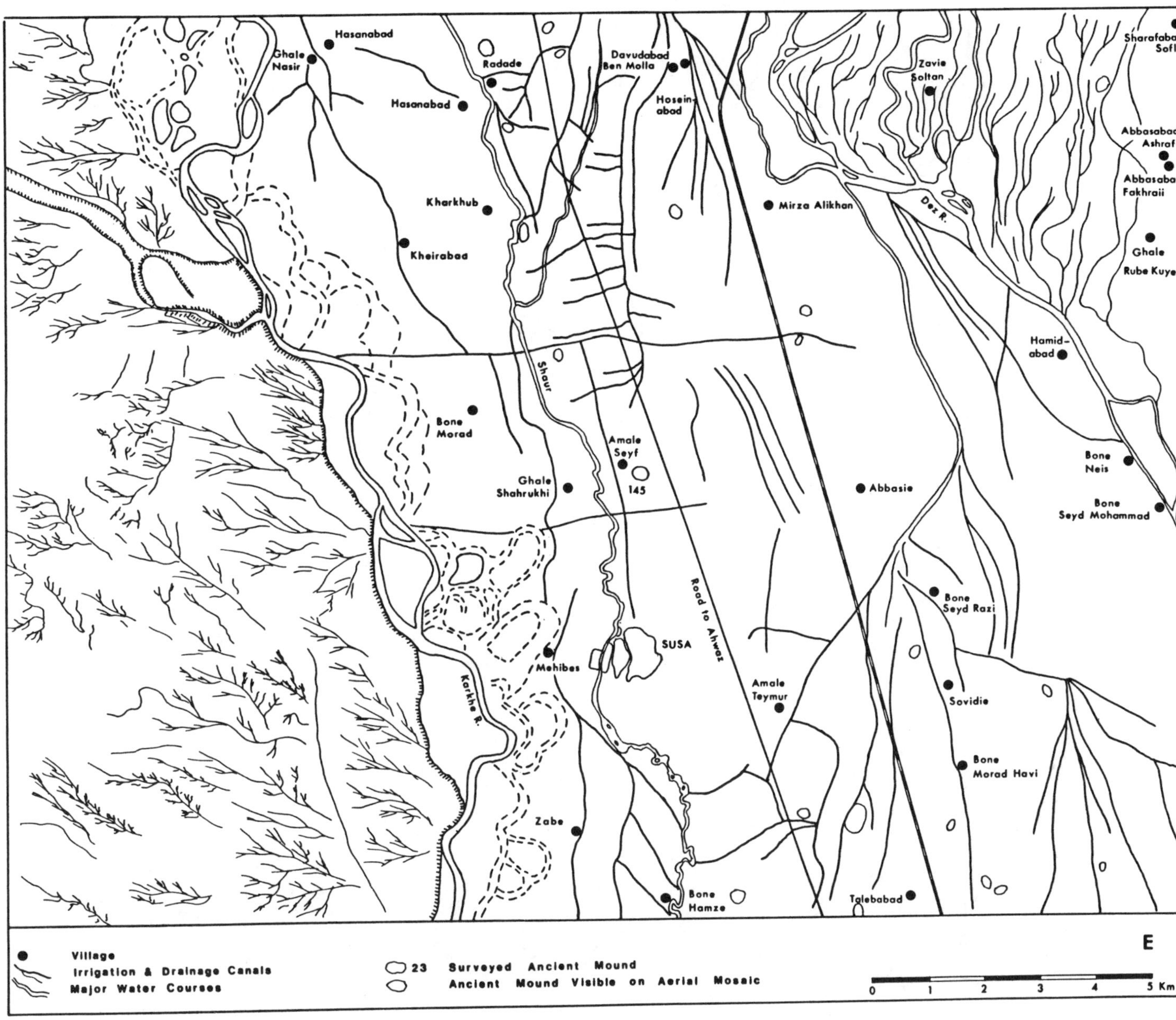

Figure 16. Detailed map of villages, ancient sites, and irrigation canals in Mosaic E.

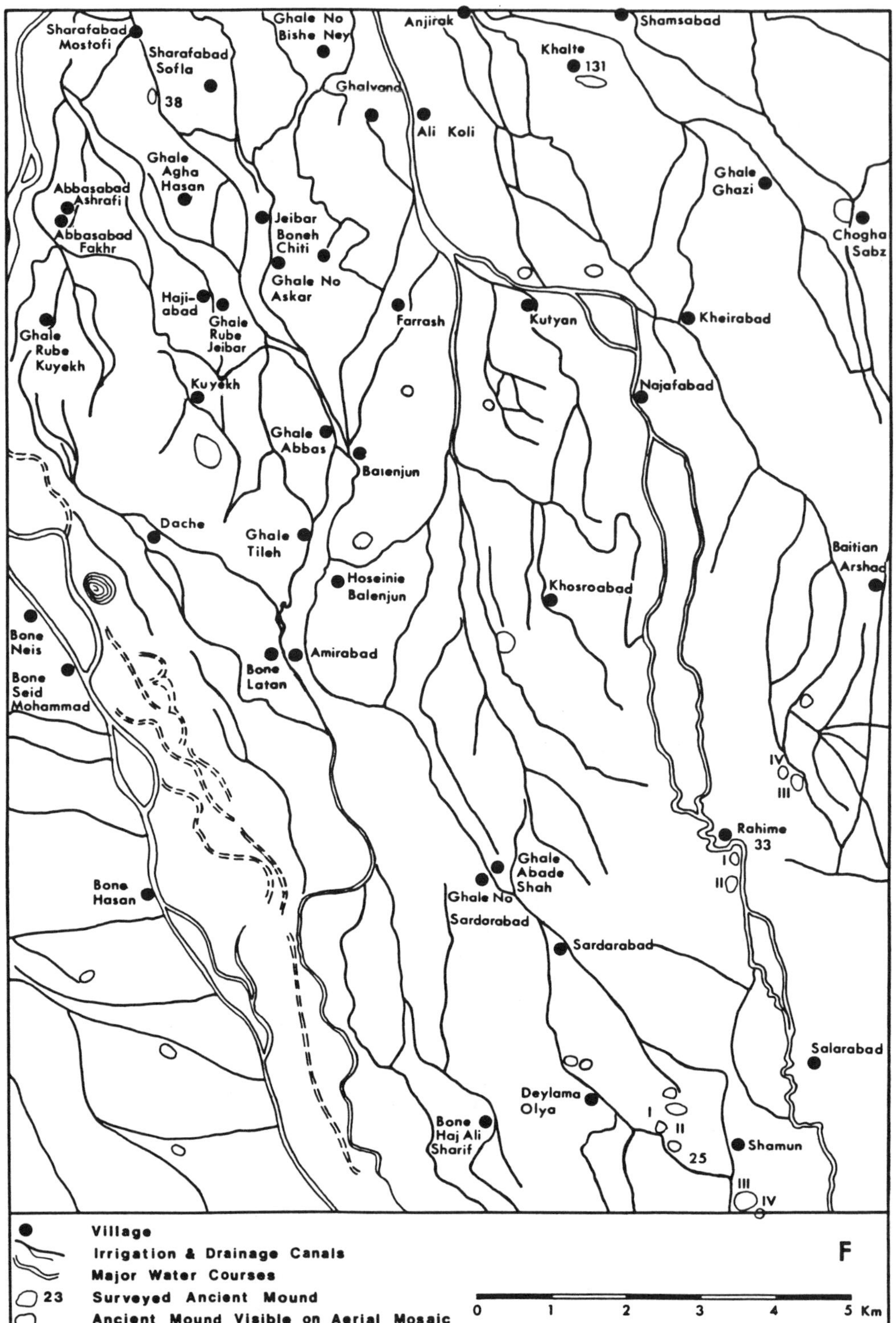

Figure 17. Detailed map of villages, ancient sites, and irrigation canals in Mosaic F.

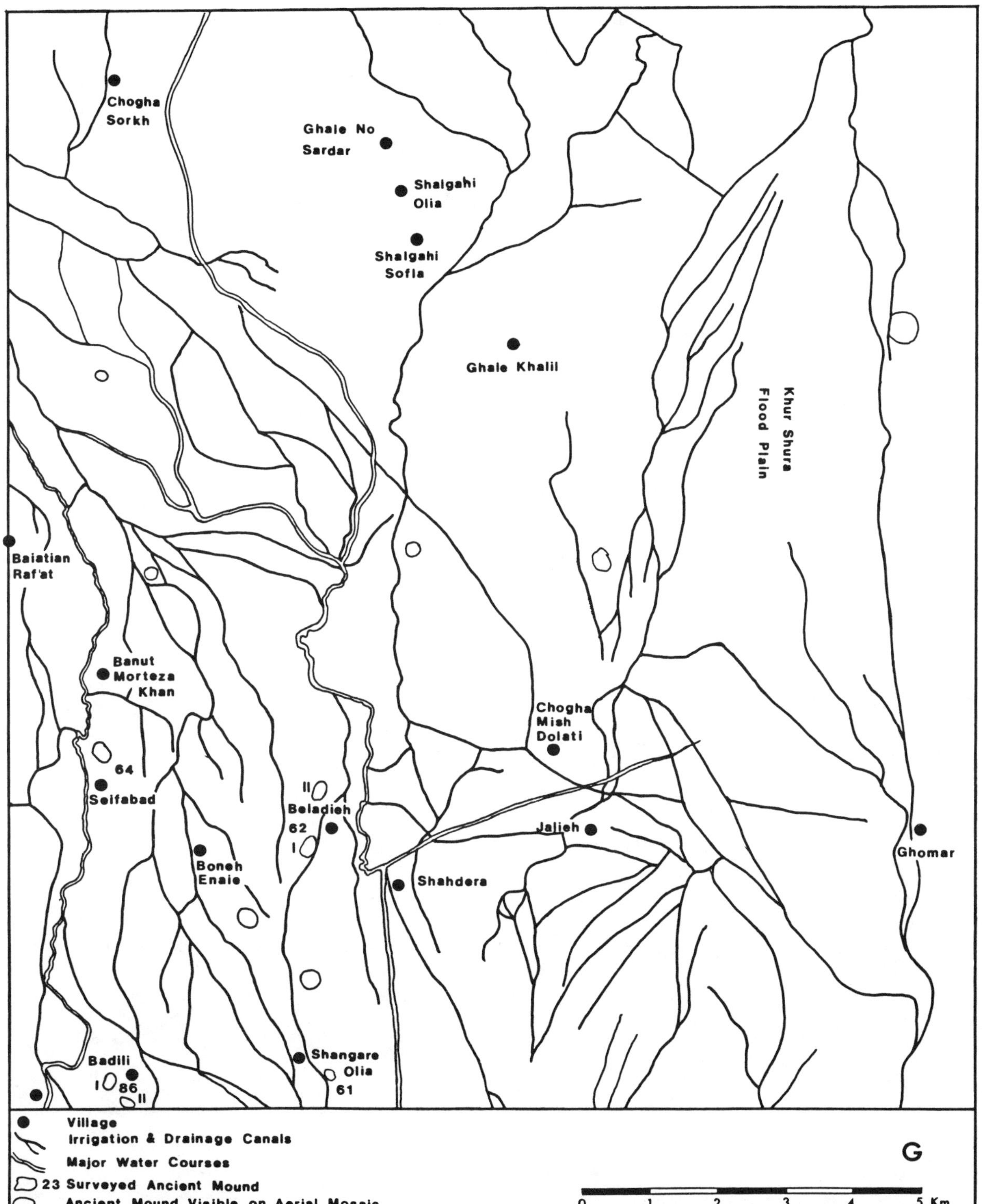

Figure 18. Detailed map of villages, ancient sites, and irrigation canals in Mosaic G.

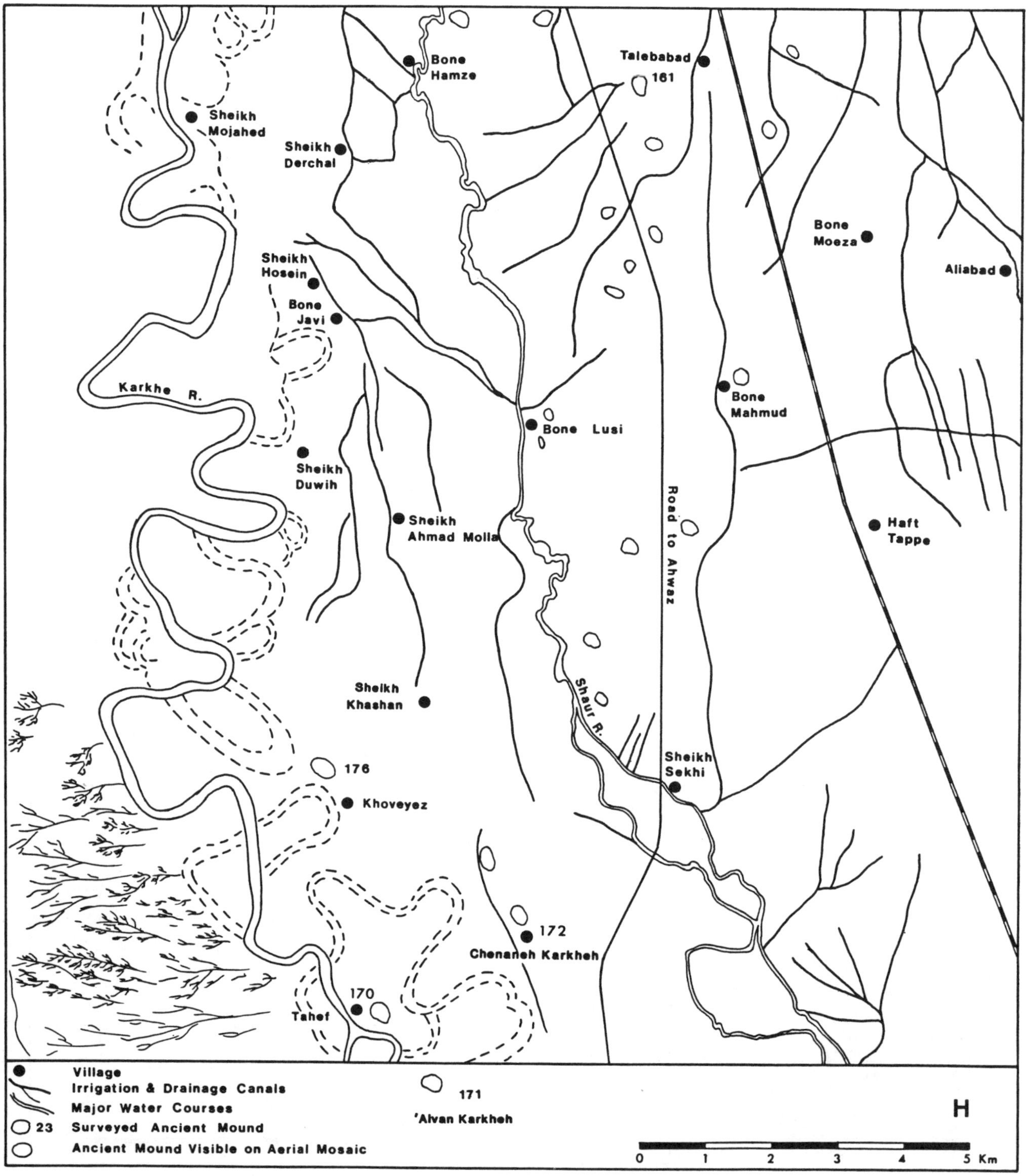

Figure 19. Detailed map of villages, ancient sites, and irrigation canals in Mosaic H.

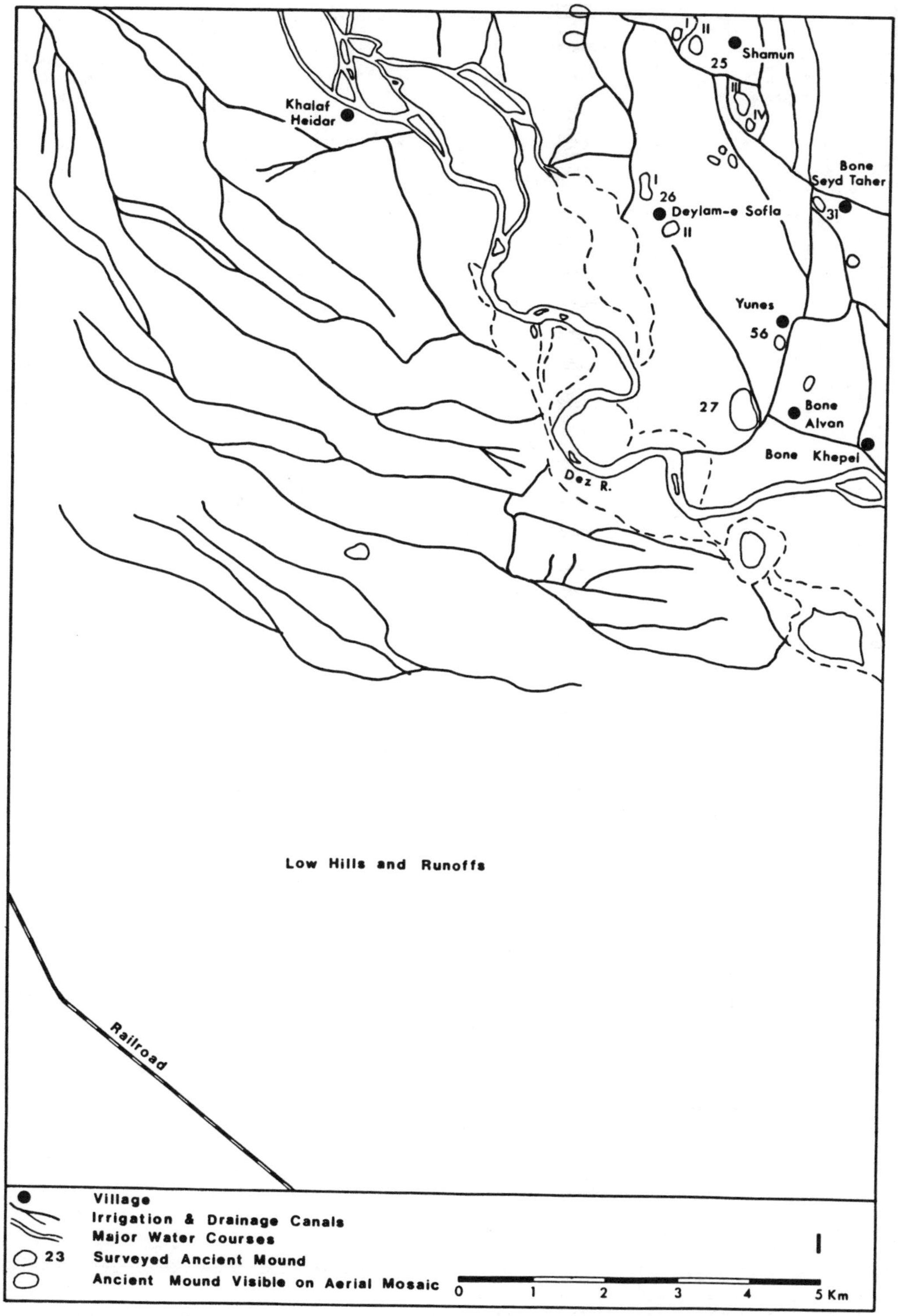

Figure 20. Detailed map of villages, ancient sites, and irrigation canals in Mosaic I.

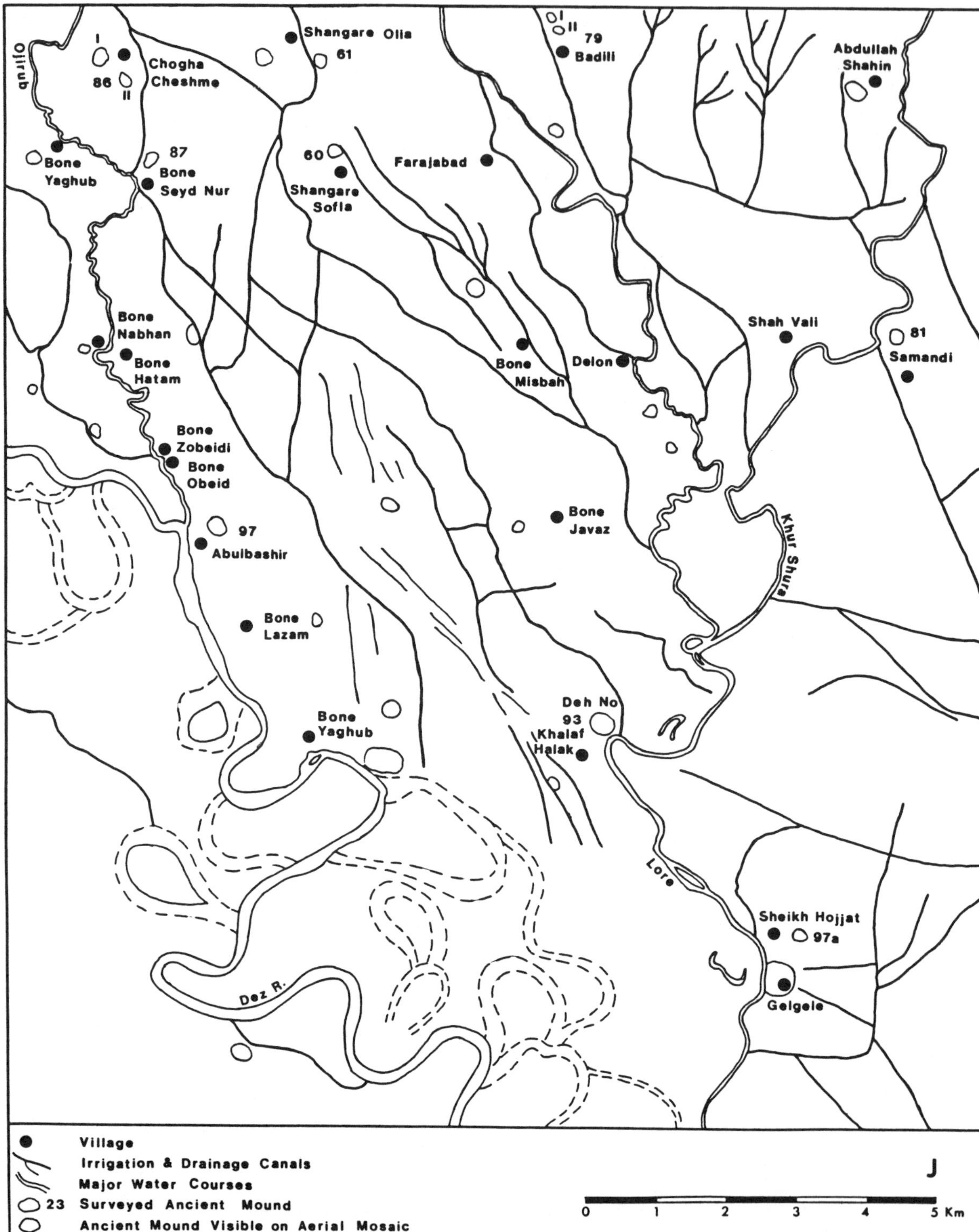

Figure 21. Detailed map of villages, ancient sites, and irrigation canals in Mosaic J.

Figure 22. Detailed map of villages ancient sites, and irrigation canals in Mosaic K.

5

THE SUSIANA PLAIN IN THE PREHISTORIC PERIODS

Formative Susiana

The earliest evidence of human activities in the plain of Susiana comes from only one site, Chogha Banut. The initial phase seems to have been aceramic with hearths, flint blades, and stone vessels (Kantor 1977:23). The following period, Formative Susiana, is characterized by simple pottery, known as Film-painted ware (Kantor 1977:23; 1979:39). Although very little is known about this early phase of settlement in Susiana, its existence is important in the study of the origins of agriculture and village life in Susiana and its relation to similar developments in the Zagros mountains.

Archaic Susiana 1-3

This period is rarely represented in surface surveys and is primarily known from the excavations at Tulaii, Chogha Mish, Boneh Fazili, and Chogha Banut. Tulaii, Chogha Mish, and Boneh Fazili were founded in this period. The latter two sites and Chogha Banut are very close to one another, whereas Tulaii, known as a campsite, is situated some 40 km to the northwest, between Deh Luran and Susiana (Hole 1974). The early deposits at Chogha Mish and Tulaii are not associated with substantial architecture; however, there is evidence at Chogha Banut of cigar-shaped bricks which became common during the AS period (Kantor 1977:22-23). The presence at Chogha Mish of solid walls made of long, cigar-shaped mudbricks, dating to the AS 3 phase, provides evidence for the continuity of a long settled life in the Susiana plain shortly after the Formative period.

The AS period is characterized by the presence of a plain, vegetal-tempered ware. The occurrence of this ware throughout the entire Archaic sequence without any major changes in fabric or in shape suggests that AS represents a developing culture with no break. The stratified succession of a series of decorated wares, however, has been used to distinguish three phases. Based on stratigraphic position and stylistic analysis of the archaeological materials, the Archaic Susiana period is divided into three phases, AS 1-3 (Kantor 1973:17-18). The earliest, AS 1, was found at Chogha Mish, Chogha Banut, and Boneh Fazili. It is marked by a decorated, straw-tempered ware, which is termed "painted burnished," usually slipped and highly burnished (Kantor 1976:184). The Red-line ware marks the succeeding AS 2 phase. It has a dense sandy fabric and is decorated with a fugitive red paint. The most frequent motif is chevron bands bordered by solid triangles. The Matt-painted and the Close-line, two wares entirely different both in fabric and decoration, represent the final phase of the AS period. The former ware has a vegetal inclusion, and the latter has fine mineral tempering. The Matt-painted ware is related to the earlier Archaic Susiana wares, but the Close-line ware has no antecedent in the earlier phases. The Close-line ware also appeared in Deh Luran, where it is known as "Chogha Mami Transitional." Although in general, this ware shows affinities with the ceramic of the Samarra period in upper Mesopotamia, recent excavations at Tell Oueili, near Larsa in southern Mesopotamia, have revealed stratified layers that predate 'Obaid 1/Eridu and contain pottery similar to the Close-line ware of Chogha Mish (Calvet 1983, 1985, 1986).

Little is known about the nature of the changes that took place during the AS 3 phase. The appearance of the new pottery in Deh Luran has been linked to the arrival of a new people in the "Chogha Mami

Transitional" phase and to a number of economic, demographic, and, ultimately, social changes (Hole 1987:35). However, the continuity of other artifacts during this phase, as in Susiana, suggests that such developments took place without violence or displacement of the local population. In Deh Luran, the appearance of the Close-line ware coincided with the introduction of "six-row hulled barley, free threshing hexaploid wheat, large-seeded lentil and flax, and cattle and dogs" (ibid.).

Except for the pottery sequence of this period, and the simple food production and tool-making techniques, little is known about the origins of these early inhabitants of the Susiana plain and their relations with the earlier and contemporary highland populations. These early communities practiced a mixed economy of farming and animal husbandry, supplemented by hunting and gathering. Their egalitarian nature is suggested by the archaeological evidence. Except for obsidian as a common denominator material among the early communities of the Near East, there is not much evidence of contact between communities. However, material culture from Tappeh Sang-e Chakhmaq (Masuda 1972), in northeastern Iran, shows affinities to the Archaic pottery assemblage, suggesting, perhaps, a common origin if not contact.

Early Susiana

A hybrid of the AS 1-2 ceramics and the Close-line tradition was developed in the ES period. Early Susiana pottery is a clear descendant of AS 3 ceramics, with the Close-line as main source of inspiration. The reserved areas in the painted designs retained their importance and continued, but the finely drawn parallel lines, so typical of the AS 3 phase, had become sloppy and almost coalesced. Others designs, such as the alternating triangles bordered with solid bands, continued even into the much later Late Susiana period (cf., for example, Fig. 28D and Dollfus 1975, Fig. 22:2; also see references to Fig. 28D in the Appendix).[1] Although the ES ceramic has many similarities with that of Eridu ('Obaid 1) in southern Mesopotamia, many ES painted forms and the dominant plain flanged vessels are not paralleled there. Despite a great number of similarities among the potteries of Susiana, Deh Luran, and southern Mesopotamia, regional developments along separate lines existed. It was not until the following MS 3 phase that the Susiana pottery became distinct from that of contemporary Mesopotamia and developed along different lines.

In the ES period, the population was still low. The some sixteen sites reported from other surveys (Hole 1987:40, Fig. 9c) and the seven sites reported here may not even have been occupied simultaneously (ibid.). The evidence from Jafarabad 6-4 suggests that people raised sheep, goats, and cattle, and grew domesticates such as wheat, barley, lentils, and peas. This diet was supplemented by hunting boars and turtles, fishing, and gathering shellfish (Dollfus 1975:61). The only comprehensive architectural plan of this period comes from Jafarabad (ibid., Figs. 6-8). It indicates a nucleated community which lived in units with large rooms and storage facilities, but without much open space in between. After three major rebuildings, the site was deserted by the end of Early Susiana period.

Middle Susiana

During the MS 1 phase, there was still an inter-regional pottery tradition, since close parallels still existed between the ceramics of Susiana, Deh Luran ("Khazineh Phase") and southern Mesopotamia ('Obaid 2/Haji Mohammad and Eridu XII-IX, Safar et al. 1981:176, Figs. 85-89). The MS period was a time of population increase in southwestern Iran, as indicated by this and other surveys (Adams 1962, Hole 1987, Dittmann 1984). It was also a period of expansion/migration from Mesopotamia to more marginal regions, such as those along the Persian Gulf coast (Oates et al. 1977). By the middle of the period, the number of sites reached a maximum. Chogha Mish grew to be the largest settlement, a development paralleled in Deh Luran, where at least two sites grew more than three hectares (Hole 1987:37, 40). The sheer size of Chogha Mish, about 15 hectares, indicates that it attained a central position in the Susiana plain. Though the architecture is mostly residential, the evidence of a 10 X 15 m monumental building with thick plastered walls (1.50 m thick) suggests the existence of a nondomestic architecture as well. The stacks of jars found in a back room of this building imply storage facilities and perhaps distribution of goods, but the presence of many complete flint blades, flint chips and nodules gives an indication of a workshop (Kantor 1976:27-28).

The Middle Susiana period may have been ended by violence, as suggested by the evidence of fire at Chogha Mish. This large Middle Susiana center, along with some contemporary sites, were abandoned, not to be reoccupied for perhaps several generations. Similar developments occurred in Deh Luran. Helbaek used botanical analysis to look for environmental factors in the termination of the Bayat phase in Deh Luran (Hole et al. 1969:364). Helbaek postulates that millennia of land use in the area had caused salinization which forced the population to search for new lands. However, Kirkby argues that the plain is not subject to drastic salinization (1977:255). Whatever the local causes for the desertion of some sites in Susiana and Deh Luran, there must have been some interregional factors which contributed to such developments in the mid-fifth millennium in southwestern Iran.

Late Susiana

The results of the present survey indicate that there was a slight decrease in the population size in this phase. The number of sites dropped from 41 to 38 in the LS 1 phase and from 38 to 35 in the LS 2 phase. Other surveys indicate that this steady decline continued until the number of sites dropped to 18 just before the Protoliterate period (Hole 1987:42). By the end of the LS 2 phase, the population of the plain must have been very small. Except for Susa, most of the sites were less than two hectares to under one hectare (ibid.)

By the end of the MS period, the interregional contact between southwestern Iran and Mesopotamia seems to have ceased. There appears to have been a reorientation of interregional contacts. The LS was a period of increasing contact with the highland, as suggested by the general similarities among the regional ceramics of southwestern Iran. A general westward shift of the settlements in Susiana also occurred. Large cemeteries of Hakalan and Parchineh, in the Zagros mountains, appeared during this period (Vanden Berghe 1970, 1973, 1975). These cemeteries were not associated with any settlement and are located in an area unsuitable for grain agriculture, suggesting their use by mobile pastoralists. Similar cemeteries of later historical periods in this region reinforce this attribution (idem, 1973). It is, therefore, tempting to link the destruction of the Burnt Building at Chogha Mish, its desertion, the westward movement of the population in the lowland, the similarities among the regional ceramics in southwestern Iran, and the appearance of the isolated highland cemeteries. Admittedly, the evidence is not strong and much research is needed to warrant such linkage.

The presumed relation between the increased activities of mobile pastoralists and the westward shift of Susiana settlements becomes more attractive when we note that the eastern part of the Susiana plain traditionally has been, and still is, the locus of the winter pasture for the mobile pastoralists of the region. If this environmental niche was also used in antiquity, as one might expect, then the westward shift of the settled community may also indicate an increase in the activities of such transhuman groups in the area.

In the Late Susiana period, Susa replaced Chogha Mish as the largest site on the plain, a status that Susa retained for several millennia. A massive mudbrick platform was constructed probably after a short period of occupation. It was topped by a monumental building of uncertain nature. Whether this project was completed in the course of several generations or in one attempt is not known. But such an undertaking required a tremendous amount of labor, and so it must have been accomplished before the population of the plain decreased.

Towards the end of the LS period, Susa shrank in size to about 5 hectares. It has been suggested that the disappearance of the long tradition of Susiana painted pottery, marking a new era, should be explained by as yet "unresolved problems of social organization rather than strictly economic or subsistence affairs." (Johnson 1987:286). Parallel transformations in Mesopotamia and Fars suggest interregional phenomena that underlie these transformations by the middle of the fourth millennium B.C. Any attempt to explain these transformations must recognize and formulate regional and interregional contributing factors.

NOTES

1. For a detailed comparison see Kantor 1985:34-64.

6

SUMMARY AND CONCLUSION

Much of the material presented here dates to the fifth and early fourth millennia, and, as such, provides additional information for the analysis of socioeconomic and demographic developments in the prestate societies of southwestern Iran. Moreover, since the present collection, being one of the earliest surveys and, so far, the only one published in its entirety, it can provide data which may have been lost to subsequent archaeological surveys. This is particularly important because some of the sites reported here may have been destroyed by agricultural activities and road and canal construction, or may have been simply missed in subsequent surveys. Of the 43 sites listed, catalogued, and dated in this survey, for example, only five, Sham'un, Deylameh, Beladiyeh, Shangareh, and Deh No, appear in Adams' list. The rest do not appear among the sites for which he recorded names.

Given the limitations of Gremliza's survey and circumstances under which it was conducted, it might be expected to provide a picture of the settlement pattern different from those of later surveys. However, in general, the results--in terms of the relative number of sites for individual periods and relative changes in settlement patterns--are similar to the results of later surveys, despite the smaller number of sites recorded. For example, although only thirteen sites were recorded for the Greater Dez area, the data are internally consistent in terms of fluctuation in population size and number of sites, producing a similar picture to that reported by later surveys with greater number of sites. This similarity may well be fortuitous.

Only three sites (G26-II, G33-II, and G33-IV) in the Pilot Area may possibly have AS material (Fig. 17, Tables 5,8). Later surveys reported, however, 25 mounds and possibly three flint sites for this period (Hole 1987:39, Fig. 7b). Seven sites are positively dated to the ES period with two other possible additional sites, making a total of nine. Other surveys report 16 sites for this period, mostly scattered in the upper part of the plain with no particular spatial distribution pattern (ibid.:40, Fig. 7c).

In a recent study of the Susiana settlement patterns (ibid.:40-41, Table 10, Fig. 9c-d), ES and MS 1, on the one hand, and MS 3 and LS 1, on the other, have been lumped together as two long periods, Susiana c-d. In the present study, these periods are separated and sites are dated to each individual phase. The pattern that emerges is one of steady increase in the number of sites until a maximum is reached in the MS 3 phase. There is a slight drop in the number of sites in the following LS 1 phase, with no apparent change in the pattern of site distribution on the plain. Chogha Mish, which enjoyed a central position because of its sheer size and location, and which probably once had a population of 1000-1500 people, was deserted. No sites attained such status until Susa was founded. By the end of LS 2 there was a sharp drop in the number of sites.

The beginning of the MS period is marked by a sharp increase in the number of settlements. Although these settlements do not exhibit any particular pattern of clustering, sites in the eastern part of the plain seem to be much closer to one another. Security may have been a factor that contributed to the clustering of the northern and northeastern sites, but it was certainly not important in western and south central Khuzestan. With regard to the observed westward movement of the Susiana settlements and the appearance of the highland communal burials, it is interesting to mention here the observation made by Hole that "...sites were often occupied for only short periods, then abandoned for a time and reoccupied. About half of sites changed status from occupied to unoccupied or vice versa ..., implying that settlements were unstable and that land was not particularly scarce and therefore not valuable" (Hole 1987:42 [emphasis added], Table 8). This westward movement continued until the region east of the Shur river became almost completely deserted right before the Protoliterate period. Even during the PL period when there was an increase in the size of the population, only six sites are reported from this area (ibid., Fig. 10).

The founding of Susa, according to the analysis presented here, occurred sometime during the latter part of the LS 1 phase, when contacts between the lowland and the highland increased rapidly. This proposition is based partly on the similarities among regional ceramic traditions. These similarities may have been the result of increased interaction between the lowland and highland, which probably developed out of increasing demand for various local commodities of both regions. This development may have been the result of the growth of regional elite in both the lowland and the highland.

Although the socioeconomic spheres of the Susiana plain must certainly have been dominated by its sedentary population during the LS period, I have argued (Alizadeh 1988a, 1988b) that control of socioeconomic affairs in Fars during the same period may have been exercised by its mobile pastoralist population, possibly with Bakun as its center. If the highland cemeteries are evidence of developed, organized mobile pastoralist groups in southwestern Iran, one can reasonably assume that the regional centers maintained their "contact" through these mobile groups who were well suited for long distance trade as intermediaries. This suggestion is helpful in describing the mechanism through which certain ceramic traits became widespread and common in Fars, Susiana, Deh Luran, Behbahan, and the central and eastern Zagros mountains. The subsequent appearance of copper objects in Fars, Susiana, and the Zagros mountains may also be linked to this mechanism.[1] In connection with the long-distance trade between the lowland and the highland, it is important to mention here that recent archaeological surveys in the eastern Zagros mountains and west of Esfahan have discovered several sites with mixed ceramics of the LS 1 and Siyalk III 1-3.[2]

Since the mobile pastoralist way of life is an environmental and, sometimes, political adaptation, one can safely assume that until industrial life became dominant in Iran in the early 1930s, this strategy of coping with the environment had not changed drastically. This is particularly true for the vertical mobile pastoralism of the Zagros mountains, since this type of pastoralism utilizes certain migration patterns imposed by the environment and regional topography, with constant use of certain ecological niches and resources. This situation makes seasonal migration of great importance in vertical mobile pastoralism. On average, a tribal family would strike and re-pitch its tent 120 times in a year. For example, the Qashqaii make a round trip of about 1000 kilometers each year, which requires a great deal of information for the annual migration to be conducted as efficiently and peacefully as possible (see Cooper 1925; Spooner 1972:122-131). Each of the major tribes in Fars has what is called locally "Il rah", or tribal route. Each tribe travels through its own Il rah. The tribes have traditional schedules of departure and of occupation of a region, affairs that depend on several environmental and social factors (see Varjavand 1967:28 ff; Barth 1964:5-7).

These factors require very careful planning and scheduling, and maximum cooperation to minimize the violent conflicts that might arise if two or more tribes tried simultaneously either to pass an Il rah or occupy the same region while migrating.[3] This scheduling and cooperation also require a great amount of information processing and decision making. Barth argues that the tightly scheduled migration through the bottlenecks requires strong and effective coordinating authorities (Barth 1960:9).

Mobile pastoralism in southwestern Iran has been an elaborate adaptation to the sociopolitical, economic, and ecological environments. This adaptation appears to have been imposed initially more by ecological and geographical features than by external political influence.[4] But the constant need of pastoralists for information and cooperation seems to have been a factor that subsequently resulted in a centralized political system with a single office of the chief, welding together the seemingly dispersed tribes (Barth 1964:71 ff). Another factor thought to have contributed to this centralization is the existence of trade routes in territories under the pastoralists control (ibid., 130). In fact, before the introduction of modern roads in Iran, there were only a few natural and narrow passes linking southern and southwestern Iran to the central plateau and points east.

To summarize, the picture presented here to describe the general conditions in Susiana during the Late Susiana period does not illustrate a purely "stressful" situation created by interaction between mobile pastoralist and settled agriculturalist communities in southwestern Iran. Rather, it seems that the development of mobile pastoralism increased contact between various regional polities, which led to the exchange of information and goods, to the emulation among the heads of those polities in seeking status items, and to the development of pottery to also satisfy that need. The simultaneous development of the highly sophisticated and symbolic painted ceramics of Susiana (Pollock 1983; Hole 1984), Fars (Alizadeh 1988a, 1988b), and the Central Plateau seems to be one of the symptoms of the socioeconomic and political transformations during the late prehistoric period in Iran.

NOTES

1. Gerd-e Chelegah and Chogha Yord, surveyed by H. Nissen and Zagarell, are particularly rich in Bakun type ceramics. The materials from this survey are at Free University of Berlin. I am grateful to Hans Nissen for allowing me to examine the survey materials.

2. I am grateful to Mr. Chegini of the Archaeological Center in Tehran for showing me the materials from his surveys in the eastern Zagros during my visit to Iran last summer.

3. For the same situation and arrangements among the tribes of the Bakhtyari confederation see Garthwaite 1983:22.

4. Cf. Barth 1961:89-90, 102-103, 128-129 for comparisons between mobile pastoralists of the Zagros mountains with a degree of centralized organizations and those to the east who lack such offices.

BIBLIOGRAPHY

Adams, Robert McC.

1962 Agriculture and Urban Life in Early Southwestern Iran. Science 136:109-122.

1965 Land Behind Baghdad: A History of Settlement on the Diyala Plains. The University of Chicago Press. Chicago.

1966 The Evolution of Urban Society: Early Mesopotamian and Prehispanic Mexico. Aldine Publishing Co. Chicago.

1981 Heartland of Cities: Surveys of Ancient Settlement and Land Use on the Central Floodplain of the Euphrates.The University of Chicago Press. Chicago.

Adams, Robert McC. and Nissen, Hans J.

1972 The Uruk Countryside: The Natural Setting of Urban Societies. The University of Chicago Press. Chicago.

Alizadeh, Abbas

1988a Socio-economic and Political Complexity in Southwestern Iran During the Fifth and Fourth Millennia B.C.: The Evidence from Tall-e Bakun A. Iran 26:17-33.

1988b Mobile Pastoralism and the Development of Complex Societies in Southern Iran. Unpublished doctoral dissertation. Dept. of Near Eastern Languages and Civilizations. The University of Chicago. Chicago.

Bakker, J. W. et al.

1956 The Development of Khuzistan's Land and Water Resources. Food and Agricultural Organization of the United Nations. Rome.

Barth, Fredrik

1960 The Land Use Pattern of Migratory Tribes of South Persia. Norsk Geografisk Tidsskrift 17:1-11.

1964 Nomads of South Persia: The Basseri Tribes of the Khamseh Confederacy. Humanities Press. New York.

Beale, Thomas W.

1986 Excavations at Tepe Yahya, Iran, 1967-1975: The Early Periods. American School of Prehistoric Research Bulletin 38. Harvard University Press. Cambridge.

Caldwell, Joseph R.

1967 Investigations at Tal-i-Iblis. Illinois State Museum. Springfield.

1968 Tell-i Ghazir. Reallexikon der Assyriologie und vorderasiatischen Archäologie 3:348-355.

Calvet, Yves

1983 Le sondage profond en Y 27. *In* Jean-Louis Huot, ed., Larsa et 'Oueili, travaux de 1978-1981. Pp. 15-69. Éditions Recherche sur les Civilisation. Paris.

1985 Le debut de la période d'Obeid en Mésopotamie du sud. l'Indus aux Balkans (Recueil Jean Deshayes). Pp. 249-260. Éditions Recherche sur les Civilisation. Paris.

1986 La phase 'Oueili de l'époque d'Obeid. *In* Jean-Louis Huot, ed., Colloques international CNRS préhistoire de la Mésopotamie. Pp. 129-144. Éditions Recherche sur les Civilisation. Paris.

Canal, Denis

1978a La haute terrasse de l'Acropole de Suse. Paléorient 4:169-176.

1978b Travaux à la terrasse haute de l'acropole de Suse. Cahiers de la délégation archéologique française en Iran 9:11-56.

Carter, Elizabeth
1971 Elam in the Second Millennium B.C.: The Archaeological Evidence. Unpublished doctoral dissertation. Department of Near Eastern Languages and Civilizations, The University of Chicago. Chicago.

Contenau, Georges and Ghirshman, Roman
1935 Fouilles de Tépé Giyan, près de Néhavend, 1931-32. Librairie Orientaliste Paul Geuthner. Paris.

Cooper, M. C.
1925 Grass. G. P. Putnam's Sons. New York.

Dittmann, Reinhard
1984 Eine Randeben des Zagros in der Frühzeit: ergebnisse des Behbahan-Zuhreh surveys. Berliner Beiträge zum Vorder Orient. Band 3. Dietrich Reimer. Berlin.

Dollfus, Geneviève
1971 Les fouilles à Djaffarabad de 1969 à 1971. Cahiers de la délégation archéologique française en Iran 1.
1975 Les fouilles à Djaffarabad de 1972 à 1974, Djaffarabad, périodes I et II. Cahiers de la délégation archéologique française en Iran 5.
1978 Djaffarabad, Djowi, Bandebal: Contribution a l'étude de la Susiane au Ve millénaire et au début du IVe millénaire. Paléorient 4:141-167.
1983a Tépé Djowi. Cahiers de la Délégation archéologique française en Iran 13:17-131.
1983b Tépé Bendebal. Cahiers de la Délégation archéologique française en Iran 13:133-275.

Egami, Namio and Masuda, Seiich
1962 Marv Dasht I: The Excavations at Tall-i Bakun 1956. The Yamakawa Publishing C., LTD. Tokyo.

Egami, Namio and Sono, Tashihiko
1962 Marv Dasht II: The Excavations at Tall-i Gap 1959. The Yamakawa Publishing Co., LTD. Tokyo.

Fisher, William B.
1968 Physical Geography. *In* William B. Fisher, ed., The Cambridge History of Iran: The Land of Iran, Vol. 1:3-110. Cambridge University Press. Cambridge.

Flannery, Kent V.
1973 The Origins of Agriculture. Annual Review of Anthropology 2:271-310.

Garthwaite, Gene R.
1983 Khans and Shahs: A Documentary Analysis of the Bakhtyari in Iran. Cambridge University Press. Cambridge.

Gautier J.-L. and G. Lampre
1905 Fouilles de Moussian. Mémoires de la Mission archéologique en Perse 8:59-147. Librairie Ernest Leroux. Paris.

Ghirshman, Roman
1938 Fouilles de Sialk, Prés de Kashan, 1933, 1934, 1937. Vol. 1. Librairie Orientaliste Paul Geuthner. Paris.

Gremliza, F. G. L.
1953 Geburtshilfe in einer Persisch-arabischen Kleinstadt. Deutsche Medizinische Wochenschrift 48:1-8.

Gremliza, F. G. L.
1959 Report on the Operations of a Mobile Field Unit and on a Public Health Survey in the Dasht-e Mishan area of Khuzestan Region. Plan Organization of Iran. Tehran.
1960 Operation of a Mobile Medical Field Unit and Public Health Survey in Dez Irrigation Project Area for the Period of September 1959-June 1960, 2 volumes. Khuzestan Development Service. Ahwaz, Iran.
1962 Ecology and Endemic Diseases in the Dez Irrigation Pilot Area: A Report to the Khuzestan Water and Power Authority and Plan Organization of Iran. Development Resource Corporation. New York.
1965 A method for Measuring the Quality of Village Conditions in Less Developed Rural Areas. American Journal of Public Health 55(1):107-115.
1966 Selected Ecological Facts on Health in the Dez Pilot Irrigation Area. Development and Resources Corporation. New York.

Hansman, John
1967 Charax and the Karkheh. Iranica Antiqua 7:21-58.

Helbaek, Hans
1969 Plant Collecting, Dry Farming and Irrigation in Prehistoric Deh Luran. *In* F. Hole, Kent Flannery, and James Neely. Prehistory and Human Ecology of the Deh Luran Plain: An Early Village Sequence from Khuzistan, Iran. Memoirs of the Museum of Anthropology 1:383-426. University of Michigan. Ann Arbor.
1972 Samarran Irrigation Agriculture at Chogha Mami in Iraq. Iraq 34(1):35-48.

Hole, Frank
1969 Report on the Survey of Upper Khuzistan. Preliminary Reports of the Rice University Project in Iran, 1968-69. Department of Anthropology mimeograph. Rice University. Houston.
1974 Tepe Tula'i, an Early Campsite in Khuzistan, Iran. Paleorient 2:219-42.
1977 Studies in the Archaeological History of the Deh Luran Plain: The Excavations of Chogha Sefid. Memoirs of the Museum of Anthropology 9. The University of Michigan. Ann Arbor.
1984 Analysis of Structure and Design in Prehistoric Ceramics. World Archaeology 15:326-47.
1987 Archaeology of the Village Period. *In* Frank Hole, ed. The Archaeology of Western Iran: Settlement and Society from Prehistory to the Islamic Conquest. Smithsonian Series in Archaeological Inquiry:29-78. Smithsonian Institution Press. Washington, D.C.

Hole, Frank, Kent V. Flannery, and James A. Neely
1969 Prehistory and Human Ecology of the Deh Luran Plain: An Early Village Sequence from Khuzistan, Iran. Memoirs of the Museum of Anthropology 1. University of Michigan. Ann Arbor.

Johnson, Gregory A.
1973 Local Exchange and Early State Development in Southwestern Iran. Anthropological Paper 51. Museum of Anthropology. University of Michigan. Ann Arbor.
1987 The Changing Organization of Uruk Administration on the Susiana Plain. *In* Frank Hole, ed. The Archaeology of Western Iran: Settlement and Society from Prehistory to the Islamic Conquest. Smithsonian Series in Archaeological Inquiry:107-140. Smithsonian Institution Press. Washington, D.C.

Kantor, Helene J.
1971 Excavations at Chogha Mish and Boneh Fazili in Khuzestan. Annual Report 1970-71: 23-30. The Oriental Institute. Chicago.

Kantor, Helene J.

1972 Excavations at Chogha Mish. Annual Report 1971-72:12-18. The Oriental Institute. Chicago.

1973 Excavations at Chogha Mish. Annual Report 1972-73:10-17. The Oriental Institute. Chicago.

1975 Excavations at Chogha Mish. Annual Report 1974-75:17-26. The Oriental Institute. Chicago.

1976 The Prehistoric Cultures of Chogha Mish and Boneh Fazili. Sixth International Symposium on the Iranian Art and Archaeology 1976:177-193. Iranian Center for Archaeological Research. Tehran.

1977 Excavations at Chogha Mish and Chogha Banut. Annual Report 1976-77:15-24. The Oriental Institute. Chicago.

1978 Chogha Mish and Chogha Banut. Annual Report 1977-78:11-19. The Oriental Institute. Chicago.

1979 Chogha Mish and Chogha Banut. Annual Report 1978-79:33-39. The Oriental Institute. Chicago.

1984 Chogha Mish. Annual Report 1983-84:25-30. The Oriental Institute. Chicago.

1985 Chogha Mish. Annual Report 1984-85:34-39. The Oriental Institute. Chicago.

Kirkby, Michael J.

1977 Land and Water Resources of the Deh Luran and Khuzistan Plains. *In* Frank Hole, Studies in Archaeological History of the Deh Luran Plain. Memoirs of the Museum of Anthropology 9:251-288. University of Michigan. Ann Arbor.

Lamberg-Karlovsky, Carl C.

1970 Excavations at Tepe Yahya, Iran: 1967-1969. American School of Prehistoric Research Bulletin 27. Harvard University Press. Cambridge.

Langsdorff, Alexander and McCown, Donald E.

1942 Tall-i Bakun A: Season of 1932. Oriental Institute Publications 54. The University of Chicago Press. Chicago.

Le Breton, Louis

1947 Note sur la céramique peinte aux environs de Suse et à Suse. Mémoires de la Mission archéologique en Perse 30:120-219. Librairie Orientaliste Paul Geuthner. Paris.

1957 The Early Periods of Susa: Mesopotamian Relations. Iraq 19:79-124.

Le Brun, Alain

1971 Recherche stratigraphiques à l'Acropole de Suse (1969-1971). Cahiers de la Délégation archéologique française en Iran 1:163-214.

1978a Suse, chantier 'Acropole 1. Paléorient 4:177-192.

1978b Le niveau 17B de l'Acropole de Suse (campagne de 1972). Cahiers de la Délégation archéologique française en Iran 9:57-145.

Lees, G. M. and N. L. Falcon

1952 The Geographical History of the Mesopotamian Plains. Geographical Journal 118:24-39.

Lilenthal, David

1963 The Journal of D. E. Lilenthal. Vol. 5, The Harvest Year. Harper and Row. New York.

Masuda, Seiichi

1972 Excavation at Tappe Sang-e Çagmaq. Proceedings of the 1st Annual Symposium of Archaeological Research in Iran. Tehran.

Mecquenem, Roland de
1928 Notes sur la céramique peinte archaique en Perse. Mémoires de la Mission archéologique en Perse 20:99-132. Librairie Ernest Leroux. Paris.
1943 Fouilles de Suse, 1933-1939. Mémoires de la Mission archéologique en Perse 29:3-161. Librairie Paul Geuthner. Paris.

Miller, Noami
1978 Preliminary Report on the Botanical Remains from Tepe Djaffarabad, 1967-74 Campaigns. Cahiers de la delegation archeologique francaise en Iran 7:49-53.

Morgan, Jacques de
1900 Fouilles à Suse en 1897-1898 et 1898-1899. Mémoires de la Mission archéologique en Perse 1. Librairie Ernest Leroux. Paris.
1912 Observations sur les couches profondes de l'Acropole de Suse. Mémoires de la Mission archéologique en Perse 13:6-26. Librairie Ernest Leroux. Paris.

Nöldke, Arnold
1932 Vierter Vorläufiger Bericht über die von der Notgemeinschaft der Deutschen Wissenschaft in Uruk. Unternommenen Ausgrabungen IV. Akademie der Wissenschaft Verlag. Berlin.

Oates, Joan
1968 Prehistoric Investigations Near Mandali, Iraq. Iraq 30:1-20.
1969 Chogha Mami 1967-68: A preliminary Report. Iraq 31:115-152.

Oates, Joan, Kamilli, and McKerrell, H.
1977 Seafaring Merchants of Ur? Antiquity 51: 221-34.

Oberlander, Theodor M.
1968 Hydrology. *In* William B. Fisher, ed. The Cambridge History of Iran: The Land of Iran, Vol. 1:264-279. Cambridge University Press. Cambridge.

Pabot, H.
1961 The Natural Vegetation of the Khuzestan Region and Headwaters. Food and Agricultural Organization of the United Nations (FAO). Rome.

Pollock, Susan
1983 Style and Information: An Analysis of Susiana Ceramics. Journal of Anthropological Archaeology 2(4):354-390.

Pottier, E.
1922 Corpus Vasorum Antiquorum. Fasicule I. Musée du Louvre. Paris.

Safar, Fuad, Mustafa, Mohammad A., and Lloyd, Seton
1981 Eridu. Ministry of Culture and Education. Baghdad.

Schroeder, J. W.
1953 Interim Report to the Government of Iran on the Geology of the Karkheh River Basin. Food and Agricultural Organization of the United Nations (FAO). Rome.

Spooner, Brian
1972 The Status of Nomadism as a Cultural Phenomenon in the Middle East. *In* William Irons and N. Dyson-Hudson, ed. Perspective on Nomadism:122-131. E. J. Brill. Leiden.

Stein, Aurel
1936 An Archaeological Tour in the Ancient Persis. Iraq 3:112-225.

Stève, M.-J. and H. Gasche

1971 L'Acropole de Suse. Mémoires de la Délégation archéologique française en Iran 46. Librairie Paul Geuthner. Paris.

Steward, Julian H.

1949 Cultural Causality and Law: A Trial Formulation of the Development of Early Civilizations. American Anthropologist 51:1-27.

Stronach, David

1961 Excavations at Ras al'Amiya. Iraq 23(2):95-137.

Vanden Berghe, Louis

1970 La necropole de Kalleh Nisar. Archéologia 32:64-73.

1973 Le Luristān avant l'Âge du Bronze: La nécrople de Hakalan. Archéologia 57:49-58.

1974 La Lurestān avant l'âge du Bronze. La nécropole de Hakalan. Proceedings of the 2nd Annual Symposium on Archaeological Research in Iran, 1973:66-79. Iranian Center for Archaeological Research. Tehran.

1975 Luristān: La nécropole de Dum-Gār-Pārchinah, IX campagne (1973). Archéologia 79:46-61.

Varjavand, Parviz

1967 Bamadi: A Bakhtiari Tribe. The University of Tehran Press. Tehran (in Persian).

Voigt, Mary M.

1983 Hajji Firuz Tepe, Iran: The Neolithic Settlement. University Museum Monograph 50. Philadelphia.

Weiss, Harvey

1976 Ceramics for Chronology: Discriminant and Cluster Analysis of Fifth Millennium Ceramic Assemblages from Qabr Sheykheyn, Khuzestan. Doctoral thesis published by University Microfilms International. Ann Arbor.

Wenke, Robert J.

1976 Imperial Investments and Agricultural Developments in Parthian and Sasanian Khuzestan: 150 B.C. to A.D. 640. Mesopotamia 10-11:13-221.

Wittfogel, Karl A.

1957 Oriental Despotism: A Comparative Study of Total Power. Yale University Press. New Haven.

Wright, Henry T.

1981 An Early Town on the Deh Luran Plain: Excavations at Tepe Farukhabad. Memoirs of the Museum of Anthropology 13. University of Michigan. Ann Arbor.

1987 Susiana Hinterlands During the Era of Primary State Formation. *In* Frank Hole, ed. The Archaeology of Western Iran: Settlement and Society from Prehistory to the Islamic Conquest. Smithsonian Series in Archaeological Inquiry:141-156. Smithsonian Institution Press. Washington, D.C.

n.d. Archaeological Survey in Areas of Ram Hormuz, Shushtar and Gutvand. Mimeographed Manuscript.

Wright, Henry T. et al.

1972 A Consideration of Interregional Exchange in Greater Mesopotamia: 4000-3000 B.C. *In* Social Exchange and Interaction. Edwin Wilmsen (ed.). Anthropological Papers, Museum of Anthropology, No. 46. The University of Michigan. Ann Arbor.

1979 Archaeological Investigations in Northeastern Xuzestan, 1976. Technical Reports of the Museum of Anthropology 10. The University of Michigan, Ann Arbor.

Wright, Henry T. and Johnson, Gregory
1975 Population, Exchange and Early State Formation in Southwestern Iran. American Anthropologist 77:267-289.
1985 Regional Perspectives on Southwest Iranian State Development. Paléorient 11(2): 25-30.

Wright, Henry T. and Perrot, Jean
1985 The Evolution of Complex Societies in Southwestern Iran. Paléorient 11/2.

Zagarell, Allen.
1982 The Prehistory of Northeast Baḫtiyārī Mountains, Iran. The Rise of a Highland Way of Life. Beihefte zum Tübinger Atlas des Vorderen Orients B (Geisteswissenschaften) 42. Wiesbaden.

Ziegler, Carl
1953 Die Keramik von der Qal'a des Haǧǧi Moḥammed. Ausgrabungen der Deutschen Forschungsgemeinschaft in Uruk-Warka 5. Berlin.

APPENDIX
CATALOGUE OF THE SURVEY MATERIAL

Figures 23-73 illustrate the representative pottery of each site. The pottery from sites G-I and G-X could not be found. Some sites, such as G33 and G-IV, are represented by a handful of sherds and others, for example G86, by several boxes of potsherds. Thus, not every site appears to have been surveyed with the same intensity. It is equally possible that sites with little painted pottery had a substantial overlay of plain wares of later periods.

For my illustrations, I have selected and drawn typical samples representing individual periods at a site; I have also included less known, unknown, and rare pieces for reference purposes. When only a few sherds are available for a site, all are shown. Pottery wasters are not illustrated; but their presence is indicated by an asterisk following site numbers in the catalogue. Whenever possible, I arranged the pottery chronologically in each figure, i.e., the latest on the top, the earliest on the bottom. Occasionally this arrangement proved both difficult to do and awkward in appearance, particularly when little material was available. Therefore, in some figures this chronological arrangement is ignored for aesthetic and practical reasons. The potsherds from Sites G31 and G172 are illustrated together in one figure because only a handful of sherds from these sites were available.

The parallels cited from Chogha Mish have been taken from the pottery catalogue of Chogha Mish I, OIP 101, forthcoming. But since the catalogue is in the process of completion, I have not been able to give complete citations for the parallels.

Figure 23	SITE G-II		*Scale*: 2/5
	DESCRIPTION	REFERENCES	PERIOD
A	Greenish buff, no visible inclusion, thick, greenish brown paint.	Susa, Pottier 1922, Pl. 2:8	LS 2
B	Buff, scattered fine grits, creamy buff slip,dark brown paint.	Chogha Mish MS, Delougaz & Kantor, nd.	MS
C	Buff, no visible inclusion, greenish brown paint.	Qabr-e Sheikhein, Weis 1976, Fig. 15:57.	LS 1
D	Greenish buff, no visible inclusion, green paint.	Qabr-e Sheikhein, Weiss 1976, Fig. 15:46.	LS 1
E	Buff, scattered grits, dark brown paint.		MS 3-LS 1
F	Buff, dark grits inclusion, shaved face, gritty face, brown paint.	Jawi II, L 10, Dollfus 1983, Fig. 33:17.	MS 3
G	Buff, fine grits inclusion, brown paint.		MS 3
H	Buff, no visible inclusion, brown paint.	Bandebal II, levels 16, 23, Dollfus 1983, Figs. 17:1, 71:17, Chogha Mish MS, Delougaz & Kantor, nd.	MS 3
I	Greenish buff, grits inclusion, greenish brown paint.	Jawi II, L 11, Dollfus 1983, Fig. 31:10; Chogha Mish MS, Delougaz and Kantor, nd.	MS 3
J	Buff, gritty ware, gritty face brown paint.		MS 3
K	Buff, grits inclusion, brown paint.	Chogha Mish MS, Delougaz & Kantor, nd.	MS 3
L	Buff, grits inclusion, prob. slipped, brown paint.	Chogha Mish MS, Delougaz & Kantor, nd.	MS 1

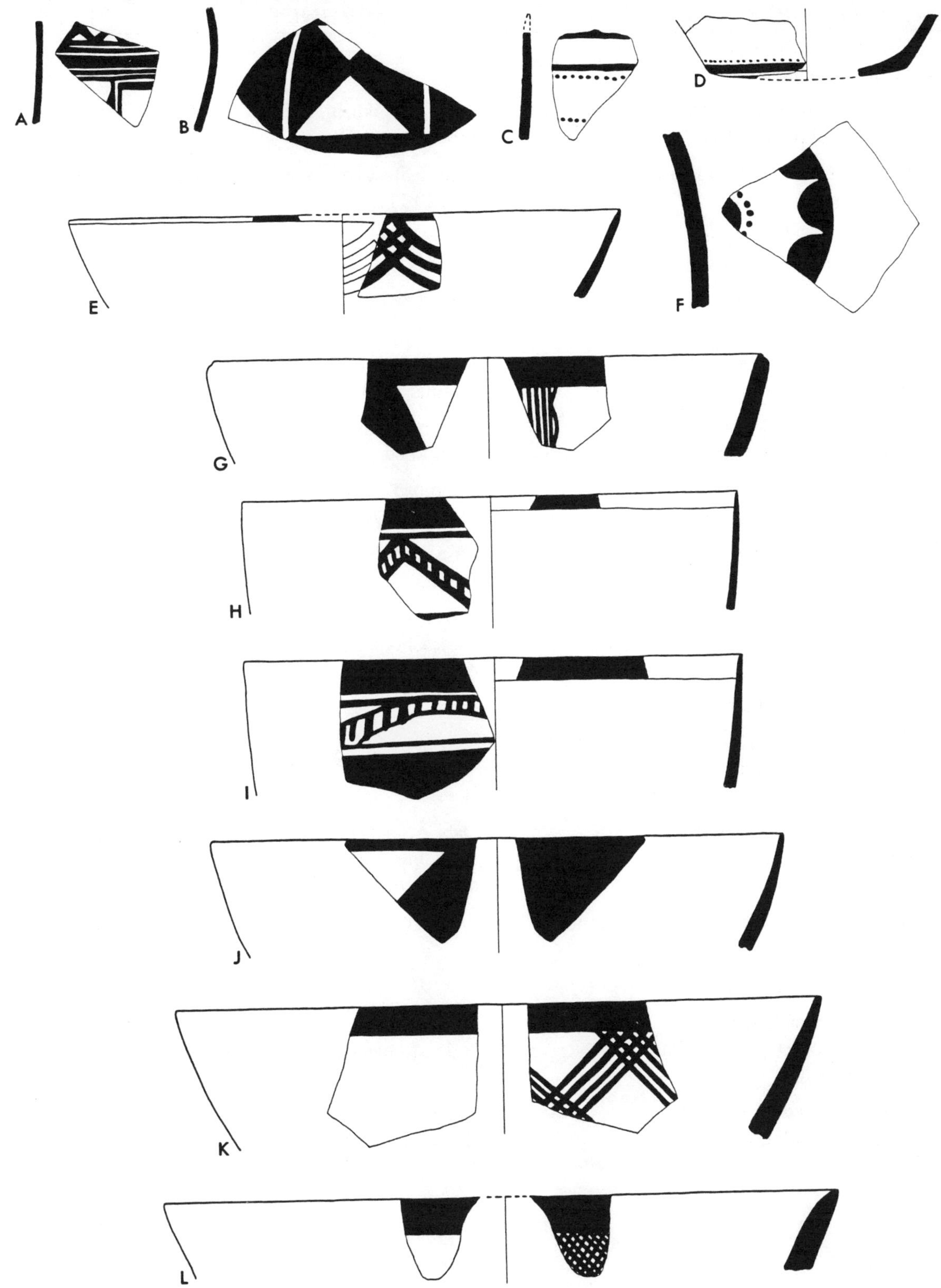
A
B
C
D
E
F
G
H
I
J
K
L

Figure 24 SITE G-III A-H; SITE G-IV I-Q *Scale*: 2/5

	DESCRIPTION	REFERENCES	PERIOD
A	Green buff, no visible inclusion, greenish paint.		LS 2
B	Buff, no visible inclusion, yellowish brown paint.	Qabr-e Sheikhein, Weiss 1976, Fig. 15:50	LS 1
C	Green buff, no visible inclusion, brown paint.	Qabr-e Sheikhein, Weiss Fig. 20:111.	LS 1
D	Buff, no visible inclusion, brown paint.		LS 1?
E	Buff, no visible inclusion, thick brown paint.	Qabr-e Sheikhein, Weiss 1976, Fig. 17:70	LS 1
F	Buff, grits inclusion, gritty face, brown paint.	Motif: Jawi II, L. 11, Dollfus 1983, Fig. 31:11.	MS 3
G	Buff, no visible inclusion, Some air pockets, brown paint.	Chogha Mish MS, Delougaz & Kantor, nd.	MS 3
H	Green buff, scattered grits face, greenish brown paint.	Jafarabad 3m-n/Jawi II, Dollfus 1978, Fig. 16:10	MS 3
I	Buff, scattered red grits, some chaff, brown paint.	Susa, de Morgan 1900 Pl. 20.	LS 2
J	Buff, scattered grits, brown paint.	Jawi I, Dollfus 1978, Fig. 14:4; Chogha Mish MS, Delougaz & Kantor, nd.	MS 3
K	Buff, no visible inclusion, reddish brown paint.		MS 3?
L	Buff, girts inclusion, pinkish core, brown paint.		MS 3?
M	Buff, no visible inclusion, thick shiny, brown paint.	Qabr-e Sheikhein, Weiss 1976, Fig. 23:160; Susa, de Mecquenem 1943, Pl. V:3, 7.	LS 2
N	Buff, no visible inclusion, brown paint.		LS 1
O	Green buff, no visible inclusion, greenish brown paint.		LS I
P	Green, no visible inclusion, some air pockets, green paint, over-fired.	Susa, de Morgan 1900, Pl. 19:4, 7; de Mecquenem 1943, Pl. 5:4.	LS 2
Q	Buff, scattered grits inclusion, over-fired, dark green	Chogha Mish LS, Delougaz & Kantor, nd; Jafarabad, Le Breton 1947, Fig. 15:10.	LS

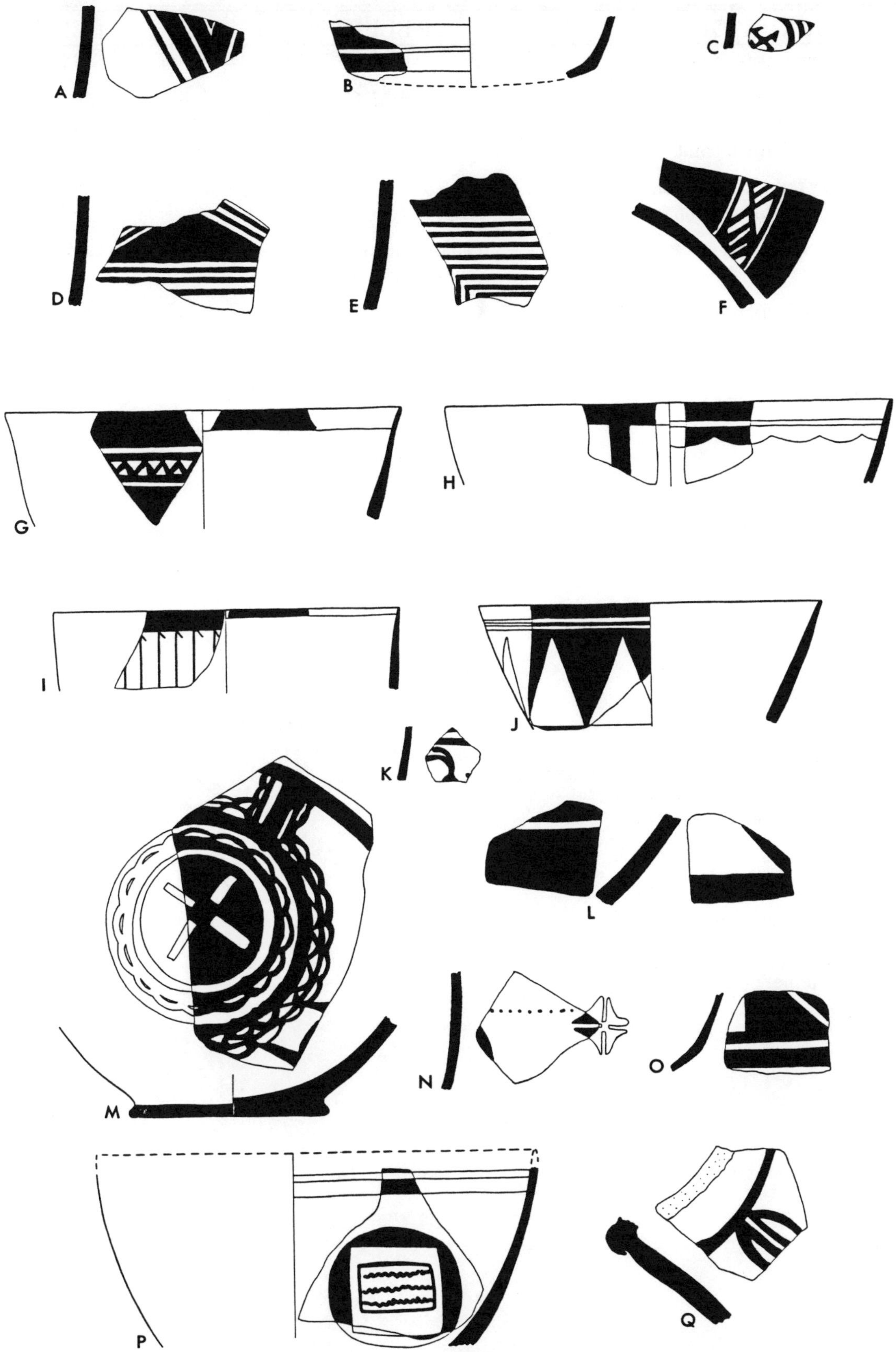
A
B
C
D
E
F
G
H
I
J
K
L
M
N
O
P
Q

Figure 25 SITE G-V A-D; SITE G-VI E-N *Scale*: 2/5

	DESCRIPTION	REFERENCES	PERIOD
A	Buff, scattered grits, brown paint.	Bandebal 16-11, Dollfus 1978, Fig. 17:9.	MS 3-LS 1
B	Greenish buff, scattered grits, greenish brown paint.		MS 3?
C	Buff, bricky red core, fine dark grits included, dark brown paint.		MS 3?
D	Green buff, no visible inclusion, green paint.	Qabr-e Sheikhein, Weiss 1976, Fig. 15:50.	LS 1
E	Buff, no visible inclusion, dark brown paint.	Qabr-e Sheikhein, Weiss 1976, Fig. 15:46.	LS 1
F	Creamy buff, no visible inclusion, brown paint.	Susa, de Morgan 1900, Pl. 20. LS 2 goblets with 'cranes' appeared at Bandebal first in L. 10, when 'dot motifs' disappeared.	LS 2
G	Buff, no visible inclusion, brown paint.	acropole 2, levels 11-7, Canal 1978, Fig. 25:1; Jafarabad 3n, Dollfus 1975, Fig. 50:6; Chogha Mish MS, Delougaz & Kantor, nd.	MS 3-LS
H	Creamy buff, no visible inclusion, brown paint.	Chogha Mish MS, Delougaz & Kantor, nd.	LS 2
I	Green buff, no visible inclusion, light brown paint.		LS 1?
J	Buff, no visible inclusion, maroon paint.	Similar: Qabr-e Sheikhein, Weiss 1973, Fig. 20:111.	LS 1
K	Greenish buff, no visible inclusion, sunken greenish brown paint.		LS 1?
L	Greenish buff, no visible inclusion, thick brown paint.	Chogha Mish MS, Delougaz & Kantor, nd.	MS 3
M	Buff, scattered grits, brown paint, prob. burnished.		MS 3
N	Animal figurine, buff ware, brown paint.		MS-LS

A
B
C
D
E
F
G
H
I
J
K
L
M
N
O
P
Q
R
S
T
U
V
W

Figure 25 SITE G-VII* O-W *Scale: 2/5*

	DESCRIPTION	REFERENCES	PERIOD
O	Greenish buff, scattered grits, some air pockets, brown paint.		MS 3
P	Creamy buff, no visible inclusion greenish paint.	Bandebal 16-11, Dollfus 1978, Fig. 17:6.	LS 1
Q	Greenish buff, grits inclusion, gritty face, greenish brown paint.		MS 3
R	green buff, small-medium grits, brown paint.		LS 1
S	Creamy buff, no visible grits, dark brown paint.		LS 1
T	Creamy buff, no visible inclusion, brown paint.		MS 3
U	Buff, no visible inclusion, brown paint, some air pockets.		LS 2
V	Creamy buff, no visible inclusion, dark brown paint.	Qabr-e Sheikhein, Weiss 1976, Fig. 15:46.	LS 1
W	Animal figurine (dog?), buff, brown paint.		MS 3-LS

Figure 26 SITES G-VIII A-J; SITE G-IX K-V *Scale*: 2/5

	DESCRIPTION	REFERENCES	PERIOD
A	Green buff, no visible inclusion, dark brown paint.	Qabr-e Sheikhein, Weiss 1976, Fig. 20:111.	LS 1
B	Greenish buff, no visible inclusion, dark brown paint.	Qabr-e Sheikhein, Weiss 1976, Figs. 15:46.	LS 1
C	Green buff, no visible inclusion, light brown paint.	Qab-e Sheikhein, Weiss 1976, Fig. 12:3.	LS 2
D	Green buff, no visible inclusion, thick shiny brown paint.	Qab-e Sheikhein, Weiss 1976, Fig. 12:3.	LS 1?
E	Buff, no visible inclusion, dark brown paint.	Qabr-e Sheikhein, Weiss 1976, Fig. 15:54.	LS 1
F	Greenish buff, scattered red and dark grits, greenish brown paint.	Qabr-e Sheikhein, Weiss 1976, Fig. 22:133-34. Tall-e Gerd-e Rahim, Fars, Stein 1936, Pl. 23:74.	LS 1
G	Buff, grits included, gritty face, brown paint.		MS 3?
H	Greenish buff, scattered grits, sunken greenish brown paint.	Bandebal II, levels 23, 16, Dollfus 1983, Fig. 71:17.	MS 3
I	Greenish buff, no visible inclusion, light green brown paint.	Qabr-e Sheikhein, Weiss 1976, Fig. 27:227.	LS 1
J	Greenish buff, scattered grits, thick, shiny greenish brown paint.		LS 2?
K	Greenish buff, no visible inclusion, greenish brown paint.	Qabr-e Sheikhein, Weiss 1976, Fig. 21:128; Susa, Steve & Gasche, 1973, Pl. 40:13.	MS 3-LS
L	Creamy buff, no visible inclu brown paint.	Chogha Mish MS, Delougaz & Kantor, nd; Qabr-e Sheikhein, Weiss 1976, Fig. 22:143.	MS 3-LS 1
M	Buff, no visible inclusion, dark brown paint.	Qabr-e Sheikhein, Weiss 1976, Figs. 13:20	LS 1
N	Buff, no visible inclusion, maroon paint.	Bakun A, Langsdorff & McCown 1942, Pl. 70:6; Behbahan, Dittmann 1984, Fig. 29:7,9.	LS 1
O	Buff, no visible inclusion, dark brown paint.		MS 3-LS
P	Greenish buff, no visible inclusion, brown paint.	Qabr-e Sheikhein, Weiss 1976, Fig. 22:133-134. Tall-e Gerd-e Rahim, Fars, Stein 1936, Pl. 23:74.	LS 1
Q	Cream buff, no visible inclusion, green brown paint.	Langsdorff & McCown 1942, Pls. 70:15, 71:1-7.	LS 1
R	Greenish buff, no visible inclusion, shaved face, greenish brown paint.		MS 3?
S	Greenish buff, no visible inclusion, greenish brown paint.		LS 1
T	Buff, scattered grits, slipped brown paint.	Bandebal II, L 16, Dollfus 1983, Fig. 76:10-11.	MS 3
U	Greenish buff, scattered grits, greenish paint.		MS 3-LS
V	Frag. of a "lizard-head" figurine, buff, no visible inclusion, brown paint (eroded).	Bakun A, Langsdorff & McCown 1942, Pl. 6:24, 26.	LS

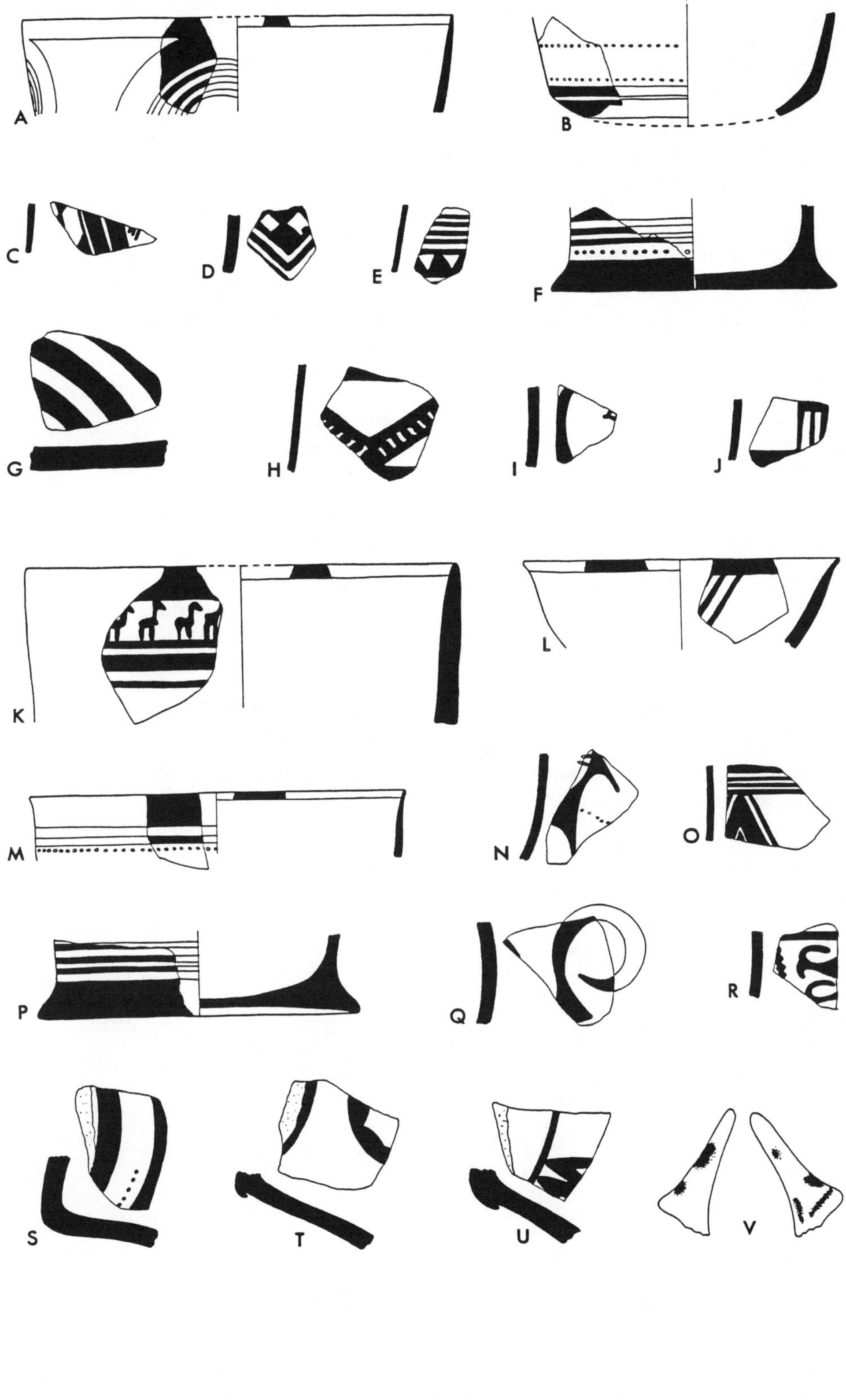
A
B
C
D
E
F
G
H
I
J
K
L
M
N
O
P
Q
R
S
T
U
V

	Description	References	Period
A	Buff, no visible inclusion, thick brown paint.	Susa, de Morgan 1900, Pl. 20.	LS 2
B	Buff, no visible inclusion, slipped, brown paint.	Susa, de Mecquenem 1928, Fig. 5:3; Jawi, Le Breton 1947, Fig. 30:7.	MS 3-LS
C	Green buff, no visible inclusion, slipped, greenish brown paint.		LS 1?
D	Buff, no visible inclusion, regular striation on the interior, burnished exterior, dark brown paint.	Chogha Mish MS, Delougaz & Kantor, nd.	MS 3
E	Buff, no visible inclusion, regular striation on the interior, burnished exterior, dark brown paint.	Similar: Chogha Mish MS, Delougaz & Kantor, nd.	MS 3
F	Buff, no visible inclusion, light brown paint.	Susa, de Mecquenem 1928, Fig. 19:9; Steve & Gasche 1971, Pl. 35:21,26.	LS 2
G	Buff, no visible inclusion, slipped, thick brown paint.	Qabr-e Sheikhein, Weiss 1976, Fig. 13:20.	LS 1
H	Creamy buff, no visible inclusion, slipped, light brown paint.	Qabr-e Sheikhein, Weiss 1976, Fig. 17; Jawi II, Dollfus 1983, Fig. 38:7; Chogha Mish MS, Delougaz & Kantor, nd.	MS 3
I	Buff, no visible inclusion, slipped, thick brown paint.	Qabr-e Sheikhein, Weiss 1976, Fig. 13:20.	LS 1
J	Greenish buff, dark grits inclusion, slipped, greenish brown paint.	Qabr-e Sheikhein, Weiss 1976, Fig. 29:3	LS 1
K	Buff, grits inclusion, gritty face, burnished exterior, thick brown paint.	Qabr-e Sheikhein, Weiss 1976, Fig. 18:91; Jawi, Le Breton 1947, Fig. 27:9.	MS 3

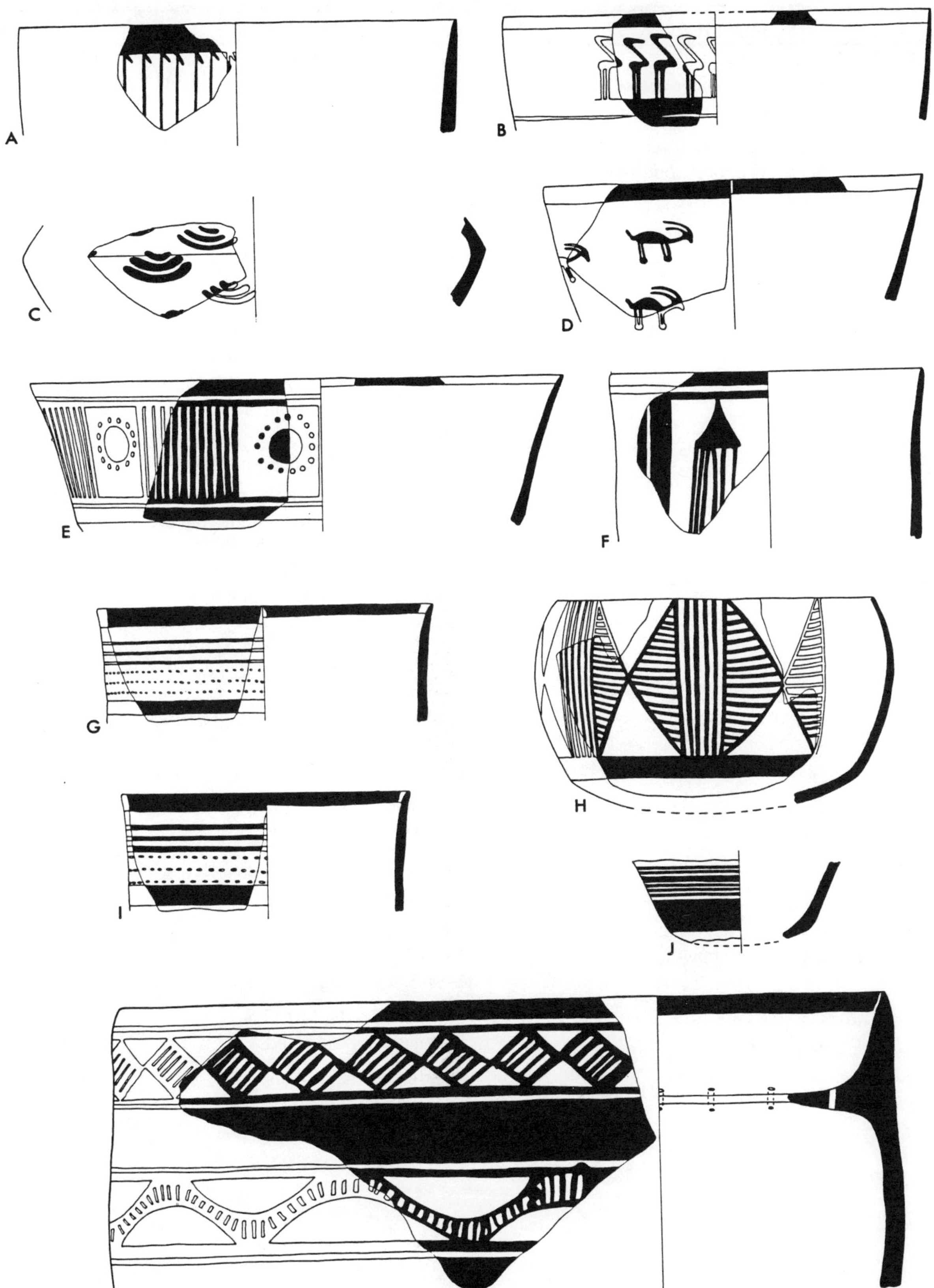
A
B
C
D
E
F
G
H
I
J
K

	DESCRIPTION	REFERENCES	PERIOD
A	Buff, dark grits inclusion, thick brown paint. Inner rim pierced with six hole.	Jafarabad 3m-n, Dollfus 1975, Fig. 52:13,17.	LS
B	Buff, fine red and dark grits inclusion, slipped, prob. burnished, thick dark br. paint.	Chogha Mish MS, Delougaz & Kantor, nd.	MS 3
C	Buff, no visible inclusion, dark brown paint.	This shape appeared in MS 3 and continued into LS 2 with various painted decorations. Jafarabad 3m-n, Dollfus 1978, Fig. 16:19; Bandebal II, L 16, Dollfus 1983, Fig. 75:14. (See also Chogha Mish, op. cit. Pl. 152:P, but without carination; Susa, Pottier 1922, nos 8,15,21.)	MS 3-LS
D	Buff, no visible inclusion,	The shape first appeared in MS3 but the painted design occurred as early as ES, continued into the Late Susiana period. Buhalan, de Mecquenem 1943, fig. 112:24-25, Damghar Par Chineh, Tomb A 30, Vanden Berghe 1975, Fig. p. 56. See also Jafarabad ES, L 4, Dollfus 1975, Fig. 22:2; Jawi I, MS 1, Dollfus 1978, Fig. 14:2. At Susa, this design appears on a similar jar with carination; Pottier 1922, No. 15.	MS 3-LS 1
E	Buff, scattered grits, slipped, thick, dark brown paint.	Susa, Steve & Gasche 1973, Pl. 40:9.	LS 2
F	Buff, no visible inclusion, thick, shiny dark brown paint.	Chogha Mish, LS, Delougaz & Kantor, nd.	MS-LS
G	Buff, scattered grits, prob. slipped, dark brown paint.	Qabr-e Sheikhein, Weiss 1976, Fig. 27:237, Chogha Mish LS, Delougaz & Kantor, nd.	MS 3-LS
F	Buff, scattered dark grits, thick, dark brown paint.	Similar: Chogha Mish LS, Delougaz & Kantor, nd.	MS 3-LS
H	Buff, no visible inclusion, dark brown paint.	Qabr-e Sheikhein, Weiss 1976, Fig. 21:128.	MS 3?

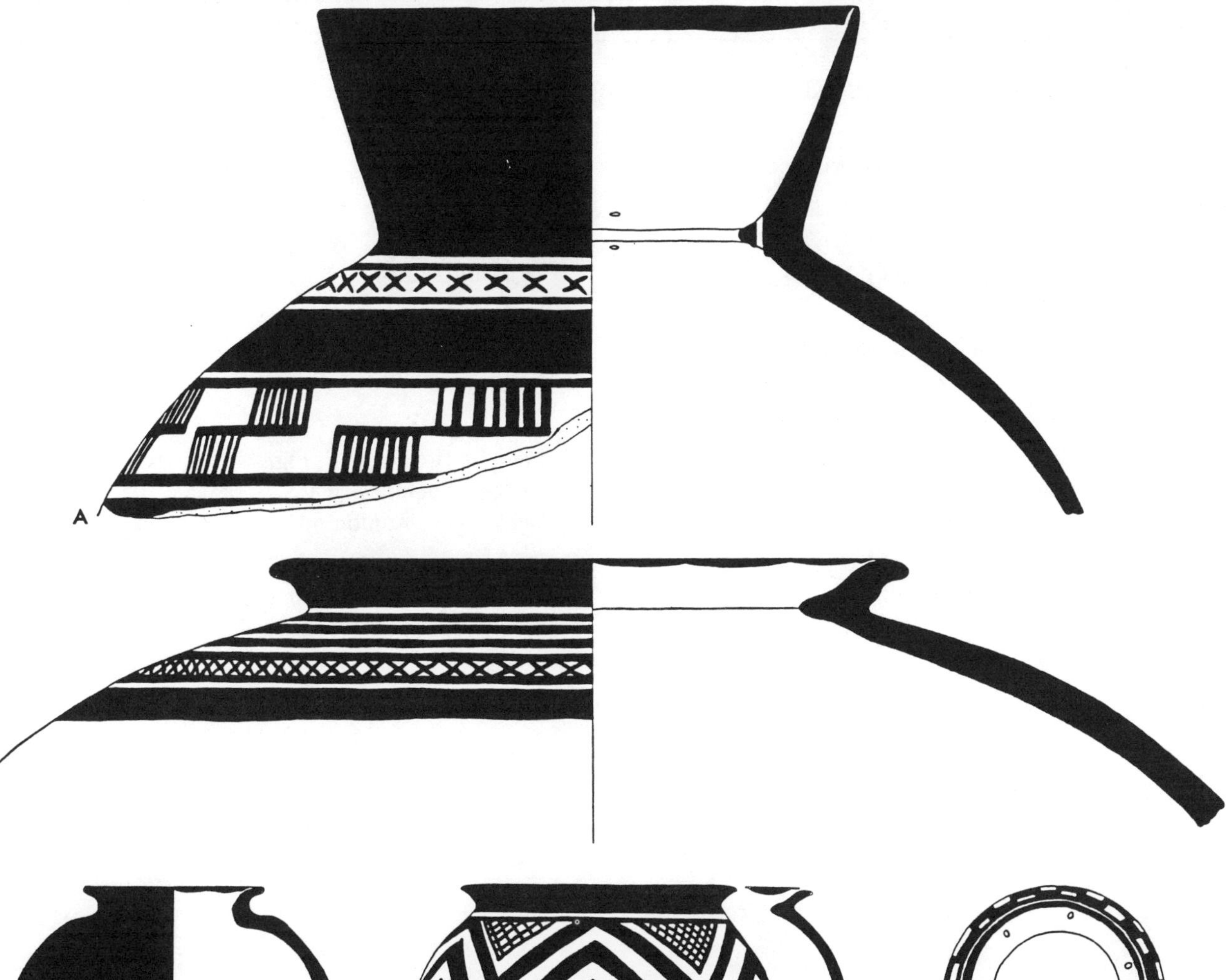
A
B
C
D
E
F
G
H

Figure 29	SITE G25-I		*Scale*: 2/5
	DESCRIPTION	REFERENCES	PERIOD
A	Greenish buff, dark & red grits, gritty face, prob. slipped, thick dark paint.	Jafarabad 3m-n, Dollfus 1978, Fig. 16:10.	MS 3
B	Greenish buff, dark grits inclusion, greenish brown paint.	Chogha Mish MS, Delougaz & Kantor, nd.	MS 3
C	Buff, scattered grits, creamy buff slipped, dark greenish brown paint.	Qabr-e Sheikhein, Weiss 1976, Fig. 22:142.	MS 3
D	Greenish buff, scattered fine dark grits, regular striations interior, slipped, thick dark brown paint.	Chogha Mish MS, Delougaz & Kantor, nd.	MS 3
E	Buff, dark grits inclusion, dark brown paint.	Jawi, Le Breton 1947, Fig. 23:15; Chogha Mish MS, Delougaz & Kantor, nd.	MS 3
F	Buff, red and dark grits, greenish dark paint.	Jawi I, L 15, Dollfus 1983, Fig. 14:5; Haji Mohammad, Ziegler 1961, Pl. 11:a,i	MS 1

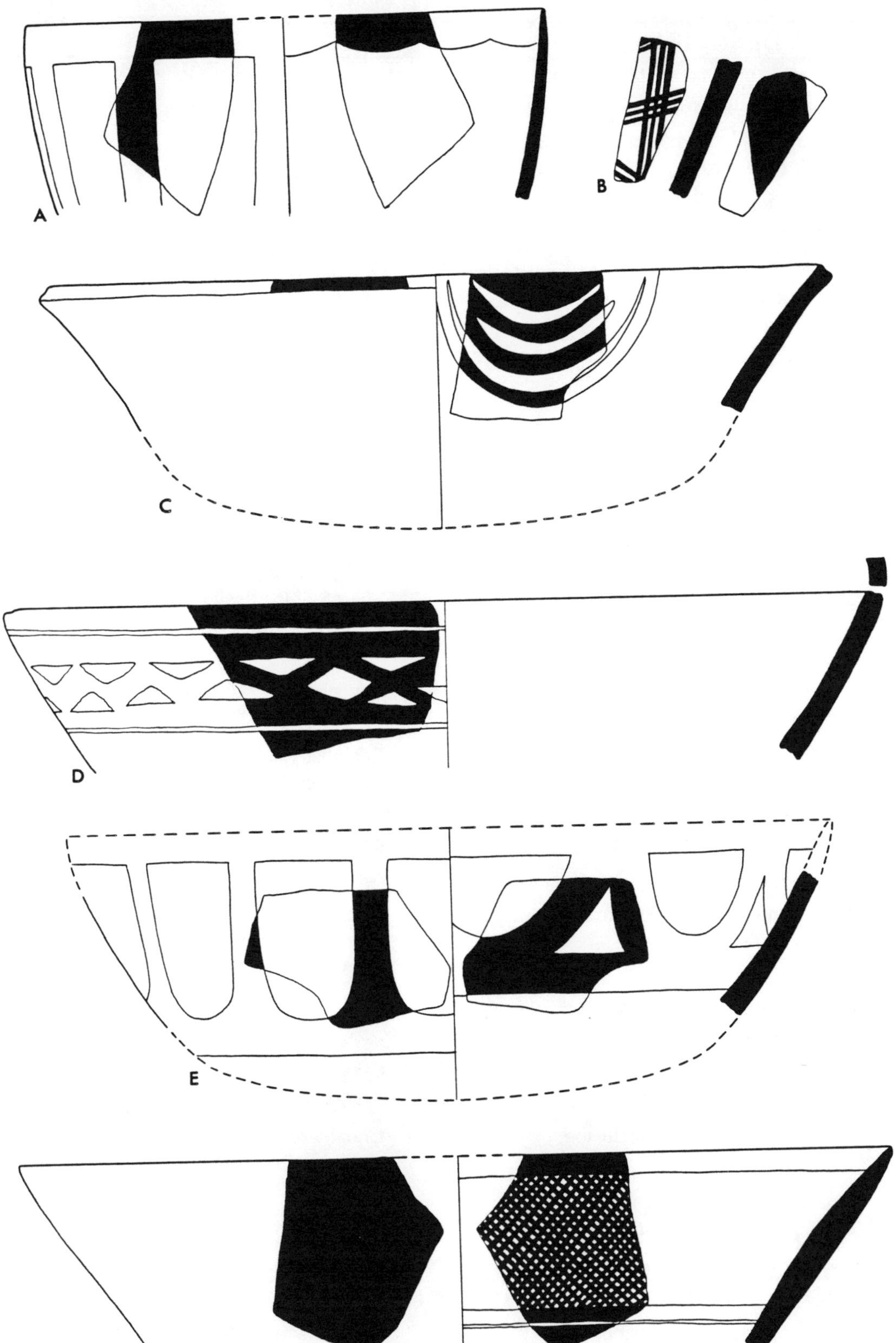
A
B
C
D
E
F

	DESCRIPTION	REFERENCES	PERIOD
A	Creamy buff, no visible inclusion, brown paint.	Chogha Mish LS, Delougaz & Kantor, nd.	LS 2
B	Warm buff, no visible inclusion, dark brown paint.	Susa, Pottier 1922, Pl. 1	MS 3-LS
C	Green buff, no visible inclusion, thick dark brown paint.	Chogha Mish LS, Delougaz & Kantor, nd.	LS 2
D	Creamy buff, cream slip, no visible inclusion, flaky, dark brown paint.	Chogha Mish LS, Delougaz & Kantor, nd.	LS
E	Buff, dark grits inclusion, buff slip, flaky, thick brown paint.		MS 3
F	Buff, no visible inclusion, dark brown paint, traces of the painted design of a similar vessel on interior.		LS 1?
G	Buff, no visible inclusion, brown paint.	Bakun A, Langsdorff & McCown 1942, Pl. 75:16. It is not easy to determine the stance of this piece from striations. Therefore the design may represent the 'kite/mask' motif of MS 3, though 'kite' motifs are not usually superimposed.	LS 1
H	Creamy buff, no visible inclusion, thick, dark brown paint.	Bandebal II, L 16, Dollfus 1983, Fig. 76:1.	MS 3-LS 1
I	Warm buff, scattered grits, thick, dark paint; ext. covered with paint.	Jafarabad, de Mecquenem 1928, Fig. 20:2.	MS 3
J	Warm buff, no visible inclusion, dark brown paint.	Chogha Mish MS, Delougaz & Kantor, nd.	MS 3
K	Buff, no visible inclusion, dark brown paint.	Chogha Mish MS, Delougaz & Kantor, nd; Ras el-Amyia, Stronach 1961, Pls. 46:4, 47:8.	MS 1
L	Buff, scattered grits, cream slip, brown paint.		MS 1
M	Buff, scattered grits, slipped, dark maroon paint.	Chogha Mish MS, Delougaz & Kantor, nd.	MS 3
N	Greenish buff, grits inclusion, brown paint.	Chogha Mish MS, Delougaz & Kantor, nd.	MS 2
O	Greenish buff, dark grits, slipped, greenish paint.		MS 3
P	Buff, red grits inclusion, dark brown paint.	Chogha Mish MS, Delougaz & Kantor, nd.	MS 1
Q	Buff, dark grits inclusion, maroon paint, prob. slipped.	Chogha Mish MS, Delougaz & Kantor, nd.	MS 3
R	Greenish buff, dark grits inclusion, greenish brown paint.		MS 3

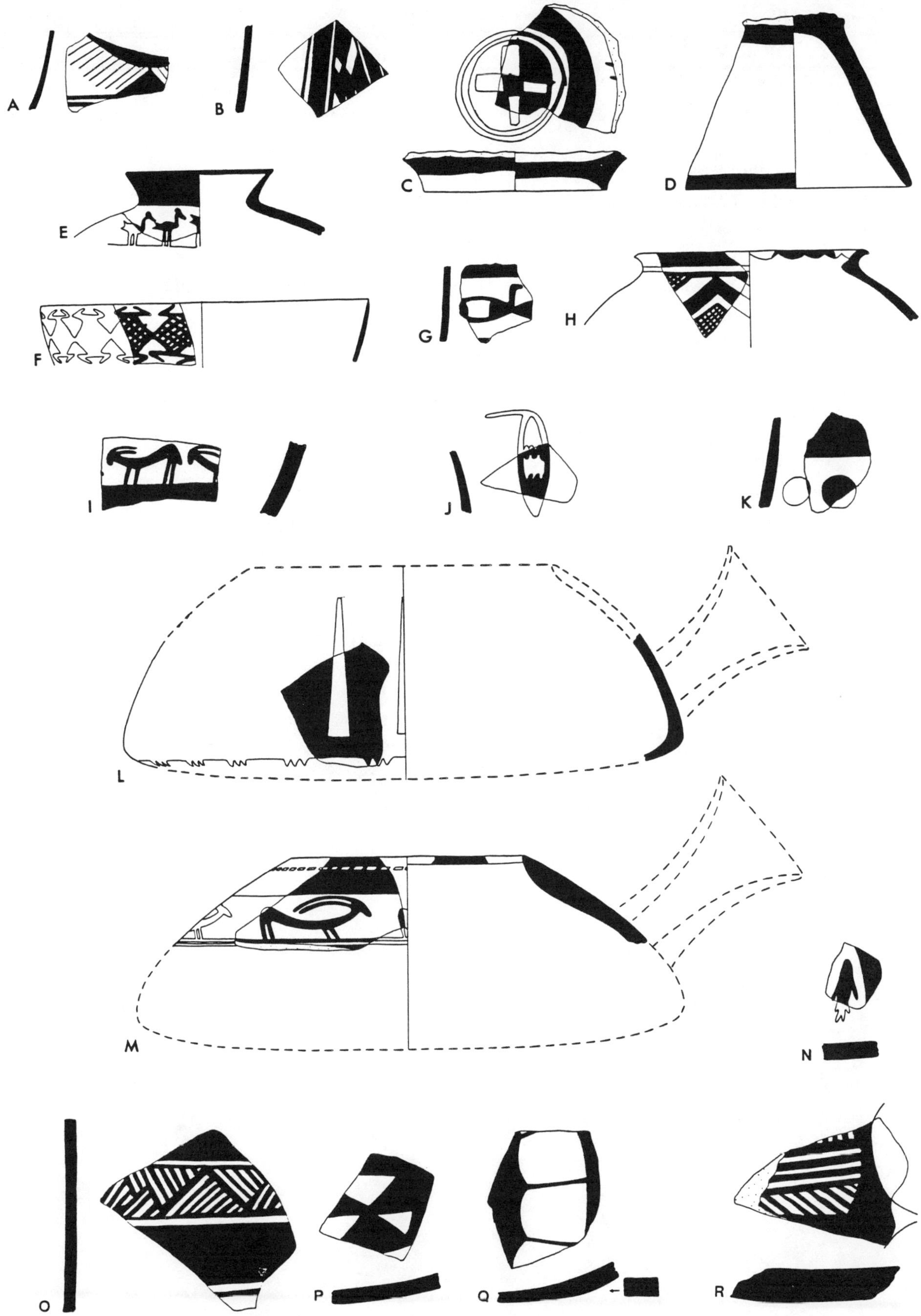
A
B
C
D
E
F
G
H
I
J
K
L
M
N
O
P
Q
R

Figure 31	SITE G25-II		*Scale*: 2/5
	DESCRIPTION	REFERENCES	PERIOD
A	Buff, no visible inclusion, slipped, brown paint.	Susa, Steve & Gasche 1971, Pl. 35:1-3.	LS 2
B	Buff, scattered dark grits, slipped, shiny dark br. paint.		MS 3
C	Buff, no visible inclusion, light brown paint.		MS 3
D	Buff, no visible inclusion, buff slipped, brown paint.	The design is similar to MS 3 forms with vertical columns of motifs.	MS 3
E	Buff,no visible grits, prob. slipped, thick greenish brown paint.	Chogha Mish MS, Delougaz & Kantor, nd.	MS 3
F	Greenish buff, no visible inclusion, greenish br. paint.		MS 3?
G	Buff, scattered grits, greenish brown paint.		MS 3?
H	Buff, scattered grits inclusion, brown paint.	Chogha Mish MS, Delougaz & Kantor, nd; Jawi II, L 11, Dollfus 1983, Fig. 31:1-3.	MS 3
I	Buff, scattered grits inclusion, dark brown paint.		MS 3
J	Buff, scattered grits inclusion, creamy buff slip, thick, shiny brown paint.	Chogha Mish LS, Delougaz & Kantor, nd; Susa, Le Breton 1947, Fig. 15:10.	LS
K	Frag. of a pedestal base or a spindle whorl. Buff, grits chaff inclusion, probably buff slipped, dark black paint.	Jafarabad 5a, Dollfus 1975, Fig. 19:10.	ES
L	Buff, dark and red grits inclusion, gritty face, black paint.		MS 1?
M	Buff, grits inclusion.		LS 2

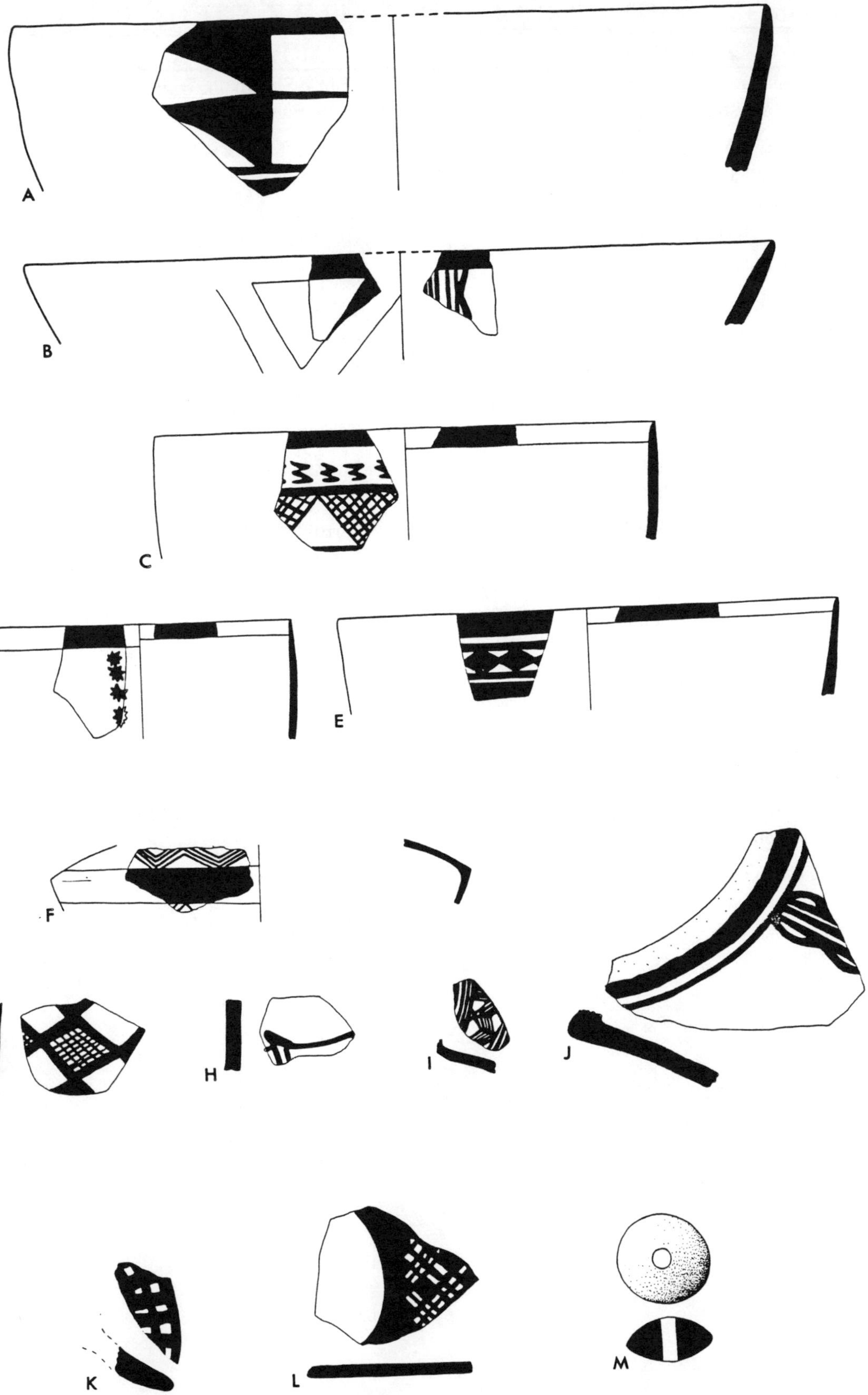
A
B
C
D
E
F
G
H
I
J
K
L
M

Figure 32 SITE G25-II A-G; SITE G25-III H-K; SITE G25-IV L-M *Scale*: 2/5

	DESCRIPTION	REFERENCES	PERIOD
A	Buff, no visible inclusion, cream slip, brown paint.	Qabr-e Sheikhein, Weiss 1976, Figs. 13:20, 14:21.	LS 1
B	Buff, no visible inclusion, cream slip, dark maroon paint, some air pockets.	Chogha Mish LS, Delougaz & Kantor, nd.	LS
C	Lid. Buff, red & dark grits, greenish brown paint.	Bandebal II, L 14, Dollfus 1983, Fig. 82:9.	MS 3
D	Buff, grits inclusion, brown paint.		AS 3
E	Buff, grits & Chaff inclusion, yellowish buff slip, black paint.	Chogha Mish ES, Delougaz & Kantor, nd.	ES
F	Buff, grits & chaff inclusion yellowish buff slip, dark brown paint.	Chogha Mish ES, Delougaz & Kantor, nd.	ES
G	Buff, grits & chaff inclusion, cream slip, dark brown paint.	Jafarabad 5, Dollfus 1975, Fig. 23:3.	ES
H	Buff, red & dark grits, cream slip, brown paint.	Farrukhabad, Wright 1981, Fig. 18:a-d.	MS 3-LS 1
I	Buff, scattered grits, buff slip, dark brown paint.	Bandebal II, L 16, Dollfus 1983, Fig. 71:2.	MS 3-LS 1
J	Buff, no visible inclusion, dark brown paint.		LS 1
K	Buff, scattered dark grits, thick dark brown paint.	Jawi II, Dollfus 1983, Fig. 31:10; Bandebal II, L 23-19, Dollfus 1983, Pl. 15:11.	MS 3
L	Buff, no visible inclusion, cream slip, brown paint.	Bandebal II, L 14, Dollfus 1983, Fig. 81:12.	LS 1?
M	Buff, no visible inclusion, cream slip, green brown paint.	Chogha Mish MS, Delougaz & Kantor, nd.	MS 3

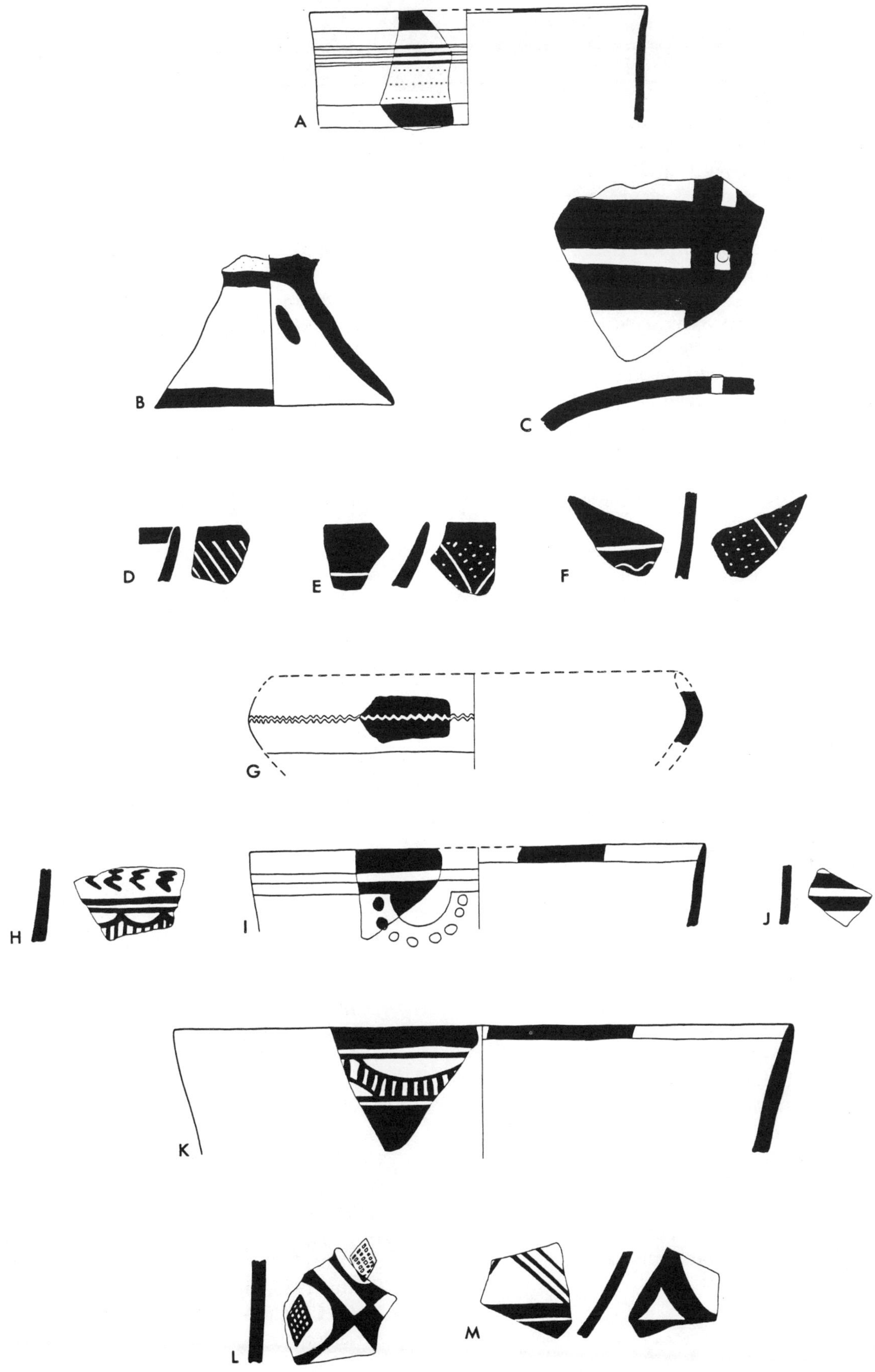
A
B
C
D
E
F
G
H
I
J
K
L
M

Figure 33	SITE G26-I A-H; SITE G26-II I-V	*Scale*: 2/5

	DESCRIPTION	REFERENCES	PERIOD
A	Buff, no visible inclusion, buff slipped, brown paint.		LS
B	Buff, no visible inclusion, buff slipped, brown paint.	Farrukhabad, Wright 1981, Fig. 17:e.	LS 1
C	Greenish buff, no visible inclusion, brown paint. 18:5-9.	Susa, de Morgan 1900, Pl.	LS 2
D	Greenish buff, scattered grits, brown paint.	Bakun A, Langsdorff & McCown 1942, Pl. 70:15; Qabr-e Sheikhein, Weiss 1976, Fig. 29:3-4.	LS 1
E	Buff, no visible inclusion, cream slip, brown paint.	Qabr-e Sheikhein, Weiss 1976, Fig. 27:237.	LS 1?
F	Creamy buff, medium dark grits inclusion, slipped, greenish brown paint.		LS 1?
G	Buff, no visible inclusion, buff slipped, brown paint.	Qabr-e Sheikhein, Weiss 1976, Fig. 23:149; Bakun A, Langsdorff & McCown 1942, Pls. 28-29.	MS 3-LS 1
H	Green, no visible inclusion, green paint, overfired.	Qabr-e Sheikhein, Weiss 1976, Fig. 15:57.	LS 1
I	Greenish buff, no visible inclusion, brown paint.	Susa, Pottier 1922, Pl. 1.	LS 2
J	Buff, no visible inclusion, buff slipped, dark br. paint.	Susa, Pottier 1922. Pl. 3:8.	LS 2
K	Buff, no visible inclusion, light brown paint.	Susa, Steve & Gasche 1971, Pl. 40:9.	LS 2
L	Cream buff, no visible inclusion, brown paint.	Jawi II, L 10, Dollfus 1983, Fig. 33:17.	MS 3
M	Buff, no visible inclusion, dark brown paint.	Susa, de Morgan 1900, Pl. 18:12,15.	LS 2
N	Buff, no visible inclusion, brown paint.	Qabr-e Sheikhein, Weiss 1976, Fig. 15:46.	LS 1
O	Warm buff, no visible inclusion, brown paint.	Qabr-e Sheikhein, Weiss 1976, Fig. 20:111.	LS 1?
P	Creamy buff, no visible inclusion, greenish brown paint.	Chogha Mish MS, Delougaz & Kantor, nd.	MS 3
Q	Buff, grits inclusion, prob. slipped, brown paint.	Chogha Mish, MS, Delougaz & Kantor, nd; Jawi II, L 12, Dollfus 1983, Fig. 26:8.	MS 3
R	Buff, no visible inclusion, brown paint.	Qabr-e Sheikhein, Weiss 1976, Fig. 27:227.	LS
S	Buff, grits inclusion, brown paint.	Jawi, Le Breton 1947, Fig. 24:4; Bandebal II, L 16, Dollfus 1983, Fig. 75:17.	MS 3-LS
T	Buff, scattered grits inclusion, thick brown paint.	Chogha Mish MS, Delougaz & Kantor, nd.	MS 3
U	Buff, grits inclusion, greenish brown paint.	Jafarabad 4-5d, Dollfus 1975, Fig. 27:6, 8-9.	AS 3-ES
V	Buff, scattered grits inclusion, brown paint.	Bandebal II, levels 23, 16, Dollfus 1983, Figs. 56:4-5, 71:17; Chogha Mish MS, Delougaz & Kantor, nd.	MS 3

A
B
C
D
E
F
G
H
I
J
K
L
M
N
O
P
Q
R
S
T
U
V

	DESCRIPTION	REFERENCES	PERIOD
A	Buff, no visible inclusion, brown paint.	Bandebal II, L 16, Dollfus 1983, Fig. 73:2.	MS 3-LS
B	Cream buff, no visible inclusion, dark brown paint.	Susa, de Mecquenem 1943, Pl. 4:4.	LS 2
C	Buff, no visible inclusion, brown paint.	Susa, Steve & Gasche 1971, Pl. 35:21,26.	LS 2
D	Greenish buff, no visible inclusion, brown paint.		LS 1?
E	Buff, no visible inclusion, greenish brown paint.	Susa, Steve & Gasche 1971, Pl. 40:9.	LS 2
F	Buff, no visible inclusion, prob. slipped, brown paint.	Chogha Mish LS, Delougaz & Kantor, nd.	LS 2
G	Buff, scattered grits, reddish brown paint.	Chogha Mish LS, Delougaz & Kantor, nd.	LS 2
H	Buff, no visible inclusion, cream slip, greenish brown paint.	Bandebal II, levels 11-12, Dollfus 1983, Fig. 87:2.	LS 1
I	Greenish buff, no visible inclusion, greenish brown paint.	Qabr-e Sheikhein, Weiss 1976, Fig. 14:21.	LS 1
J	Warm buff, no visible inclusion, brown paint.		LS 1?
K	Buff, no visible inclusion, cream slip, brown paint.	Bakun A, Langsdorff & McCown, Pl. 70:15; Qabr-e Sheikhein, Weiss 1976, Fig. 22:139.	LS 1
L	Buff, grits inclusion, cream slip, thick shiny brown paint.		MS 3-LS 1?
M	Buff, no visible inclusion, cream slip, dark brown paint.	Qabr-e Sheikhein, Weiss 1976, Fig. 22:143.	MS 3-LS 1
N	Buff, scattered grits, dark brown paint.	Chogha Mish MS, Delougaz & Kantor, nd.	MS 3
O	Buff, no visible inclusion, dark brown paint.	Bandebal II, L 23, Dollfus 1983, Fig. 56:4-5.	MS 3
P	Buff, red & dark grits inclusion, brown paint.	Qabr-e Sheikhein, Weiss 1976, Fig. 16:76.	MS 3
Q	Greenish buff, no visible in dark green paint.	Chogha Mish MS, Delougaz & Kantor, nd.	MS 1

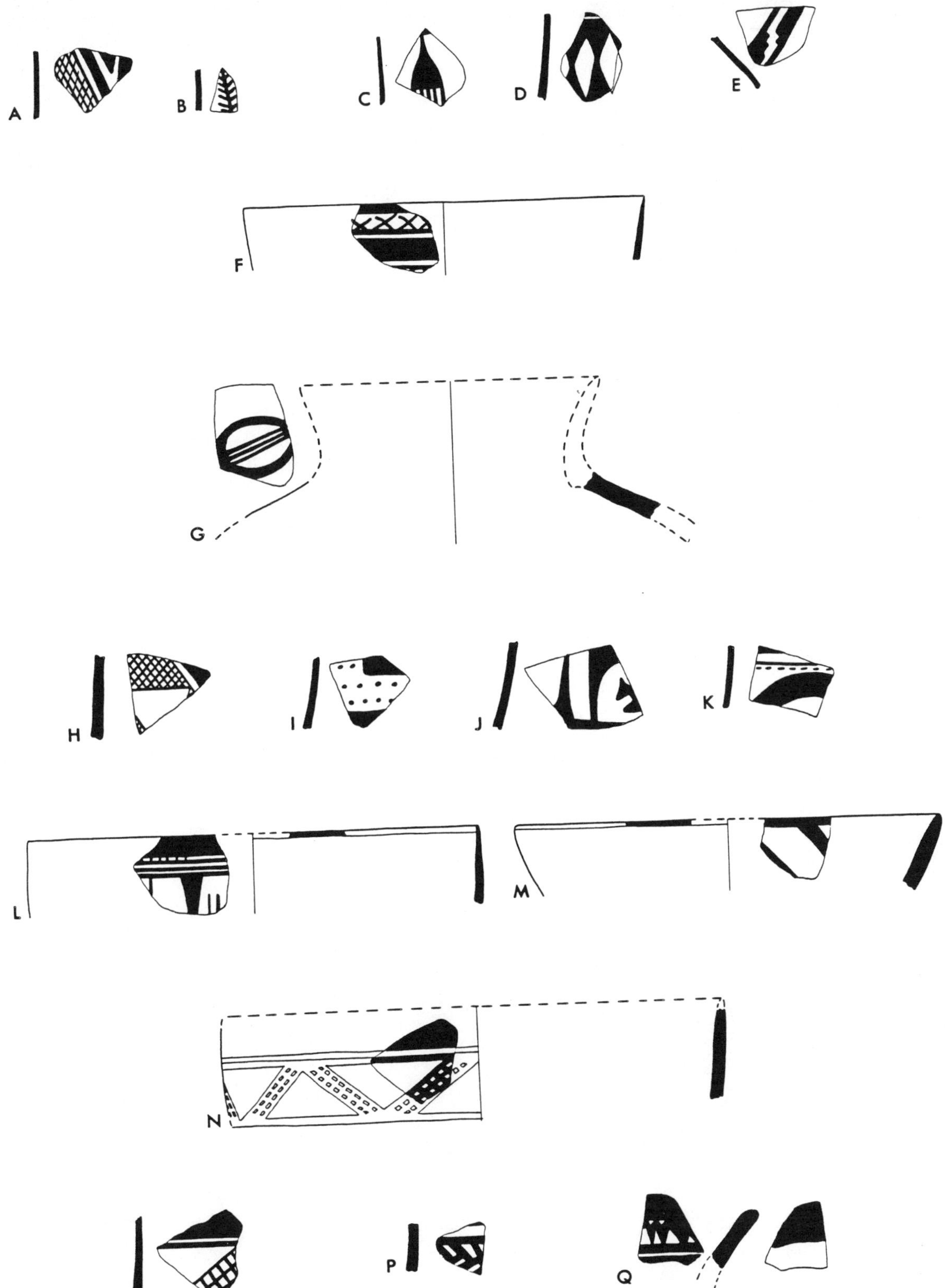
A
B
C
D
E
F
G
H
I
J
K
L
M
N
O
P
Q

Figure 35 SITE G31 A-F; SITE G172 G-I *Scale*: 2/5

	DESCRIPTION	REFERENCES	PERIOD
A	Buff, grits inclusion, slipped, brown paint.		LS?
B	Buff, no visible inclusion, brown paint.		LS
C	Buff, no visible inclusion, dark brown paint.		LS
D	Buff, no visible inclusion, greenish brown paint.		LS?
E	Pinkish buff, dark grits inclusion, slipped, brown paint.		MS 3?
F	Base frag. Reddish buff, dark grits inclusion, brown paint.		MS 3-LS
G	Buff, grits inclusion, dark brown paint.	Farrukhabad, Wright 1981, Fig. 24:a; Bandebal II, L 16, Dollfus 1983, Fig. 76:14.	MS 3-LS 1
H	Buff, scattered grits, brown paint.	Chogha Mish MS, Delougaz & Kantor, nd; Qabr-e Sheikhein, Weiss 1976, Fig. 18:91.	MS 3
I	Buff, grits inclusion, dark brown paint, much worn.		MS 3

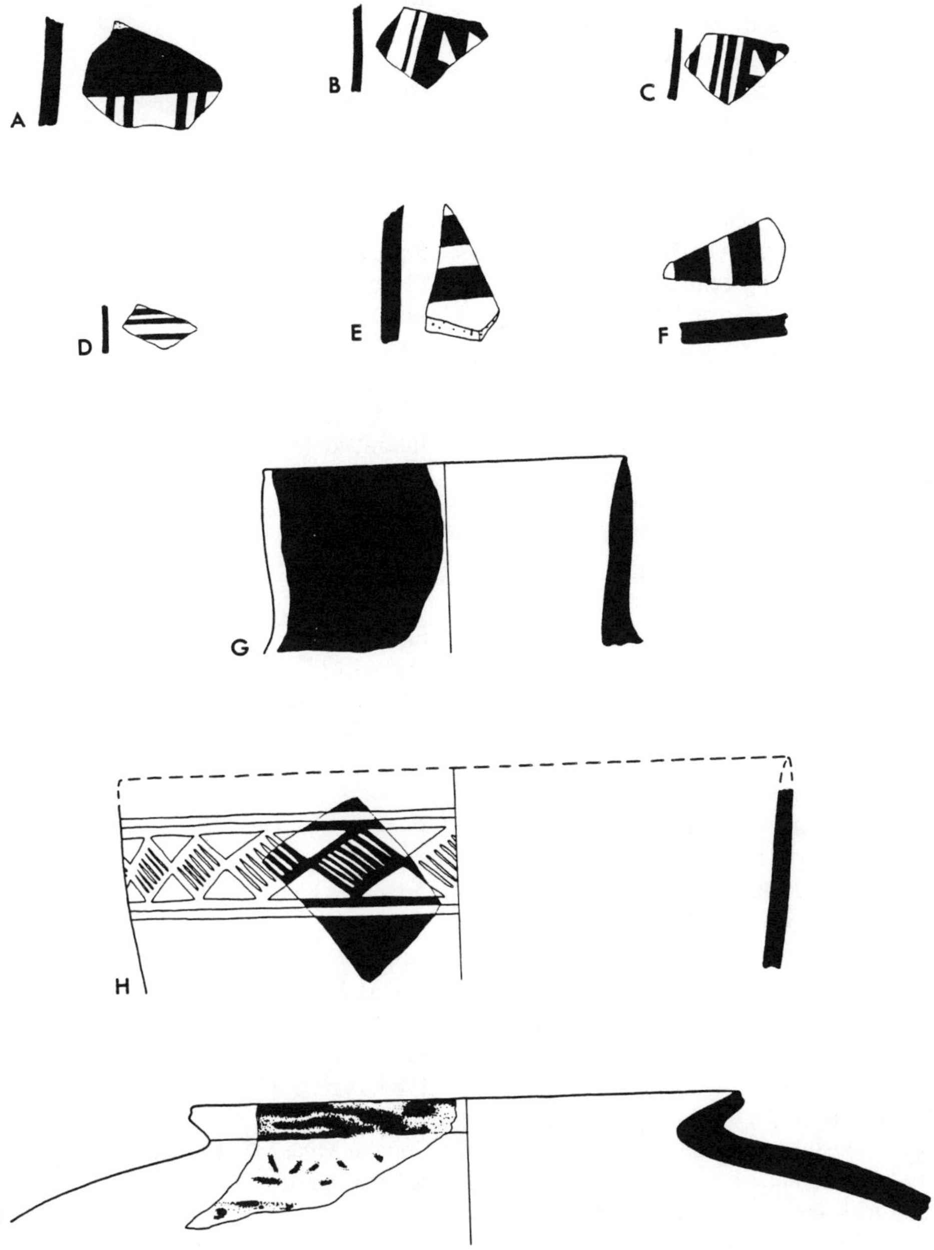
A
B
C
D
E
F
G
H
I

Figure 36 SITE G33-I* A-J; SITE G33-III* K-T; SITE G33-IV* U-AA *Scale*: 2/5

	DESCRIPTION	REFERENCES	PERIOD
A	Buff, no visible inclusion, cream slip, dark brown paint.	Qabr-e Sheikhein, Weiss 1976, Fig. 13:12; Bandebal II, L 12, Dollfus 1983, Fig. 87:4.	LS 1
B	Greenish buff, scattered grits, some air pockets, greenish brown paint, over-fired.		MS 3-LS 1
C	Buff, no visible inclusion, cream slip, thick, dark brown paint.	Chogha Mish LS, Delougaz & Kantor, nd.	LS 2
D	Token (?) Buff, no visible inclusion.		MS?
E	Jar shoulder frag. Buff, no visible inclusion, some air pockets, dark brown paint.		LS
F	Jar shoulder frag. Greenish buff, no visible inclusion, greenish paint.	Susa, Steve & Gasche 1971 Pl. 35:5.	LS 2
G	Jar shoulder frag. Green buff, no visible inclusion, brown paint, shaved interior.	Jafarabad 3d-1, Dollfus 1978, Fig. 19:23.	LS 2
H	Buff, grits & chaff inclusion, slipped, brown paint.	Jafarabad 5, Dollfus 1975, Fig. 19:2-3.	ES
I	Buff, dark grits & chaff inclusion, yellowish buff slip, dark brown paint.	Jafarabad 4, Dollfus 1975, Fig. 21:17.	ES
J	Greenish buff, dark grits & chaff inclusion, dark brown paint.	Chogha Mish ES, Delougaz & Kantor, nd.	ES
K	Buff, grits inclusion, slipped, incised decoration.		PL
L	Buff, no visible inclusion, cream slip, incised decoration, regular striations on interior.	Farrukhabad, Wright 1981, Fig. 44:1; Uruk, Noldke 1932, Pl. 19D:b.	PL
M	Buff, grits inclusion, prob. slipped, incised decoration, regular striations on interior.	Uruk, Noldke 1932, Pl. 19D:b.	PL
N	Mosaic cone. Pink buff, no visible inclusion.		PL
O	Buff, red & dark grits inclusion, cream slip, light brown paint.		MS 3
P	Buff, grits and chaff inclusion, regular striations on interior.	Adams & Nissen 1972, Fig. 76:20.	PL
Q	Spout. Buff, scattered grits, regular striations on interior.	Susa, L 17B, Le Brun 1978, Fig. 31:6,9.	PL
R	Spout. Buff, scattered grits, slipped.	Adams & Nissen 1972, Fig. 64:17.	PL
S	Creamy buff, dark grits inclusion, dark brown paint.	Jawi II, L 10, Dollfus 1983, Fig. 33:7.	MS 3
T	Mosaic cone. Buff, no visible inclusion.		PL
U	Buff, no visible inclusion, dark brown paint.	Chogha Mish MS, Delougaz & Kantor, nd.	MS 3
V	Buff, grits & chaff inclusion, red paint.		AS?
W	Buff, red & dark grits inclusion, greenish brown paint.	Jawi II, L 12, Dollfus 1983, Fig. 26:8.	MS 3
X	Base frag. Buff, red & dark grits inclusion, dark brown paint.		MS 3
Y	Base frag. grits inclusion, green brown paint.		MS 3
Z	Jar shoulder frag. Greenish buff, grits inclusion, dark green paint.	Chogha Mish MS, Delougaz & Kantor, nd.	MS 3
AA	Jar shoulder frag. Greenish buff, no visible inclusion, brown paint.	Qabr-e Sheikhein, Weiss 1976, Fig. 23:	MS 3-LS

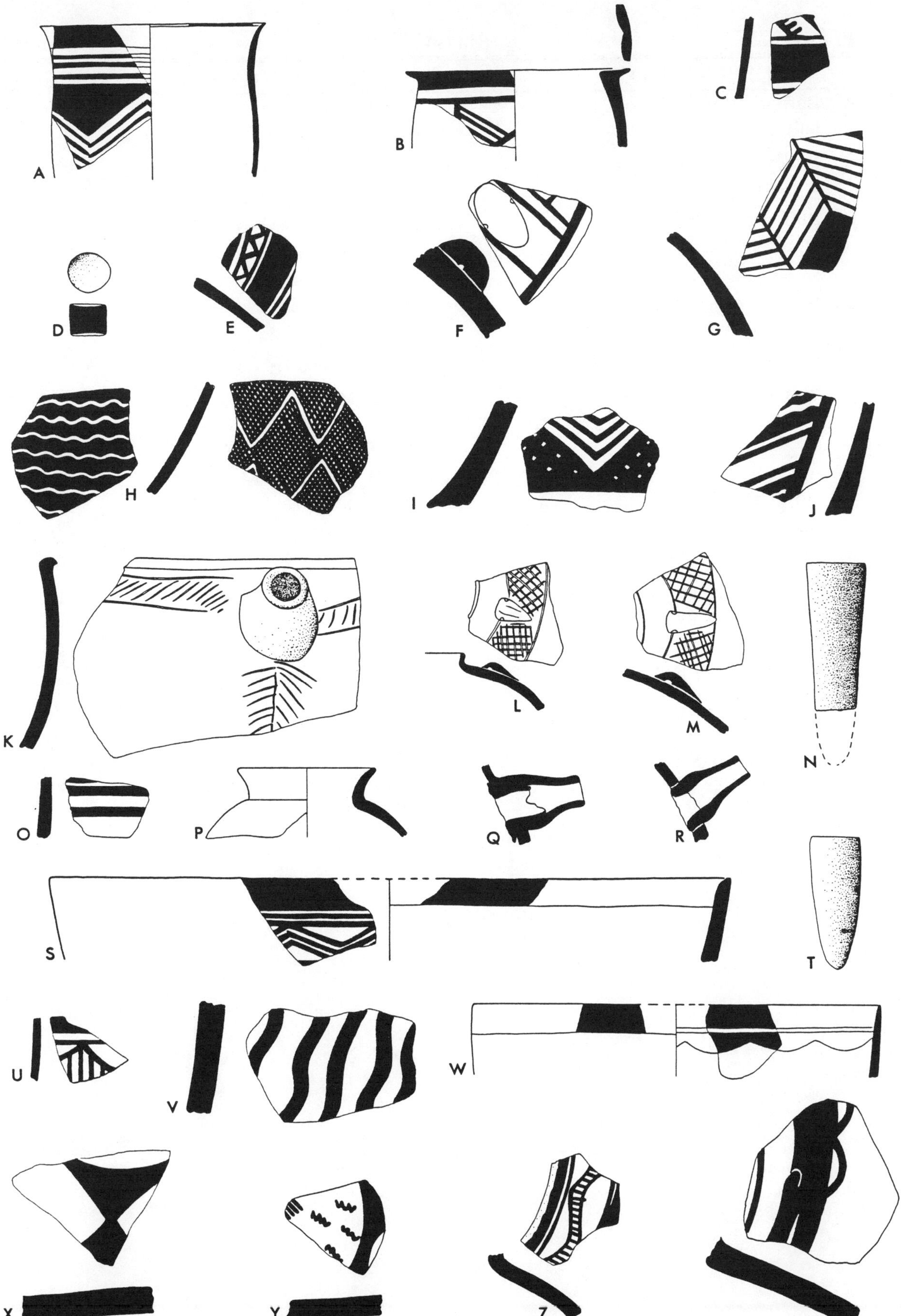
A
B
C
D
E
F
G
H
I
J
K
L
M
N
O
P
Q
R
S
T
U
V
W
X
Y
Z
AA

Figure 37 SITE G33-II* *Scale*: 2/5

	DESCRIPTION	REFERENCES	PERIOD
A	Buff, no visible inclusion, buff slipped, brown paint.	Jafarabad 3m-n, Jawi II, Dollfus 1978, Fig. 16:10.	MS 3
B	Buff, no visible inclusion, brown paint.	Bandebal II, L 11, Dollfus 1983, Pl. 19:3.	LS 1
C	Buff, reg & dark grits inclusion, greenish brown paint.	Jawi, Le Breton 1947, Fig. 23:13; Qabr-e Sheikhein Weiss 1976, Fig. 22:142.	MS 3-LS 1
D	Buff, no visible inclusion, greenish brown paint.	Bandebal III, L 10, Dollfus 1983, Fig. 88:8.	LS 2
E	Buff, grit inclusion, brown paint.	Jawi, Le Breton 1947, Fig. 23:15.	MS 3
F	Buff, no visible inclusion, brown paint.	Chogha Mish MS, Delougaz & Kantor, nd; Bandebal II, L 24, Dollfus 1983, Fig. 57:8.	MS 3
G	Buff, scattered grits inclusion, brown paint.	Jawi II, L 10, Dollfus 1983, Fig. 33:17.	MS 3
H	Buff, no visible inclusion, brown paint.	Chogha Mish MS, Delougaz & Kantor, nd.	MS 3-LS 1
I	Buff, dense gritty, prob. burnished on the exterior, brown paint.		ES
J	Greenish buff, white grits, inclusion, gritty face, overfired, green-brown paint.	Jawi II, L 7, Dollfus 1983, Fig. 37:3; Bandebal II, L 16, Dollfus 1983, Fig. 57:4; Chogha Mish, Delougaz & Kantor, nd.	MS 3
K	Buff, scattered grits inclusion, dark brown paint.	Chogha Mish ES, Delougaz & Kantor, nd.	ES
L	Buff, dense gritty, greenish brown paint.		MS 3

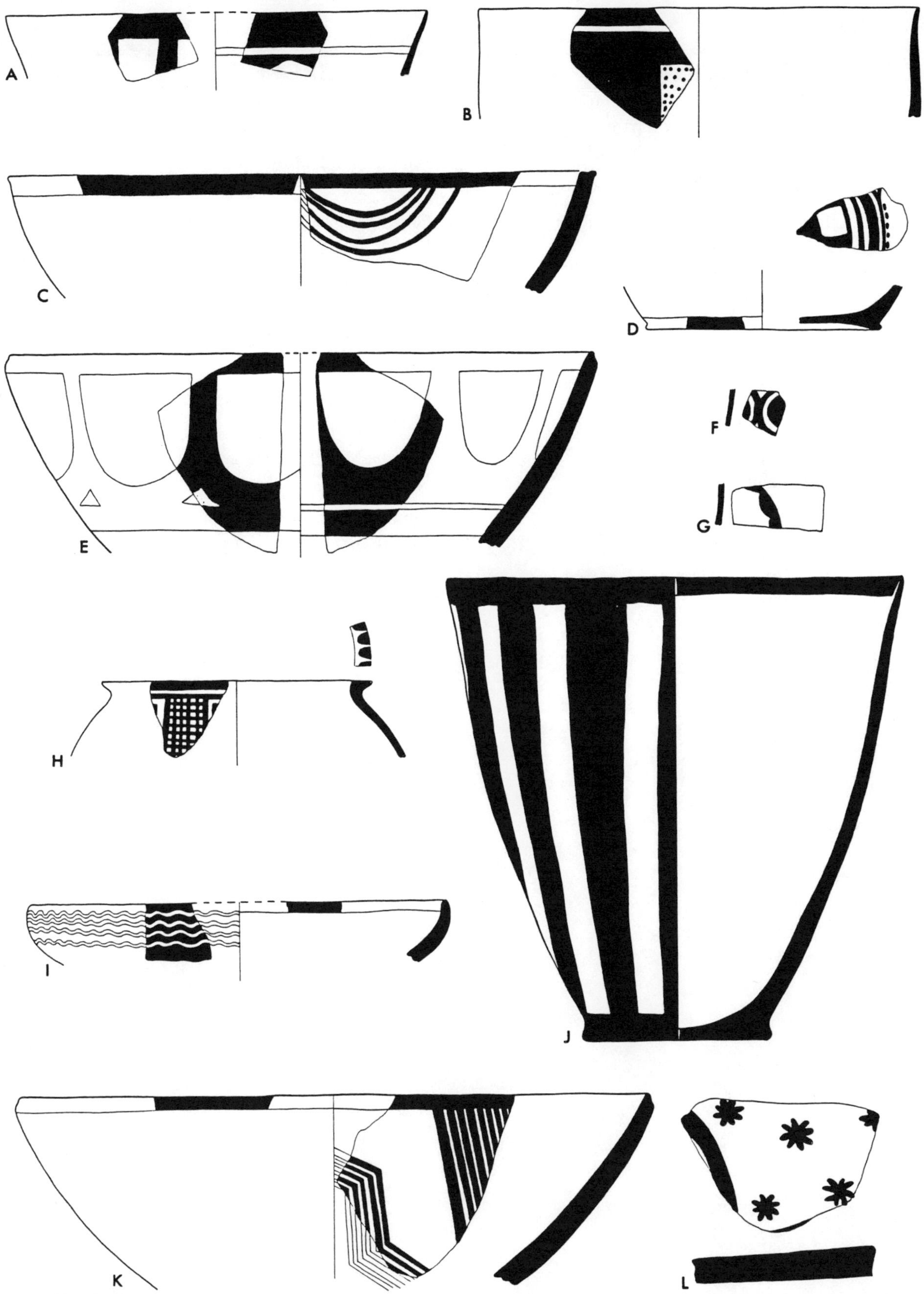
A
B
C
D
E
F
G
H
I
J
K
L

	DESCRIPTION	REFERENCES	PERIOD
A	Buff, dark grits & chaff inclusion, cream buff slip, brown paint.	Jafarabad 5b, Dollfus 1975, Fig. 21:9	ES
B	Buff, scattered grits & chaff inclusion, slipped, black paint.	Jafarabad 6, Dollfus 1975, Fig. 21:15.	ES
C	Base frag. creamy buff, no visible inclusion, thick brown paint.	Chogha Mish ES, Delougaz & Kantor, nd.	ES
D	Buff, grits & chaff inclusion, brown paint.	Chogha Mish ES, Delougaz & Kantor, nd.	ES
E	Buff, grits & chaff Inclusion, slip, black paint.	Chogha Mish ES, Delougaz & Kantor, nd.	ES
F	Buff, red & dark inclusion, cream slip, black paint.	Chogha Mish ES, Delougaz & Kantor, nd.	ES
G	Buff, grits & chaff inclusion, black paint.	Chogha Mish ES. Delougaz & Kantor, nd.	ES
H	Buff, grits & chaff inclusion, cream slip, black paint.	Similar: Jafarabad 5b, Dollfus 1975, Fig. 18:3.	ES
I	Buff, grits inclusion, black paint.		AS 3-ES?
J	Buff, dark grits & chaff inclusion, yellowish buff slip, dark brown paint.	Chogha Mish ES, Delougaz & Kantor, nd.	ES

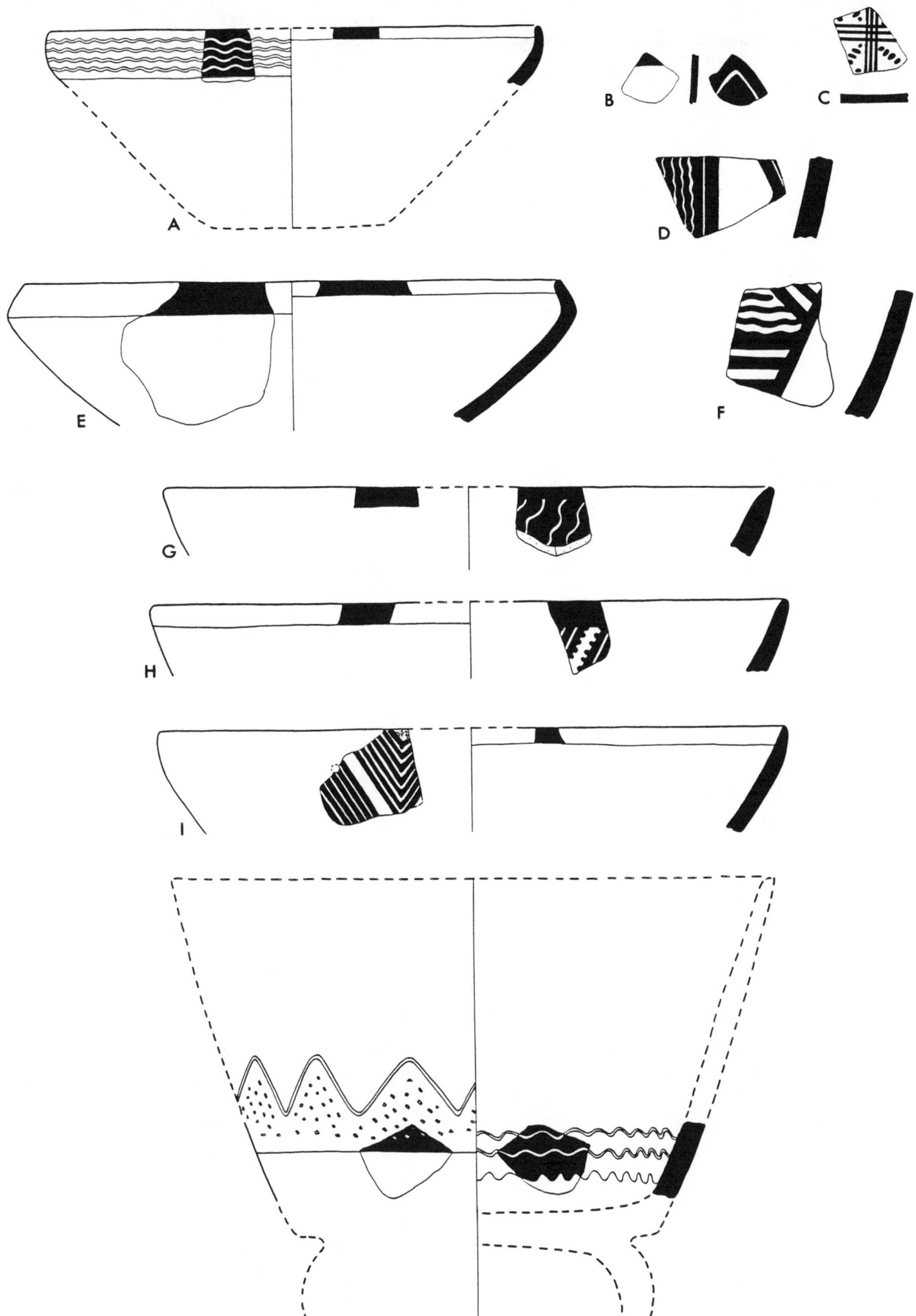
A
B
C
D
E
F
G
H
I
J

Figure 39	SITE G38*		*Scale* 2/5
	DESCRIPTION	REFERENCES	PERIOD
A	Red buff, red & dark grits inclusion, one row of impressed triangles around the neck and a cluster under the false spout on the shoulder.	Adams & Nissen 1972, Figs. 30:C, 59:31.	PL
B	Spout. Cream buff, grits inclusion, red slip.	Susa, acropole 2, L 5, Canal 1978, Fig. 26:1.	PL
C	Marble bowl.		LS-PL
D	Marble wall-cone.		PL
E	Mosaic wall-cone. Buff, no visible inclusion.		PL
F	Buff, no visible inclusion, greenish brown paint.	Qabr-e Sheikhein, Weiss 1976, Fig. 21:120; Bakun A, Langsdorff & McCown 1942, Pl. 30:12; Buhalan, de Mecquenem 1943, Fig. 109:2.	LS 1
G	Buff, no visible inclusion, thick shiny brown paint.	Susa, Steve & Gasche 1971, Pl. 36:5.	LS 2
H	Buff, no visible inclusion, dark brown paint, burnished on the interior.	Susa, de Mecquenem 1943, Pl. V:1	LS 2
I	Buff, no visible inclusion, thick brown paint.	Jafarabad 3m-n, Dollfus 1975, Pl. 20:16.	MS 3-LS
J	Buff, no visible inclusion, thick, shiny brown paint.	Qabr-e Sheikhein, Weiss 1976, Fig. 23:160; Susa, acropole 2, levels 11-7, Canal 1978, Fig. 25:4.	LS 2
K	Buff, no visible inclusion, brown paint (eroded).	Jafarabad 3m-n, Dollfus 1978, Fig. 16:9; Susa, de Morgan 1912, Pl. 3:1.	MS 3-LS
L	Buff, no visible inclusion, buff slipped, brown paint.	Susa, Pottier, Pl. 2:23.	LS 2
M	Buff, no visible inclusion, thick, shiny greenish brown paint.	Jafarabad, Le Breton 1947, Fig. 13:12; Susa, Pottier 1922, Pl. 3:11.	LS 2
N	Buff, no visible inclusion, thick, shiny dark brown paint.		LS 2
O	Buff, no visible inclusion, brown paint.	Musiyan, Gautier & Lampre 1905, Fig. 228; Chogha Mish MS, Delougaz & Kantor, nd; Buhalan, de Mecquenem 1943, Fig. 112:34; Bakun A, Langsdorff & McCown 1942, Pl. 70:6.	MS 3
P	Frag. of a spouted bowl. Buff, grits inclusion, thick dark brown paint.	Susa, Pottier 1922, Pl. 11:33. Bandebal II, L 16, Dollfus 1983, Fig. 77:11.	LS
Q	Buff, no visible inclusion, buff slipped, brown paint.	Musiyan, Gautier & Lampre 1905, Fig. 228; Chogha Mish, Delougaz & Kantor, nd.	MS 3
R	Buff, no visible inclusion, brown paint.	Chogha Mish LS, Delougaz & Kantor, nd; Bandebal III, L. 10, Dollfus 1983, Fig. 88:22-23.	LS 2
S	Buff, no visible inclusion, brown paint.	Jawi II, L 10, Dollfus 1983, Fig. 33:16, Jawi I, L 13. Fig. 23:17.	MS 3-LS
T	Greenish buff, no visible inclusion, green paint.	Bakun A, Langsdorff & McCown 1942, Pl. 70:15.	LS 1

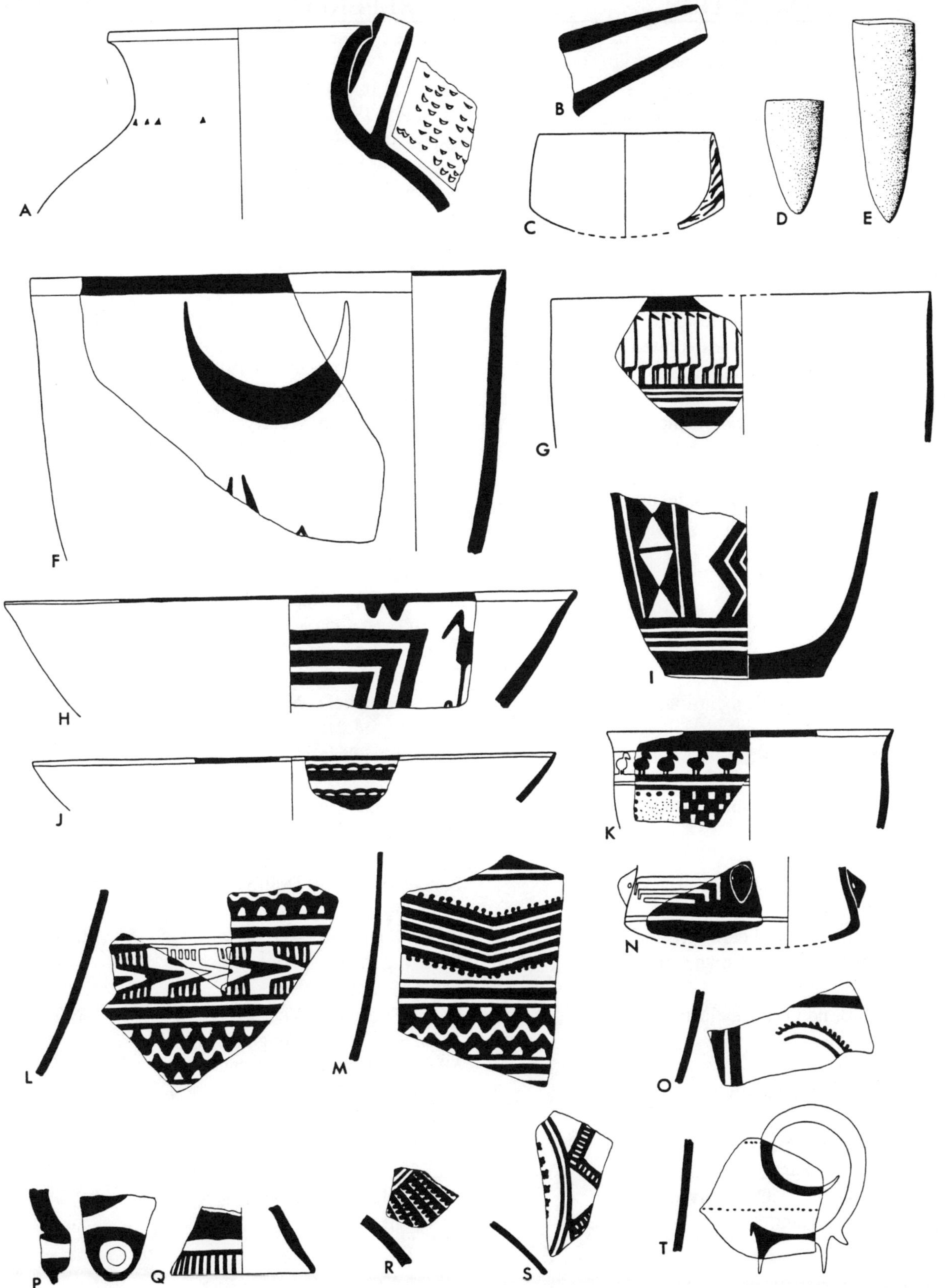
A
B
C
D
E
F
G
H
I
J
K
L
M
N
O
P
Q
R
S
T

Figure 40	SITE G38*		*Scale*: 2/5
	DESCRIPTION	REFERENCES	PERIOD
A	Greenish buff, no visible inclusion, dark brown paint.	Susa, de Morgan 1900, Pl. 18:6.	LS 1
B	Buff, no visible inclusion, greenish buff paint.	Bandebal II, L 16, Dollfus 1983, Fig. 73:4.	MS 3-LS 1
C	Buff, no visible inclusion, brown paint.	Qabr-e Sheikhein, Weiss 1976, Fig. 13:12; Ram Hurmoz, Site 18, McCown's unpublished survey.	LS 1
D	Buff, no visible inclusion, reddish brown paint, burnished exterior.	Bandebal II, L 12, Dollfus 1983, Fig. 87:4; Qabr-e Sheikhein, Weiss 1976, Fig. 13:12.	LS 1
E	Buff, no visible inclusion, regular striation on the interior, greenish brown paint.	Qabr-e Sheikhein, Weiss 1976, Fig. 16:60-61; Bandebal II, L 18, Dollfus 1983, Fig. 62:5; Tall-e Rigi (Fars) Stein 1936, Pl. 26:25.	LS 1
F	Cream buff, no visible inclusion, brown paint.	Qabr-e Sheikhein, Weiss 1976, Fig. 29:3; Bakun A, Egami & Masuda 1962, Fig. 8:2.	LS 1
G	Cream buff, no visible inclusion, burnished exterior brown paint.	Giyan Vc, Contenau and Ghirshman 1935, Pl. 48:22; Bandebal II, levels 17-16, 14, Dollfus 1983, Figs, 65: 10, 81:15, 82:8; Bakun B, Egami & Masuda 1961, Fig. 15:13; Tall-e Sang-e Siah, Fars, Stein 1936, Pl. 23:69.	LS 1
H	Buff, no visible inclusion, thick brown paint.	Qabr-e Sheikhein, Weiss 1976, Fig. 14:21.	LS 1
I	Buff, no visible inclusion, brown paint.	Qabr-e Sheikhein, Weiss 1973, Fig. 16:67.	MS 3
J	Buff, no visible inclusion, brown paint.	Qabr-e Sheikhein, Weiss 1976, Fig. 22:139; Jawi, Le Breton 1947, Fig. 29:2.	MS 3
K	Buff, grits inclusion, thick brown paint.	Bandebal II, L 24, Dollfus 1983, Fig. 56:10.	MS 3
L	Buff, scattered dark grits inclusion, thick, greenish brown paint.	Qabr-e Sheikhein, Weiss 1976, Fig. 16:67; Chogha Mish MS, Delougaz & Kantor, nd.	MS 3
M	Buff, no visible inclusion, brown paint.	Qabr-e Sheikhein, Weiss 1976, Fig. 22:139; Chogha Mish MS, Delougaz & Kantor, nd.	MS 3
N	Buff, grits inclusion, dark brown paint.	Jawi II, L 10, Dollfus 1983, Fig. 33:17.	MS 3
O	Buff, no visible inclusion, brown paint.		MS 3
P	Buff, no visible inclusion, brown paint.	Jafarabad 3m-n, Dollfus 1978, Fig. 16:11-12.	MS 3

A
B
C
D
E
F
G
H
I
J
K
L
M
N
O
P

	DESCRIPTION	REFERENCES	PERIOD
A	Green buff, no visible inclusion, greenish brown paint.	Qabr-e Sheikhein, Weiss 1976, Fig. 18:83.	MS 3
B	Buff, red & dark grits inclusion, brown paint.		MS 1?
C	Buff, scattered red & dark grits inclusion, brown paint.	Chogha Mish MS, Delougaz & Kantor, nd.	MS
D	Buff, red & dark grits inclusion, brown paint.	Jawi, Le Breton 1947, Fig. 23:15; Chogha Mish MS, Delougaz & Kantor, nd.	MS 3
E	Buff, scattered grits inclusion, black paint.	Chogha Mish MS, Delougaz & Kantor, nd.	MS 1
F	Buff, grits inclusion, dark brown paint.	Jawi I, L 15, Dollfus 1983, Fig. 14:5; Haji Mohammad, Ziegler 1961, Pl. 11:a,i.	MS 1
G	Buff, scattered grits inclusion, dark paint.	As above.	MS 1
H	Buff, scattered grits inclusion, brown paint.	Bandebal II, Dollfus 1983, Fig. 94.	MS-LS
I	Buff, no visible inclusion.	Jafarabad 3m, Dollfus 1975, Fig. 54:1.	MS-LS
J	Buff, no visible inclusion, impressed design.	Bandebal II, Dollfus 1983, Fig. 94.	MS-LS
K	Buff, scattered grits inclusion,	As above.	MS-LS
L	Buff, scattered dark grits inclusion, dark, brown paint.	Bandebal II, L 16, Dollfus 1983, Fig. 93:6.	MS-LS 1
M	Buff, no visible inclusion, brown paint.	Jawi, Le Breton 1947, Fig. 18.	MS 3-LS 1
N	Buff, red & dark grits inclusion, greenish brown paint.		MS
O	Buff, red & dark grits inclusion, green brown paint.	Jawi, Le Breton 1947, Fig. 18.	MS

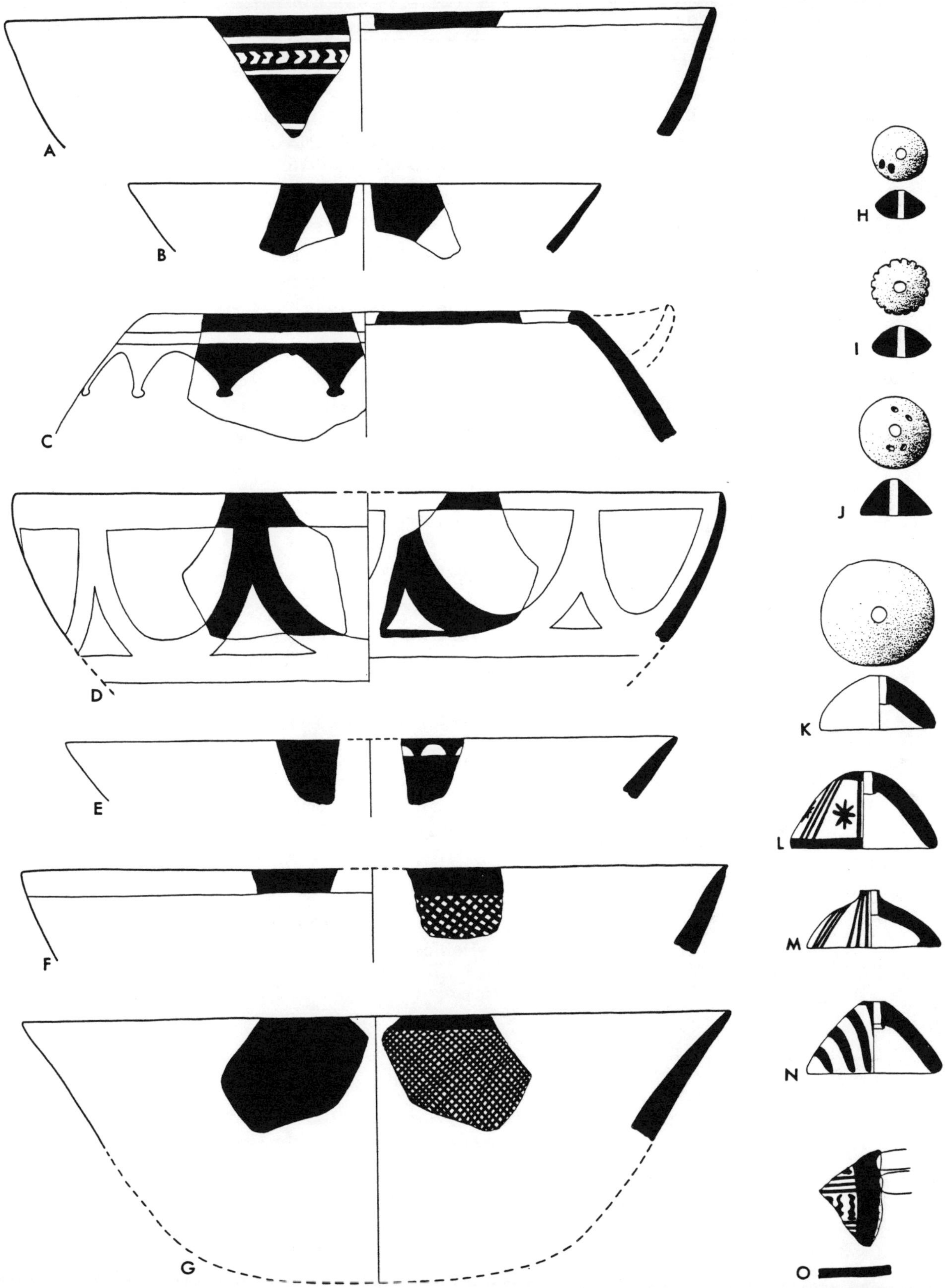
A
B
C
D
E
F
G
H
I
J
K
L
M
N
O

Figure 42		SITE G56-I	*Scale*: 2/5
	DESCRIPTION	REFERENCES	PERIOD
A	Greenish buff, no visible inclusion, brown paint.		MS 3?
B	Cream buff, no visible inclusion, brown paint.	Bandebal II, L 14, Dollfus 1983, Fig. 81:4-5; Qabr-e Sheikhein, Weiss 1976, Fig. 24:171.	MS 3-LS 1
C	Cream buff, scattered red & dark grit inclusion, green brown paint.		MS 3?
D	Greenish buff, no visible inclusion, over-fired, greenish brown paint.	Qabr-e Sheikhein, Weiss 1976, Fig. 15:50.	LS 1
E	Greenish buff, scattered red & dark grits inclusion, grayish green paint.	Qabr-e Sheikhein, Weiss 1976, Fig. 15:50.	LS 1
F	Buff, scattered grits inclusion, dark brown paint.	Bandebal II, L 11, Dollfus 1983, Fig. 86:4-5.	LS 1
G	Buff, no visible inclusion, brown paint.	Qabr-e Sheikhein, Weiss 1976, Fig. 15:46.	LS 1
H	Buff, no visible inclusion, thick, shiny brown paint.	Qabr-e Sheikhein, Weiss 1976, Fig. 17:76, Bandebal, Le Breton 1947, Fig. 37:9; Gap, Egami & Sono 1962, Fig. 23:6.	LS 1
I	Buff, red & dark grits inclusion, dark brown paint.	Farrukhabad, Wright 1981, Fig. 24:b; Qabr-e Sheikhein Weiss 1976, Fig. 25:203.	MS 3-LS 1
J	Buff, no visible inclusion, greenish brown paint.	Qabr-e Sheikhein, Weiss 1976, Fig. 12:3.	MS 3-LS 1
K	Buff, scattered fine grit inclusion, brown paint.	Bandebal, Le Breton 1947, Fig. 39; Qabr-e Sheikhein, Weiss 1976, Fig. 20:111.	LS 1
L	Buff, scattered grits inclusion, white slip, brown paint.		ES ?
M	Buff, no visible inclusion.	Jafarabad 3m/Bandebal 16, Dollfus 1975, Fig. 54:1.	MS 3-LS

A
B
C
D
E
F
G
H
I
J
K
L
M

Figure 43		SITE G60-I	*Scale*: 2/5
	DESCRIPTION	REFERENCES	PERIOD
A	Buff, no visible inclusion, brown paint.	Susa, acropole 2, L 11-7, Canal, 1978, Fig. 25:1; Chogha Mish LS, Delougaz & Kantor, nd.	LS
B	Buff, no visible inclusion, brown paint.	Chogha Mish LS, Delougaz & Kantor, nd.	LS 2
C	Buff, no visible inclusion, greenish brown paint.	Giyan Vc, Contenau & Ghirshman 1935, Pl. 55.	LS 1
D	Buff, no visible inclusion, greenish brown paint.	Susa, acropole 2, L 11-10, Canal 1978, Fig. 25:1.	LS 2
E	Green buff, scattered grits inclusion, green paint, over-fired.		LS
F	Green buff, scattered grits inclusion, dark green paint, shaved exterior.	Farrukhabad, Wright 1981, Fig. 14:b.	LS 1
G	Buff, no visible inclusion, brown paint.	Qabr-e Sheikhein, Weiss 1976, Fig. 29:3-4.	LS 1
H	Buff, no visible inclusion, greenish brown paint.	Qabr-e Sheikhein, Weiss 1976, Fig. 14:21.	LS 1
I	Buff, scattered grits inclusion, greenish brown paint.		MS 3-LS 1
J	Buff, no visible inclusion, brown paint.	Bakun A, Langsdorff & McCown 1942, Pl. 76:1.	MS 3
K	Buff, scattered grits inclusion, brown paint.	Jawi, Le Breton 1947, Fig.18.	MS
L	Buff, grits inclusion, brown paint.		LS 1?
M	Buff, no visible inclusion, greenish brown paint.	Qabr-e Sheikhein, Weiss 1976, Fig. 29:3; Bakun A, Egami & Masuda 1962, Fig. 8:2.	LS 1
N	Buff, scattered grits inclusion, over-fired, brown paint, very uneven lip.	Bandebal II, levels 16, 12, Dollfus 1983, Figs. 73:2, 87:2; Chogha Mish MS, Delougaz & Kantor, nd; Qabr-e Sheikhein, Weiss 1976, Fig. 12:3.	MS 3-LS 1

A
B
C
D
E
F
G
H
I
J
K
L
M.
N

Figure 44	SITE G60-I	*Scale*: 2/5

	DESCRIPTION	REFERENCES	PERIOD
A	Buff, red & dark grits inclusion, brown paint.	Similar:Gap, Egami & Sono 1961, Fig. 25:3.	LS 1?
B	Buff, no visible inclusion, brown paint.	Chogha Mish MS, Delougaz & Kantor, nd.	MS 3
C	Buff, red & dark grits inclusion, brown paint.	Chogha Mish MS, Delougaz & Kantor, nd.	MS 2
D	Buff, dark grits inclusion, brown paint.	Chogha Mish MS, Delougaz & Kantor, nd.	MS 3
E	Buff, dense grits inclusion, gritty face, brown paint.	Chogha Mish MS, Delougaz & Kantor, nd.	MS1-2
F	Cream buff, no visible inclusion, greenish brown paint, some air pockets.		MS 1

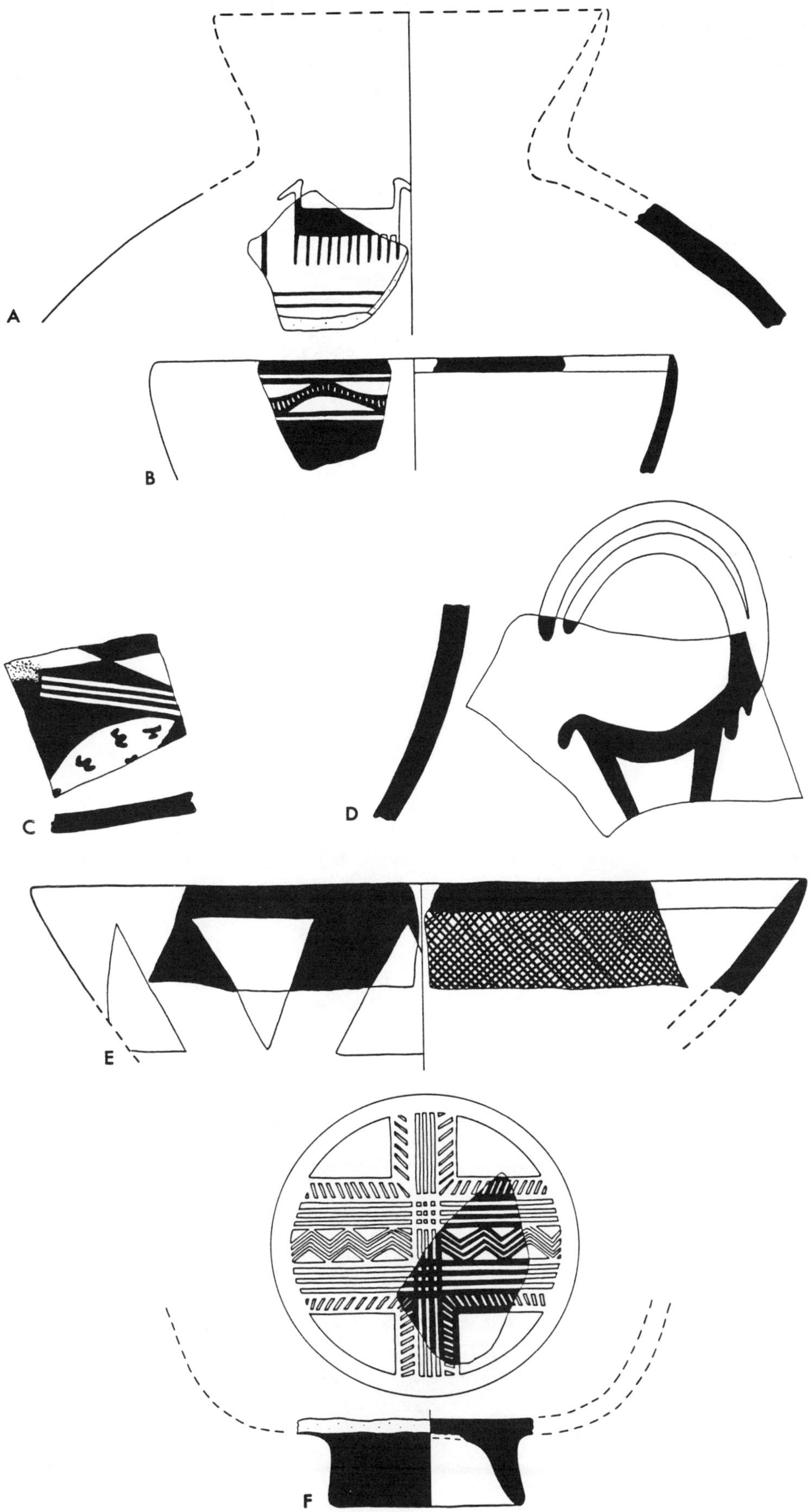
A
B
C
D
E
F

Figure 45	SITE G61		*Scale*: 2/5
	DESCRIPTION	**REFERENCES**	**PERIOD**
A	Buff, no visible inclusion, brown paint.	Bandebal II, L. 24, Dollfus 1983, Fig. 57:8; Chogha Mish, Delougaz & Kantor, nd.	MS 3
B	Buff, no visible inclusion, brown paint.	Chogha Mish LS, Delougaz & Kantor, nd; Susa, L. 21.74 m., Steve & Gasche 1971, Pl. 35:21,26-27.	LS 2
C	Buff, no visible inclusion, greenish brown paint.	Susa, Steve & Gasche 1971, Pl. 36:3-4.	LS 2
D	Buff, no visible inclusion, greenish brown paint.	Chogha Mish LS, Delougaz & Kantor, nd.	LS 2
E	Buff, no visible inclusion, brown paint.	Jawi, Le Breton 1947, Fig. 30:1; Bakun B, Egami & Masuda 1961, Fig. 15:5.	MS 3-LS 1
F	Greenish buff, no visible inclusion, greenish brown paint, over-fired.	Bandebal II, L 16, Dollfus 1983, Fig. 73:4; Bakun A, Langsdorff & McCown 1942, Pls. 40:6, 57:14.	LS 1
G	Buff, no visible inclusion, brown paint, burnished ext.		LS 1?
H	Buff, no visible inclusion, brown paint.	Bandebal II, L 12, Dollfus 1983, Fig. 85:2; Farrukhabad, Wright 1981, Fig. 15:h; Qabr-e Sheikhein, Weiss 1976, Fig. 29:3.	LS 1
I	Buff, grits inclusion, greenish brown paint.	Qabr-e Sheikhein, Weiss 1976, Fig. 24:171.	MS 3-LS 1
J	Greenish buff, no visible inclusion, thick green paint.	Chogha Mish MS, Delougaz & Kantor, nd; Bandebal II, L 22, Dollfus 1983, Fig. 60:3.	MS 3
K	Buff, no visible inclusion, greenish brown paint.	Buhalan, de Mecquenem 1943, Fig. 110:6.	LS 1?
L	Buff, scattered dark grits inclusion, greenish brown paint.	Chogha Mish MS, Delougaz & Kantor, nd.	MS 3
M	Buff, no visible inclusion, brown paint.	Bakun B, Egami & Masuda 1962, Fig. 15:5.	MS 3-LS 1
N	Buff, no visible inclusion, brown paint.	Chogha Mish MS, Delougaz & Kantor, nd.	MS 1
O	Buff, no visible inclusion, brown paint.	Susa, Pottier 1922, Pl. 5:17.	LS 2
P	Greenish grey, no visible inclusion, brown paint.	These goats do not appear at at Bandebal.	MS 3
Q	Buff, scattered grits inclusion, brown paint.	Bandebal II, L 16, Dollfus 1983, Fig. 93:6.	LS
R	Buff, red & dark grits inclusion, dark paint.	Chogha Mish MS, Delougaz & Kantor, nd.	MS 3

A
B
C
D
E
F
G
H
I
J
K
L
M
N
O
P
Q
R

Figure 46 SITE G61 *Scale*: 2/5

	DESCRIPTION	REFERENCES	PERIOD
A	Buff, dark grits inclusion, burnished exterior, thick brown paint.	Jawi II, L. 10, Dollfus 1983, Fig. 33:17.	MS 3
B	Greenish buff, scattered grits inclusion, thick shiny, greenish brown paint, over-fired.	Gap, Egami & Sono 1962, Fig. 16:9; Qabr-e Sheikhein, Weiss 1976, Fig. 17:70.	LS 1
C	Buff, no visible inclusion, creamy buff slipped, brown paint.	Bandebal II, L 16, Dollfus 1983, Fig. 71:11; Qabr-e Sheikhein, Weiss 1976, Fig. 20:170.	MS 3-LS 1

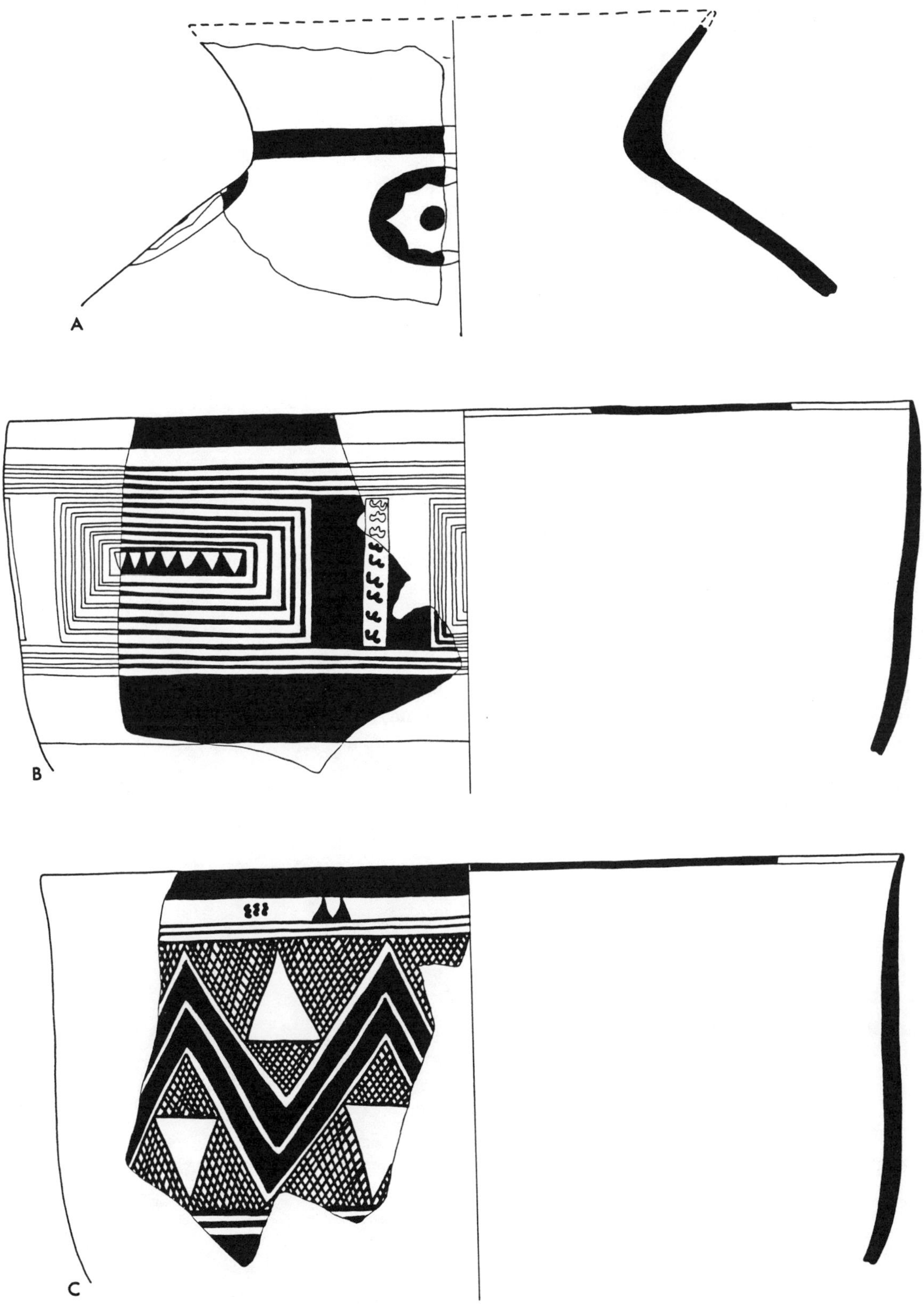
A
B
C

Figure 47	SITE G62-I*	*Scale*: 2/5

	DESCRIPTION	REFERENCES	PERIOD
A	Buff, no visible inclusion, reddish brown paint.	Susa, Steve & Gasche 1971, Pl. 36:3-4.	LS 2
B	Buff, no visible inclusion, dark brown paint.	Bakun A, Langsdorff & McCown 1942, Pl. 71:13.	LS 1?
C	Buff, no visible inclusion, greenish brown paint.		LS 1
D	Greenish buff, no visible inclusion, prob. slipped, dark brown paint.	Qabr-e Sheikhein, Weiss 1976, Fig. 18:94.	LS 1
E	Buff, no visible inclusion, dark brown paint.	Qabr-e Sheikhein, Weiss 1976, Fig. 15:46.	LS 1
F	Buff, no visible inclusion, buff slipped, brown paint.	Chogha Mish LS, Delougaz & Kantor, nd.	LS 2
G	Buff, scattered dark inclusion dark brown paint.	Gap, Egami & Sono 1962, Fig. 15:3.	MS 3-LS 1
H	Cream buff, no visible inclusion brown paint.	Qabr-e Sheikhein, Weiss 1976, Fig. 29:2; Bandebal II, L. 12, Dollfus 1983, Fig. 85: 2; Farrukhabad, Wright 1981, Fig. 15:h.	LS 1
I	Buff, no visible inclusion, brown paint.	Bandebal II, L 16, 12, Dollfus 1983, Figs. 73:2, 87:2.	MS 3-LS 1
J	Cream buff, no visible inclusion buff slipped, brown paint.	Qabr-e Sheikhein, Weiss 1976, Fig. 15:40.	LS 1
K	Buff, scattered grits inclusion thick dark paint.	Chogha Mish MS, Delougaz & Kantor, nd; Bandebal II, Dollfus 1983, L 16, Fig. 73:2, L 12, Fig. 87:2.	MS 3-LS 1

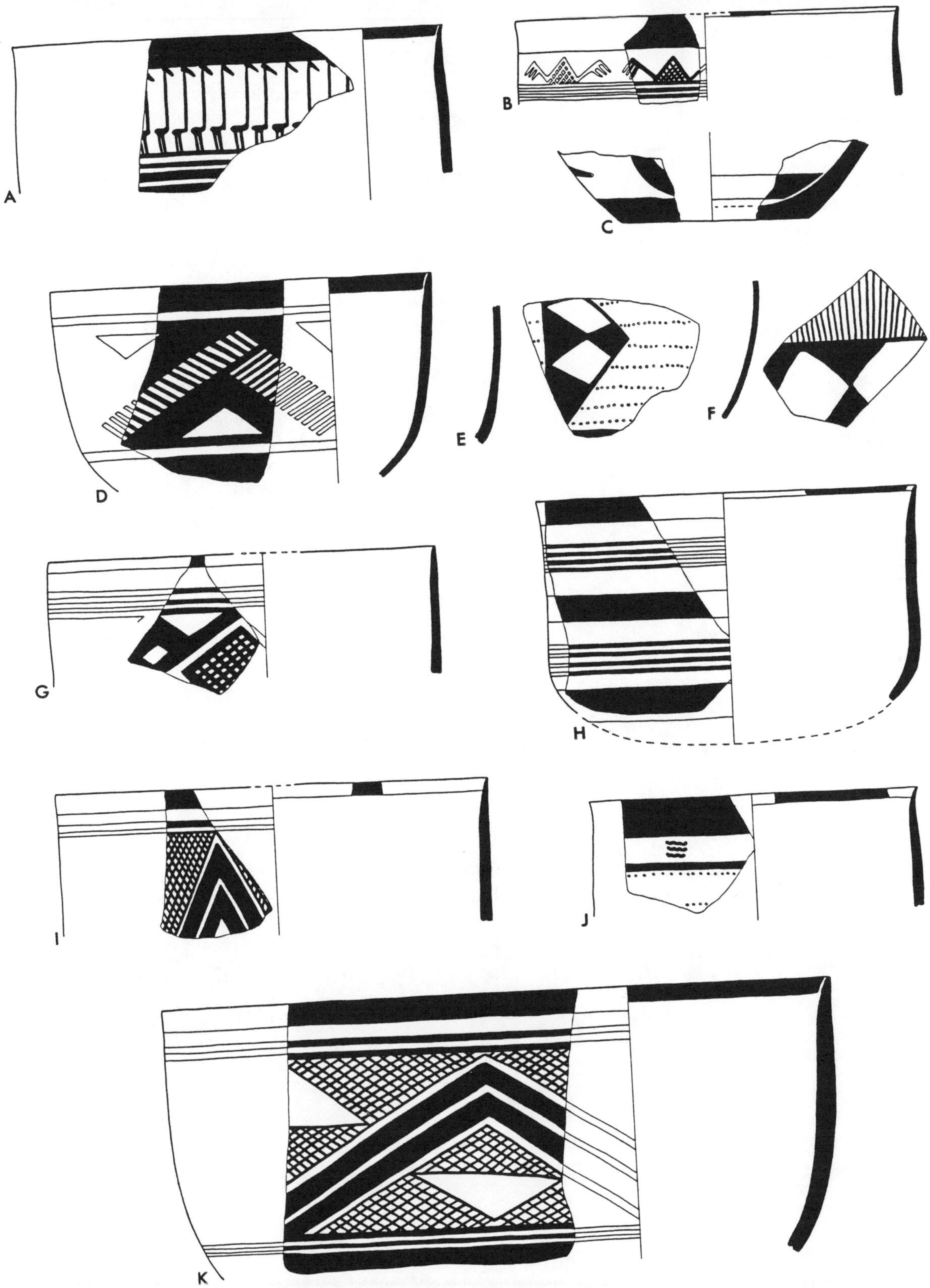
A
B
C
D
E
F
G
H
I
J
K

Figure 48		SITE G62-I*	*Scale*: 2/5
	DESCRIPTION	REFERENCES	PERIOD
A	Green, no visible inclusion, green paint, over-fired.	Bandebal, Le Breton 1947, Fig. 38:14-15.	MS 3- LS 1
B	Buff, no visible inclusion, greenish brown paint.	Fars, Sumner, unpublished survey; Chogha Mish LS, Delougaz & Kantor, nd.	LS 2
C	Buff, grits inclusion, greenish brown paint.	Jafarabad 3m, Dollfus 1975 Fig. 49:4, 6.	MS 3- LS 1
D	Buff, no visible inclusion, greenish brown paint.	Susa, Steve & Gasche 1971, Pl. 35:1-3.	LS 2?
E	Buff, red & dark grits inclusion greenish brown paint.	Qabr-e Sheikhein, Weiss 1976, Fig. 22:142-143; Bandebal II, L 14, Dollfus 1983, Fig. 81:6; Farrukhabad, Wright 1981, Fig. 23:I.	MS 3
F	Green buff, red & dark grits inclusion, greenish paint.	Giyan Vd, Contenau & Ghirshman 1935, Pl. 57:8; Musiyan, Gautier & Lampre 1905, Fig. 150; Bandebal II, L 24, Dollfus, 1983, Fig. 56:10; Jafarabad 3n, Dollfus 1975, Fig. 50:7.	MS 3
G	Buff, grits inclusion, buff slip, brown paint, exterior prob. burnished.	Chogha Mish MS, Delougaz & Kantor, nd; Jawi II, L 11, Dollfus 1983, Fig. 31:1-3.	MS 3
H	Buff, no visible inclusion, buff slipped, brown paint.	Chogha Mish MS, Delougaz & Kantor, nd; Bakun A, Langsdorff & McCown 1942, Pl. 73:1-2.	MS 3
I	Buff, grits inclusion, dark brown paint.	Jafarabad 3m-n, Dollfus 1978, Fig. 16:10.	MS 3
J	Greenish buff, grits inclusion, greenish brown paint, overfired.	Bandebal II, levels 23, 16, Dollfus 1983, Figs. 57:4, 75:5.	MS 3
K	Buff, dense grits & chaff inclusion, reserved diagonal wavy lines on dark brown paint.	Chogha Mish, ES, Delougaz & Kantor, nd.	ES

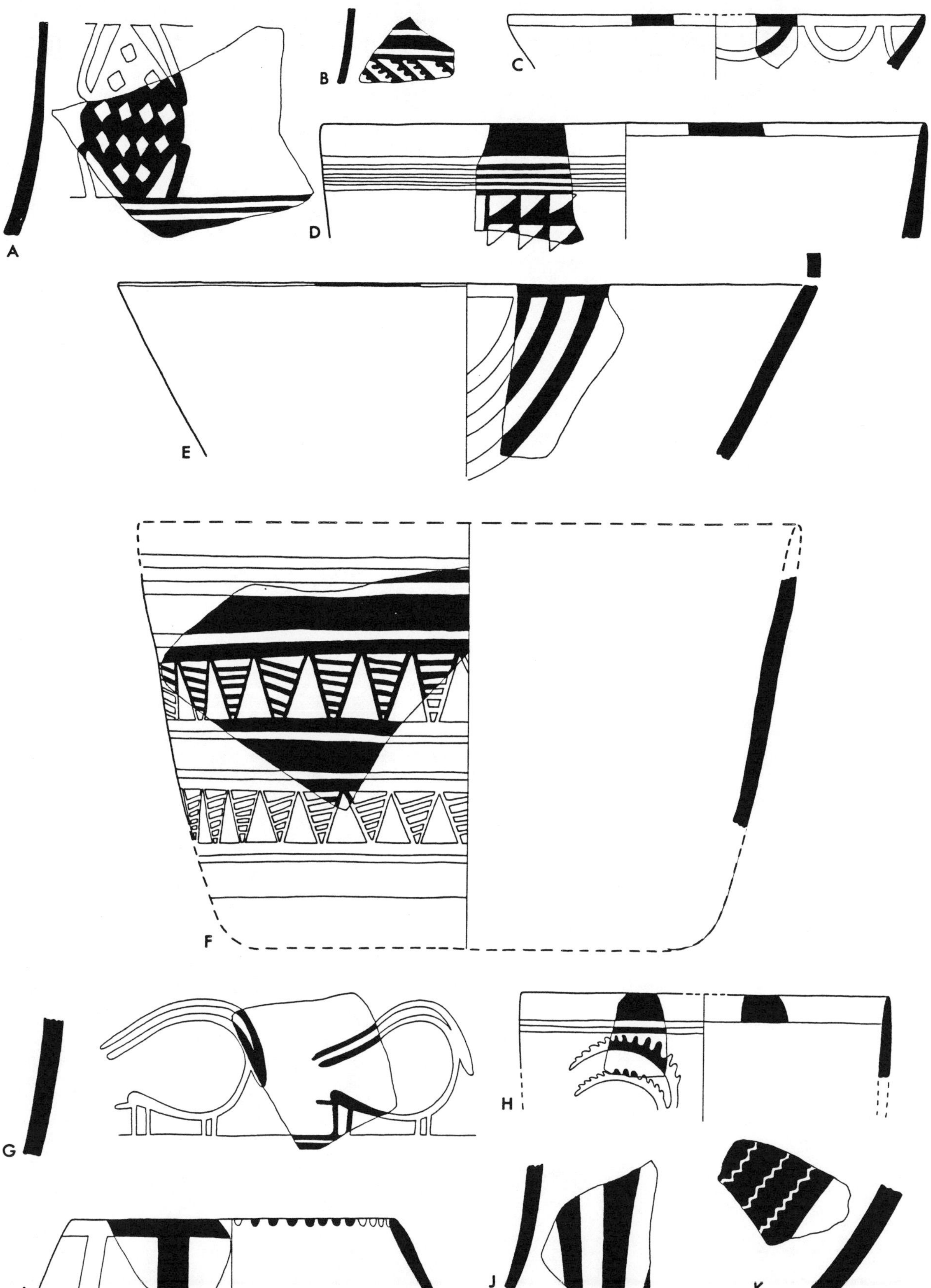
A
B
C
D
E
F
G
H
I
J
K

Figure 49	SITE G64-I	*Scale*: 2/5

	DESCRIPTION	REFERENCES	PERIOD
A	Green buff, no visible inclusion buff slipped, dark paint.	Susa, Steve & Gasche 1971, Pl. 41:13.	LS 2
B	Cream buff, no visible inclusion buff slipped, brown paint.	Susa, Steve & Gasche 1971, Pl. 41:18.	LS 2
C	Cream buff, no visible inclusion slipped, flaky brown paint.	Chogha Mish MS, Delougaz & Kantor, nd; Susa acropole 2, levels 11-7, Canal 1978, Fig. 25:1; Jafarabad 3n, Dollfus 1975, Fig. 50:6.	MS 3-LS
D	Cream buff, no visible inclusion greenish brown paint.	Chogha Mish MS, Delougaz & Kantor, nd.	MS 3
E	Greenish buff, no visible inclusion, greenish brown paint.	Bakun A, Langsdorff & McCown 1942, Pl. 71:1,3,5.	LS 1
F	Buff, no visible inclusion, thick brown paint.	Susa, de Mecquenem 1943, Pl. 4:4.	LS 2
G	Cream buff, no visible inclusion buff slipped, thick brown paint.	Susa, Pottier 1922, Pl. 1:7, 9-10.	LS 2
H	Greenish buff, no visible inclusion, greenish brown paint.		LS 1?
I	Buff, no visible inclusion, buff slipped, brown paint.	Qabr-e Sheikhein, Weiss 1976, Fig. 18:88; Giyan Vd, Contenau & Ghirshman 1935, Pl. 56:6; Fars, Site 378, Sumner, unpublished survey.	LS 1
J	Pedestal base. Buff, no visible inclusion, regular striations on the ext. & int., buff slip, grayish green paint.	Chogha Mish LS, Delougaz & Kantor, nd; Susa, Steve & Gasche 1971, Pls. 36:28, 39:20.	LS
K	Buff, no visible inclusion, buff slipped, brown paint.	Qabr-e Sheikhein, Weiss 1976, Fig. 24:163.	LS 2

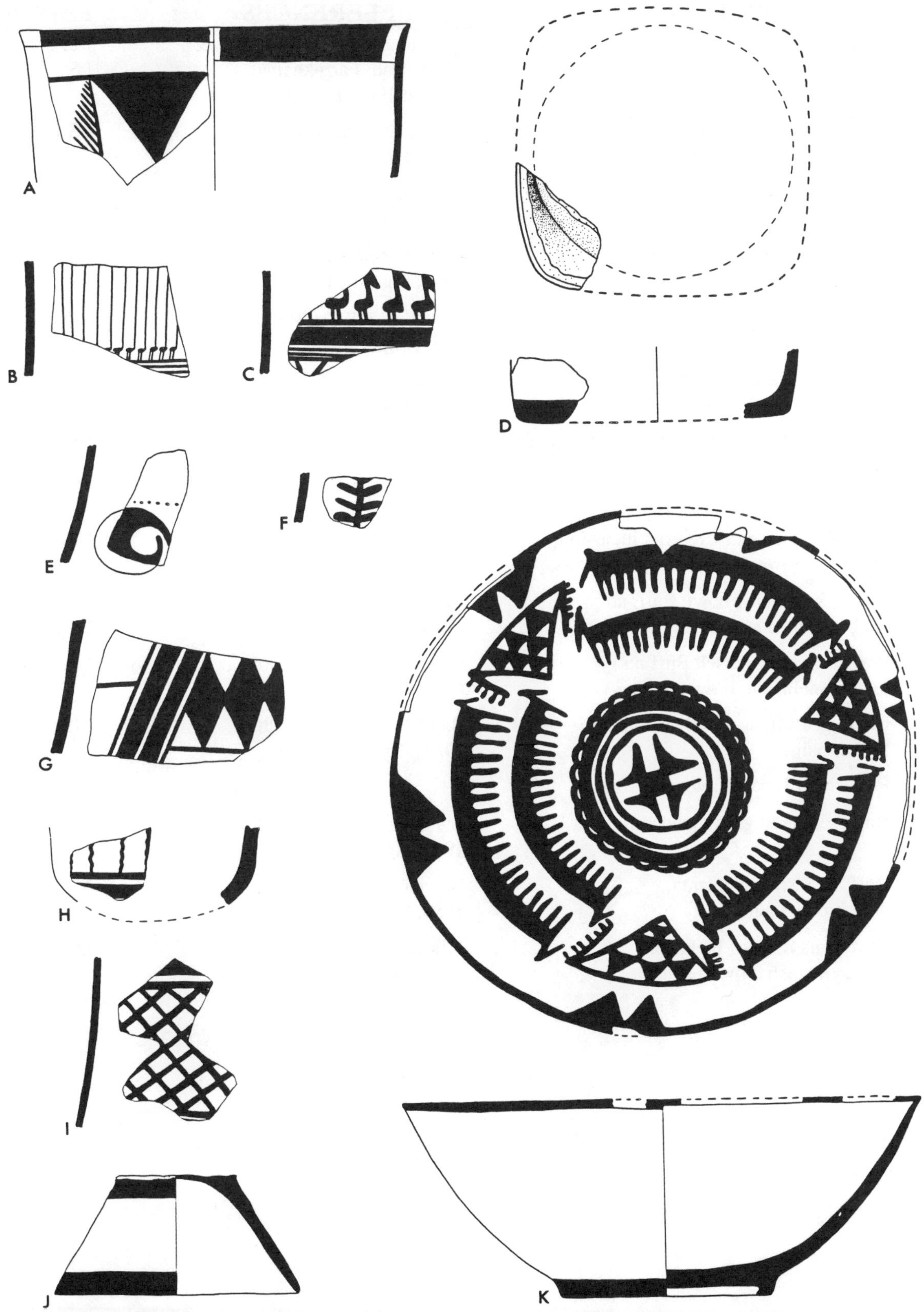
A
B
C
D
E
F
G
H
I
J
K

Figure 50	SITE G64-I		*Scale*: 2/5
	DESCRIPTION	REFERENCES	PERIOD
A	Greenish buff, no visible inclusion, dark greenish brown paint.	Chogha Mish MS, Delougaz & Kantor, nd; Farrukhabad, Wright 1981, Fig. 24:c.	MS 3-LS 1
B	Cream buff, no visible inclusion, buff slipped, brown paint.	Qabr-e Sheikhein, Weiss 1976, Fig. 14:21.	LS 1
C	Cream buff, no visible inclusion, brown paint.	Susa, Steve & Gasche 1971, Pl. 50:26.	LS 2
D	Buff, no visible inclusion, dark, greenish brown paint, eaten into the surface.	Qabr-e Sheikhein, Weiss 1976, Fig. 14:21.	LS 1
E	Buff, scattered grits inclusion, brown paint.	Jawi II, L 10, Dollfus 1983, Fig. 33:17.	MS 3
F	Cream buff, scattered grits inclusion, cream slip, black paint.	Chogha Mish LS, Delougaz & Kantor, nd.	LS
G	Buff, fine grits inclusion, thick dark paint.		MS 3
H	Cream buff, no visible inclusion, shiny brown paint.	Susa, Steve & Gasche 1971, Pl. 35:21, 26.	LS 2
I	Greenish buff, straw & grits inclusion, greenish brown paint, some air pockets.		MS ?
J	Frag. of a spouted bowl. Buff, no visible inclusion, dark brown paint.	Bandebal II, L 16, Dollfus 1983, Fig. 77:11.	MS 3-LS 1
K	Prob. a tortoise vessel. Buff no visible inclusion, brown paint.	Chogha Mish MS, Delougaz & Kantor, nd.	MS 1
L	Lid frag. Buff, no visible inclusion, brown paint.	Bandebal II, L 14, Dollfus 1983, Fig. 82:9.	MS 3
M	Pinkish buff, no visible inclusion.		LS
N	Buff, scattered grits inclusion.	Bandebal II, L 16, Dollfus 1983, Fig. 94:7.	LS
O	Buff, no visible inclusion, dark brown paint.	Bandebal II, L 16, Dollfus 1983, Fig. 93:6.	MS 3-LS 1
P	Buff, grits & chaff inclusion, dark, greenish brown paint.	Jafarabad 6-4, Dollfus 1978, Fig. 13:15.	ES

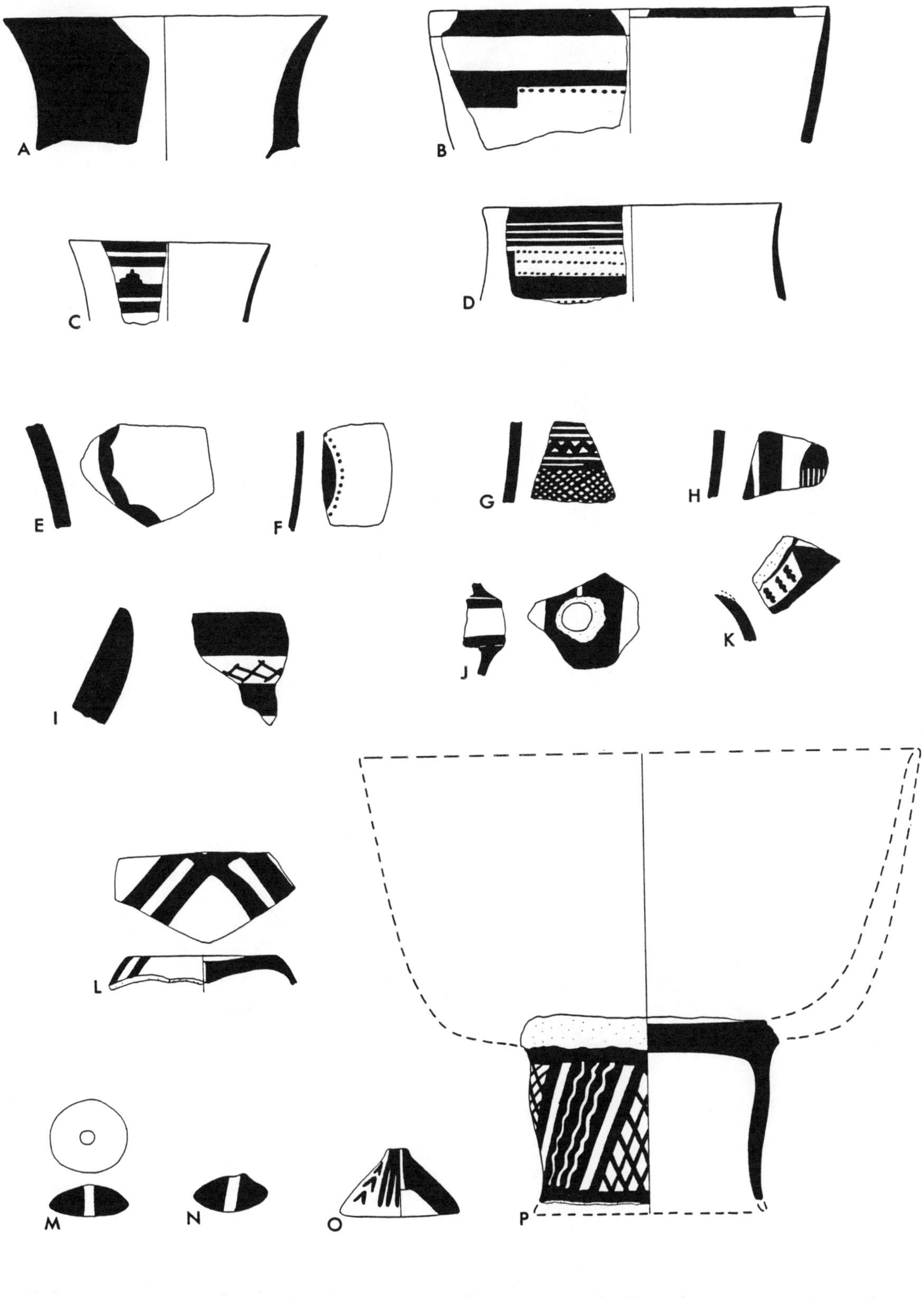
A
B
C
D
E
F
G
H
I
J
K
L
M
N
O
P

Figure 51	SITE G79-I*		*Scale*: 2/5
	DESCRIPTION	REFERENCES	PERIOD
A	Buff, no visible inclusion, brown paint.	Chogha Mish LS, Delougaz & Kantor, nd.	MS 3-LS
B	Buff, no visible inclusion, brown paint.	Susa, Steve & Gasche 1971, Pl. 40:10.	LS 2
C	Buff, scattered grits inclusion, shiny, dark brown paint, some air pockets.	Susa, Steve & Gasche, 1971, Pl. 39:14; Jafarabad 3d, Dollfus 1978, Fig. 19:23.	LS 2
D	Buff, dark grits inclusion, dark greenish brown paint.	Farrukhabad, Wright 1981, Fig. 24:a.	MS 3-LS 1
E	Cream buff, scattered grits inclusion, slip, greenish brown paint.	Ram Hormuz, Site 18, McCown, unpublished survey; Qabr-e Sheikhein, Weiss 1976, Fig. 17:70.	LS 1
F	Buff, no visible inclusion, prob. slipped, shiny greenish brown paint.	Douecye, Le Breton 1947, Fig. 2:3; Bandebal, Le Breton 1947, Fig. 36:5.	LS 1
G	Buff, no visible inclusion, brown paint.	Qabr-e Sheikhein, Weiss 1976, Fig. 13:20.	LS 1
H	Buff, no visible inclusion, thick, shiny brown paint.	Bandebal II, L 22, Dollfus 1983, Fig. 60:5; Jawi II, L 7, Dollfus 1983, Fig. 37: 7; Jafarabad, 3m, Dollfus 1975, Fig. 51:1.	MS
I	Buff, no visible inclusion, brown paint.	Similar to the 'step motif' at Farrukhabad, Wright 1981 fig. 19.	LS 1
J	Buff, no visible inclusion, buff slipped, thick, shiny brown paint.	Susa, Le Breton 1947, Fig. 46:13.	LS 2
K	Buff, scattered grits inclusion, cream slip, dark maroon paint.	Chogha Mish MS, Delougaz & Kantor, nd.	MS 3

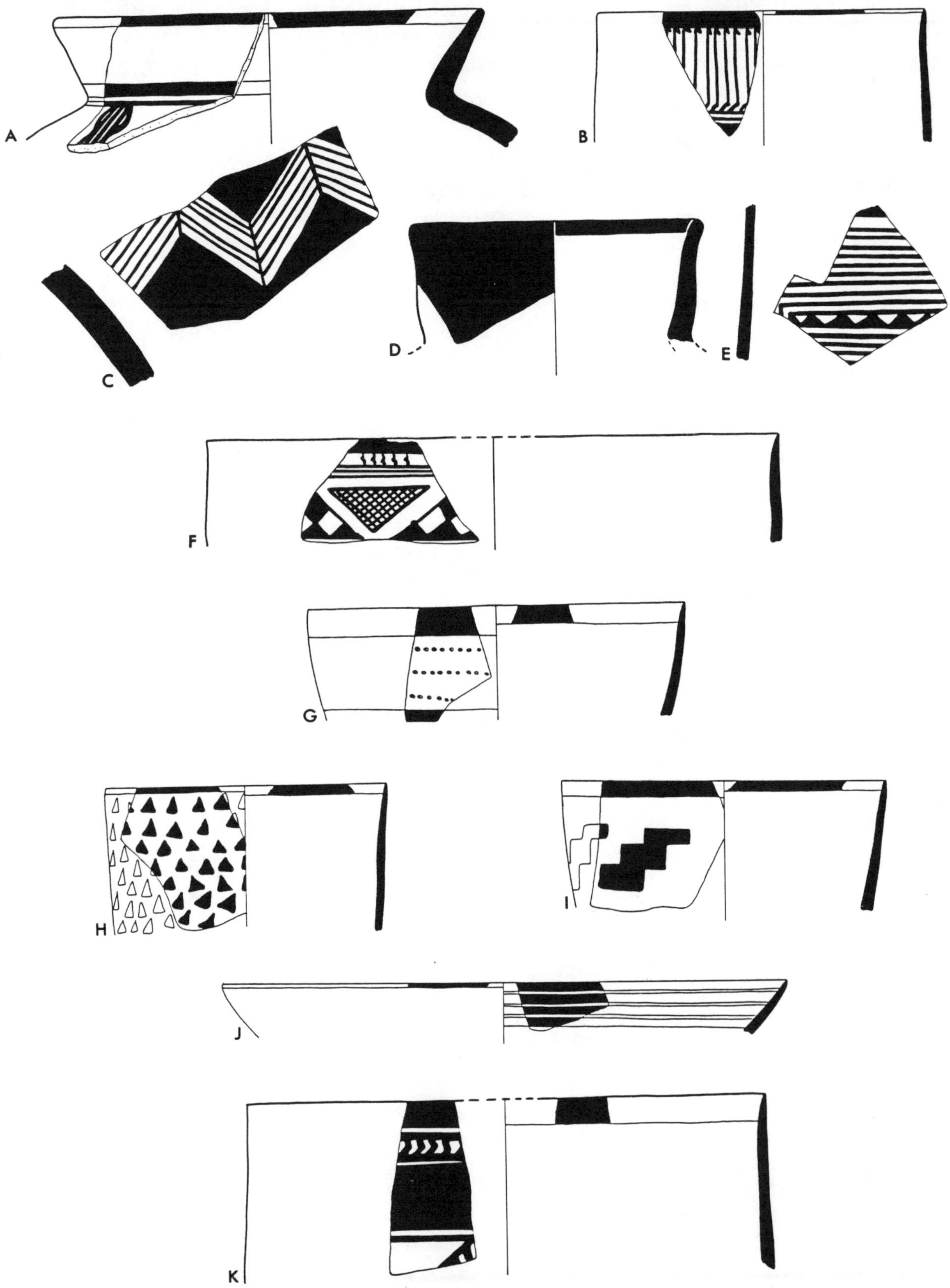
A
B
C
D
E
F
G
H
I
J
K

Figure 52	SITE G79-II		*Scale*: 2/5
	DESCRIPTION	REFERENCES	PERIOD
A	Buff, no visible inclusion, greenish brown paint.	Qabr-e Sheikhein, Weiss 1976, Fig. 14:21.	LS 1
B	Buff, no visible inclusion, brown paint.	Qabr-e Sheikhein, Weiss 1976, Fig. 23:160.	LS 2
C	Buff, no visible inclusion, buff slipped, brown paint.		LS 1?
D	Greenish buff, no visible inclusion, greenish brown paint.	Qabr-e Sheikhein, Weiss 1976, Fig. 18:94.	LS 1
E	Cream buff, scattered grits inclusion, glossy dark brown paint, some air pockets.		LS 1?
F	Buff, no visible inclusion, brown paint.		LS 1?
G	Buff, no visible inclusion, greenish brown paint.	Susa, Pottier 1922, Pl. 5:26	LS 2
H	Green buff, scattered grits inclusion, sunken green paint, over-fired.		MS 3
I	Buff, no visible inclusion, thick dark paint.		LS 1?
J	Greenish buff, scattered grits inclusion, thick dark paint, some air pockets.	Gap, Egami & Sono 1962, Fig. 16; Bandebal II. L 16, Dollfus 1983, Fig. 71:9.	MS 3-LS 1?

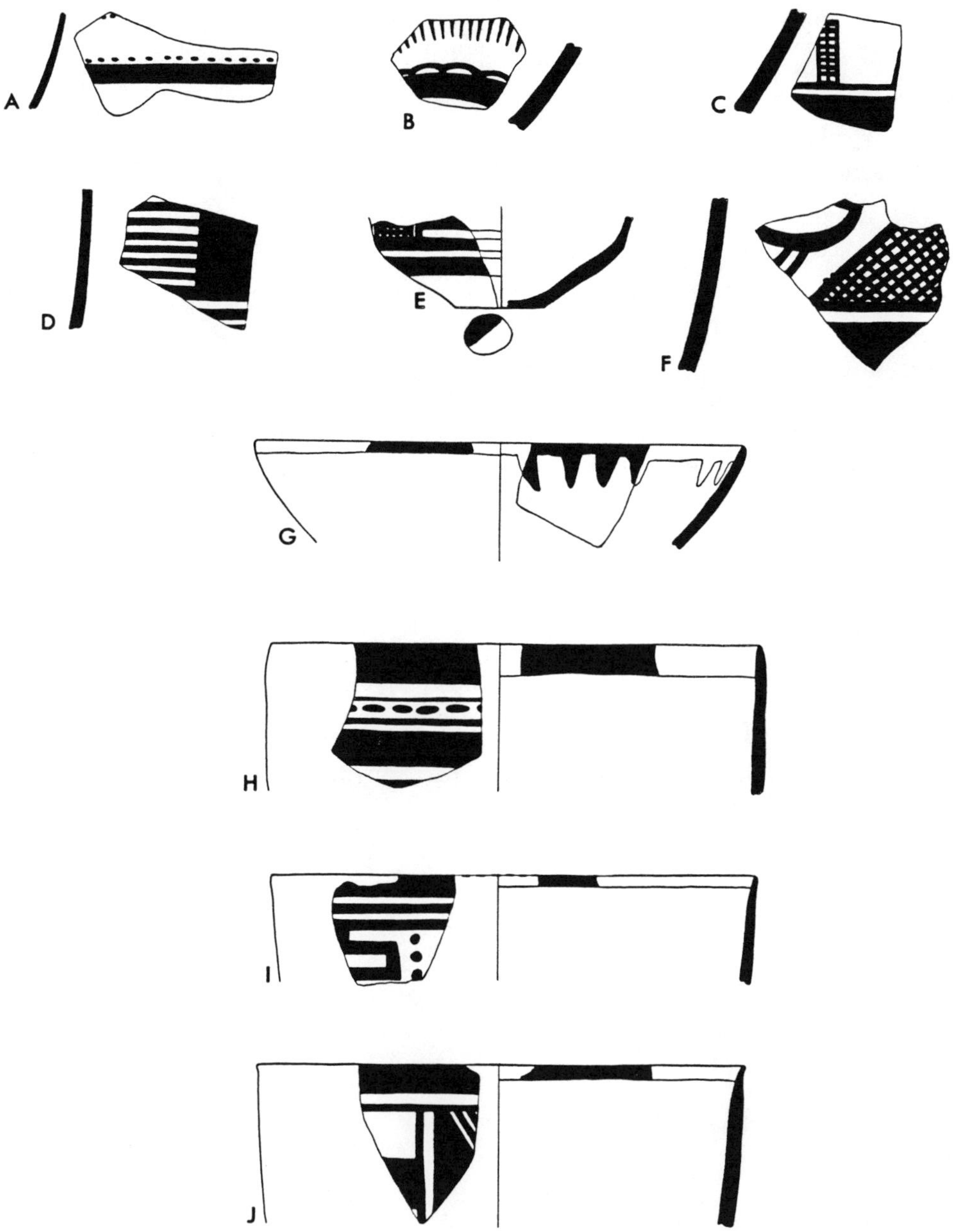
A
B
C
D
E
F
G
H
I
J

Figure 53	SITE G81*	*Scale*: 2/5

	DESCRIPTION	REFERENCES	PERIOD
A	Buff, no visible inclusion, brown paint.	Susa, acropole 2, levels 11-7, Canal 1978, Fig. 25:1; Chogha Mish MS, Delougaz & Kantor, nd.	MS 3-LS 1
B	Buff, no visible inclusion, brown paint.	Susa, Steve & Gasche 1971, Pl. 36:5.	LS 2
C	Buff, no visible inclusion, greenish brown paint.	Bakun A, Egami & Masuda 1962, Fig. 11:11.	LS 1
D	Buff, no visible inclusion, brown paint.	Susa, de Morgan 1900, Pl. 20.	LS 2
E	Green buff, scattered grits inclusion, green paint, some air pockets, over-fired.		LS
F	Buff, red & dark grits inclusion, brown paint.	Bandebal III, L 10, Dollfus 1983, Fig. 88:25.	LS 2
G	Greenish buff, scattered grits inclusion, dark brown paint.	Bakun A, Langsdorff & McCown 1942, Pl. 63:3; Giyan Vb, Contenau & Ghirshman 1935, Pl. 45:2; Kanakan (Fars), Stein 1936, Pl. 21:44.	MS 3-LS
H	Buff, grits inclusion, dark brown paint.	Chogha Mish MS, Delougaz & Kantor, nd; Farrukhabad, Wright 1981, Fig. 16:a.	MS 3
I	Buff, no visible inclusion, brown paint.	Qabr-e Sheikhein, Weiss 1976, Fig. 13:20.	LS 1
J	Buff, no visible inclusion, brown paint.	Qabr-e Sheikhein, Weiss 1976, Fig. 14:21.	LS 1
K	Buff, no visible inclusion, brown paint.		LS 1

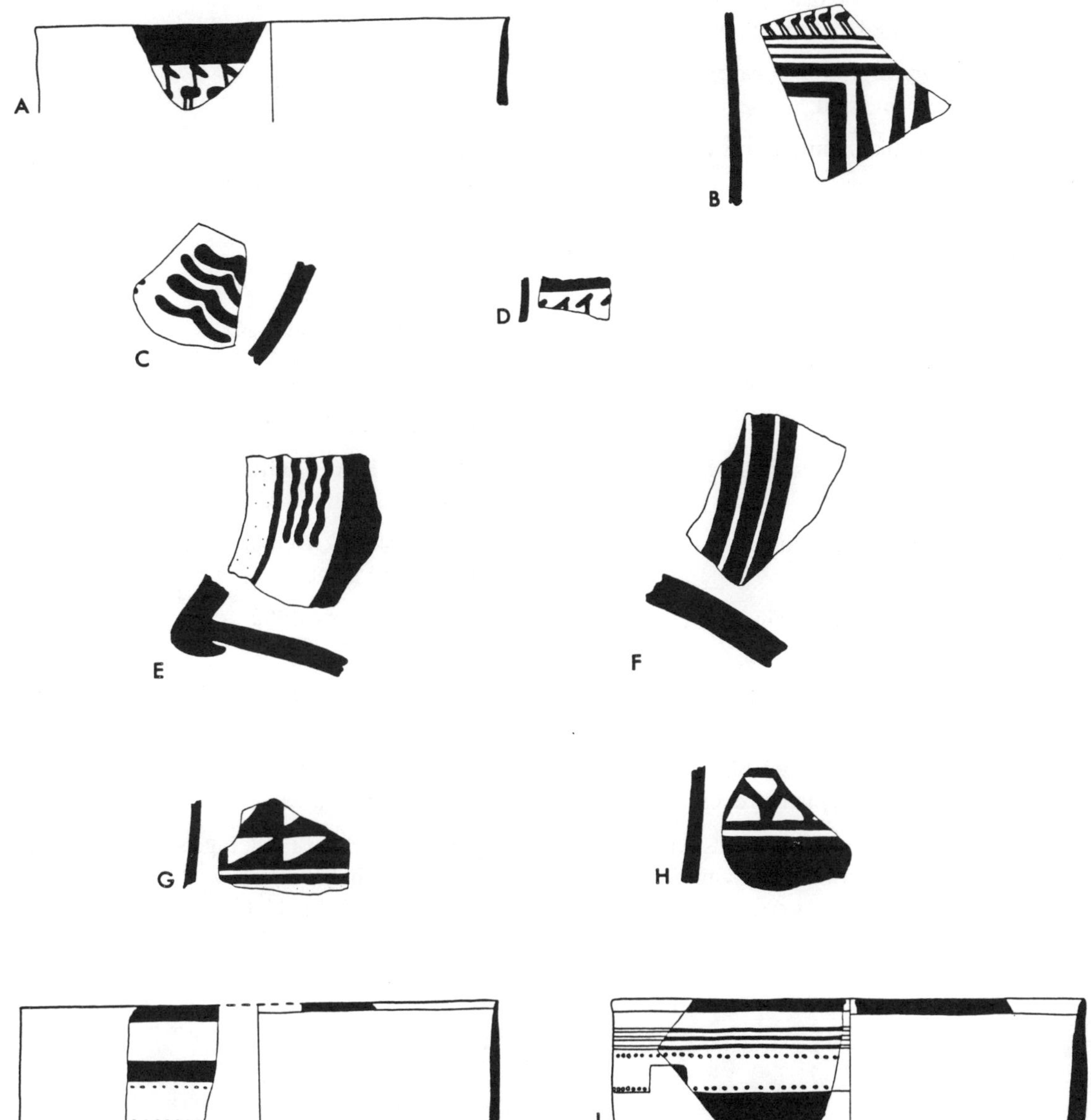
A
B
C
D
E
F
G
H
I
J
K

	DESCRIPTION	REFERENCES	PERIOD
A	Buff, no visible inclusion, dark greenish paint, over- fired, deformed, prob. a waster.		MS 3- LS 1
B	Buff, scattered grits inclusion, slipped, brown paint.		MS 3
C	Buff, no visible inclusion, brown paint.	Susa, Steve & Gasche 1971, Pl. 40:12; Susa, de Mecquenem 1928, Fig. 9.	LS 2
D	Buff, dense red & dark grits inclusion, slipped, brown paint.		MS 3
E	Buff, scattered grits inclusion thick, dark brown paint.	Chogha Mish LS, Delougaz & Kantor, nd; Jafarabad, 3d-1, Dollfus 1978, Fig. 19:23; Susa, de Mecquenem, 1943, Pl. 7:1-2.	LS 2
F	Buff, medium size grits inclusion, slipped, brown paint.	Bandebal II, L 16, Dollfus 1983, Pl. 17:7.	LS
G	Buff, no visible inclusion, brown paint.	Chogha Mish MS, Delougaz & Kantor, nd.	MS 3
H	Buff, no visible inclusion, brown paint.	Gap, Egami & Sono 1962 Fig. 24:7.	MS 3
I	Cream buff, no visible inclusion, shaved surface on ext.	Farrukhabad, Wright 1981, Fig. 14:a.	LS 1
J	Bird figurine. Buff, no visible inclusion, br. paint, pierced eyes.	Bakun A, Langsdorff & McCown 1942, Pl. 5:4-6.	LS 2
K	Greenish buff, no visible inclusion, slipped, shiny, dark brown paint.	Gap, Egami & Sono 1962, Fig. 20:4; Giyan Vb, Contenau & Ghirshman 1936, Pl. 44:15.	MS 3

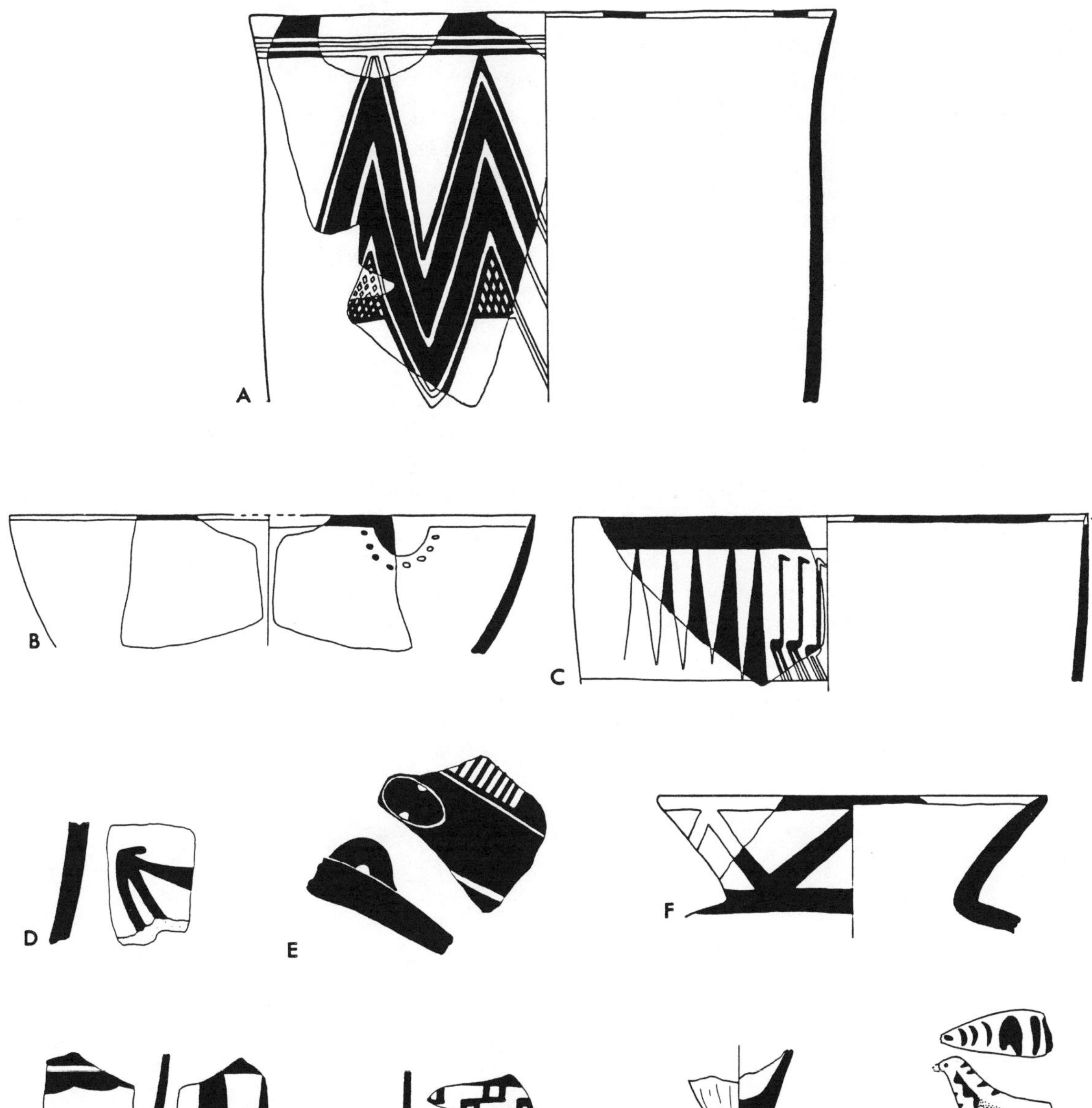
A
B
C
D
E
F
G
H
I
J
K

Figure 55	SITE G86-I	*Scale*: 2/5

	DESCRIPTION	REFERENCES	PERIOD
A	Buff, no visible inclusion, buff slipped, brown paint.	Bandebal, Le Breton 1947, Fig. 38:9; Qabr-e Sheikhein, Weiss 1976, Fig. 15:46.	LS 1
B	Cream buff, no visible inclusion (occasional straws), slipped, dark brown paint.	Qabr-e Sheikhein, Weiss 1976, Fig. 15:40.	LS 1
C	Green buff, no visible inclusion greenish brown paint.	Qabr-e Sheikhein, Weiss 1976, Fig. 20:111; Bandebal, Le Breton 1947, Fig. 38:1.	LS 1
D	Green buff, scattered grits, prob. slipped, thick, shiny, greenish brown paint, sunken in places.	Chogha Mish MS, Delougaz & Kantor, nd.	MS 1
E	Green, scattered grits inclusion, sunken green paint, over-fired.	Jawi II, L 7, Dollfus 1983, Fig. 37:3; Bandebal II, L 23; ibid., Fig. 57:4. Chogha Mish MS, Delougaz & Kantor, nd.	MS 3
F	Probably a lid. Light bricky, dense dark grits inclusion, rough int., smoothed ext., dark brown painted circle.	Bandebal II, L 20, Dollfus 1983, Fig. 58:15; L 16, Fig. 66:8; Qabr-e Sheikhein, Weiss 1976, Fig. 111:2.	MS 3?
G	Buff, scattered red & dark dark brown paint.	Jawi I, L 15, Dollfus 1983, 14:5; Ziegler 1962, Pl. 11:a,i.	MS 1

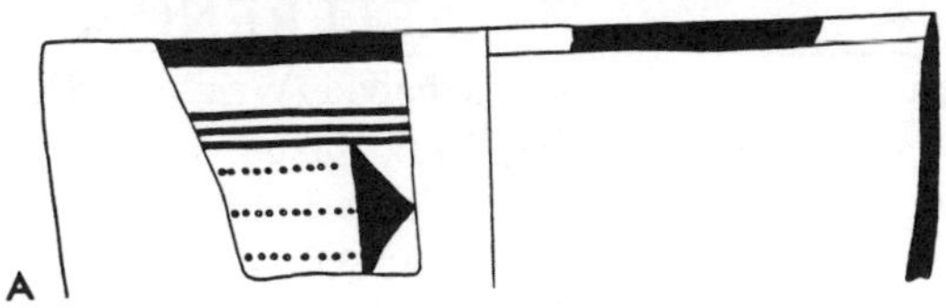
A

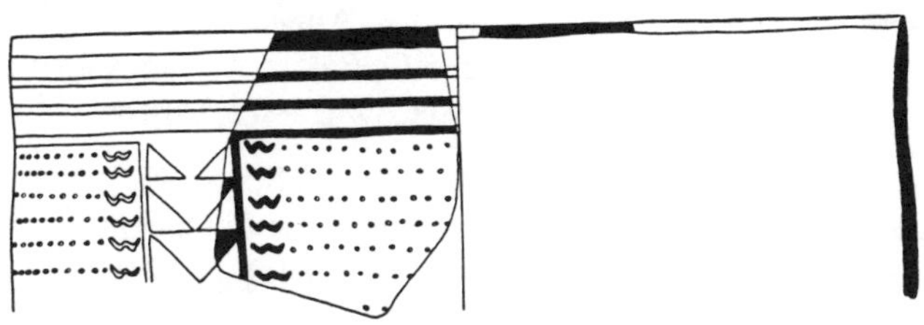
B

C

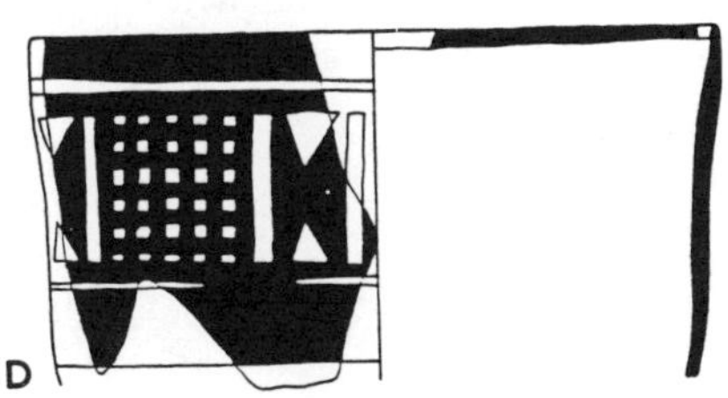
D

E

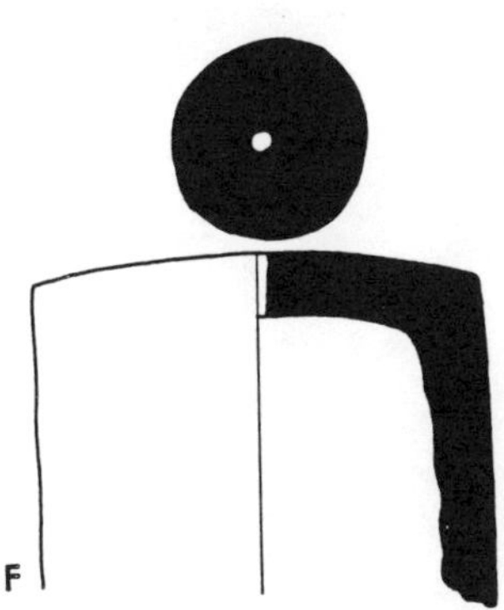
F

G

Figure 56	SITE G86-II		*Scale*: 2/5
	DESCRIPTION	REFERENCES	PERIOD
A	Buff, no visible inclusion, cream slip, thick dark brown paint.	Farrukhabad, Wright 1981, Fig. 14:6; Bakun A, Langsdorff & McCown 1942, Pls. 16:6, 36:13-14; Qabr-e Sheikhein, Weiss 1976, Fig. 29:11.	LS 1
B	Lid. Buff, red and & dark grits inclusion, cream slip, dark brown paint.		MS 3
C	Greenish buff, no visible inclusion, greenish brown paint.	Bakun A, Alizadeh 1988a, Fig. 6:C; Bakun A, Langsdorff & McCown, 1942, Pl. 16:1.	LS 1
D	Buff, red & dark grits inclusion prob. slip, dark brown paint.	Gap, Egami & Sono 1962, Fig. 28:3, Pl.37; Behbahan, Dittmann 1984, Fig. 27:2,4.	MS 3-LS 1
E	Buff, scattered grits inclusion brown paint.		MS 3
F	Greenish buff, scattered grits inclusion, wet-smoothed int. scratched wavy lines on thick dark green paint.	Chogha Mish MS, Delougaz & Kantor, nd.	MS 1

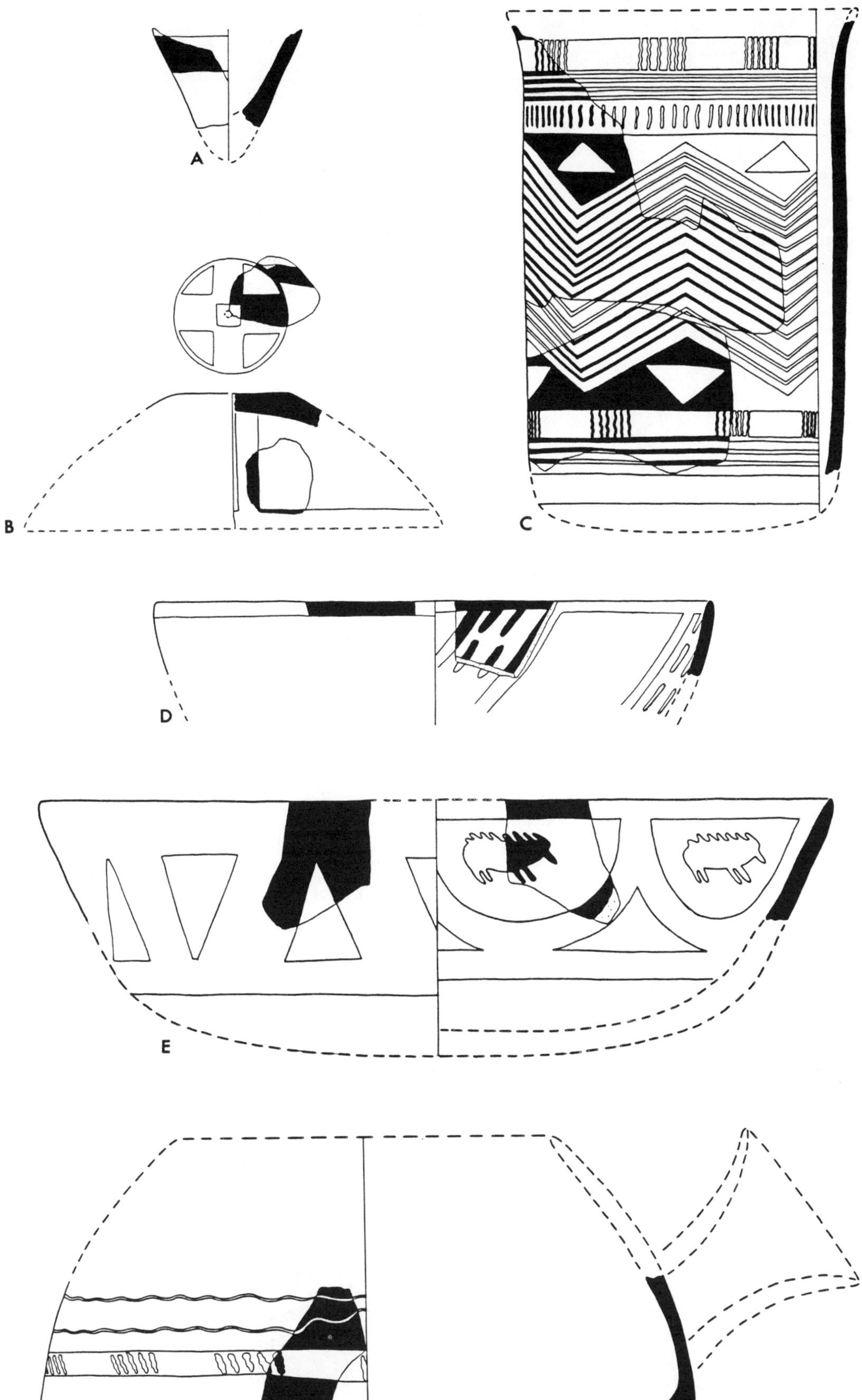
A
B
C
D
E
F

	DESCRIPTION	REFERENCES	PERIOD
A	Buff, no visible inclusion, buff slipped, thick dark brown paint.	Susa, de Mecquenem 1943, Pl. 4:4.	LS 2
B	Buff, no visible inclusion, slipped, brown paint.	Susa, Pottier 1922, Pls. 1-2.	LS 2
C	Buff, no visible inclusion, buff slipped, brown paint.	Qabr-e Sheikhein, Weiss 1976, Fig. 24:163.	LS 2
D	Buff, no visible inclusion, buff slipped, brown paint.	Jafarabad 3n, Dollfus 1975, Fig. 50:6.	MS 3
E	Buff, no visible inclusion, buff slipped, brown paint.	Qabr-e Sheikhein, Weiss 1975, Fig. 24:163.	LS 2
F	Buff, no visible inclusion, buff slipped, thick brown paint.	Susa, acropole 2, levels 11-7, Canal 1978, Fig. 25:1; Chogha Mish MS, Delougaz & Kantor, nd.	MS 3-LS
G	Buff, no visible inclusion, slipped, brown paint.	Farrukhabad, Wright 1981, Fig. 17:d. Fars: Tall-e Saku & Kanakan, Stein 1936, Pls. 28:27, 21:41. Gap, Egami & Sono 1962, Fig. 20:12. Kerman: Tall-e Eblis, Caldwell 1967, Fig. 10. Tappeh Yahya, Beale et al. 1986, Figs. 4.20:X, 4.21:C.	LS 1
H	Buff, no visible inclusion, brown paint.	Bakun A, Langsdorff & McCown 1942, Pl. 4:1.	LS 1
I	Buff, no visible inclusion, light brown paint.	Susa, Pottier 1922, Pl. 1-2.	LS 2
J	Buff, no visible inclusion, cream slip, shiny brown paint.	Gap, Egami & Sono 1962, Fig. 28:3; Qabr-e Sheikhein, Weiss 1976, Fig. 23:148.	LS 1
K	Buff, no visible inclusion, brown paint.	Chogha Mish MS, Delougaz & Kantor, nd.	MS 3
L	Buff, scattered grits inclusion probably buff slipped, brown paint.	Bakun A, Langsdorff & McCown 1942, Pl. 73:4-6	LS 1
M	Buff, no visible inclusion, cream slip, greenish brown paint.	Qabr-e Sheikhein, Weiss 1976, Fig. 23:149.	LS 1
N	Buff, scattered grits inclusion thick, dark greenish brown paint.	Chogha Mish MS, Delougaz & Kantor, nd.	MS 3
O	Pinkish buff, no visible inclusion, thick brown paint.		MS 3-LS 1
P	Buff, no visible inclusion, buff slipped, greenish brown paint.	This piece may well be the upper part of a tortoise vessel, and as such is MS 3.	MS 3
Q	Buff, no visible inclusion, buff slipped, brown paint.	Qabr-e Sheikhein, Weiss 1976, Fig. 15:35.	LS 1
R	Buff, no visible inclusion, thick brown paint.	Qabr-e Sheikhein, Weiss 1976, Fig. 24:171; Susa, acropole 2, levels 11-7, Canal 1978, Fig. 25:4.	LS

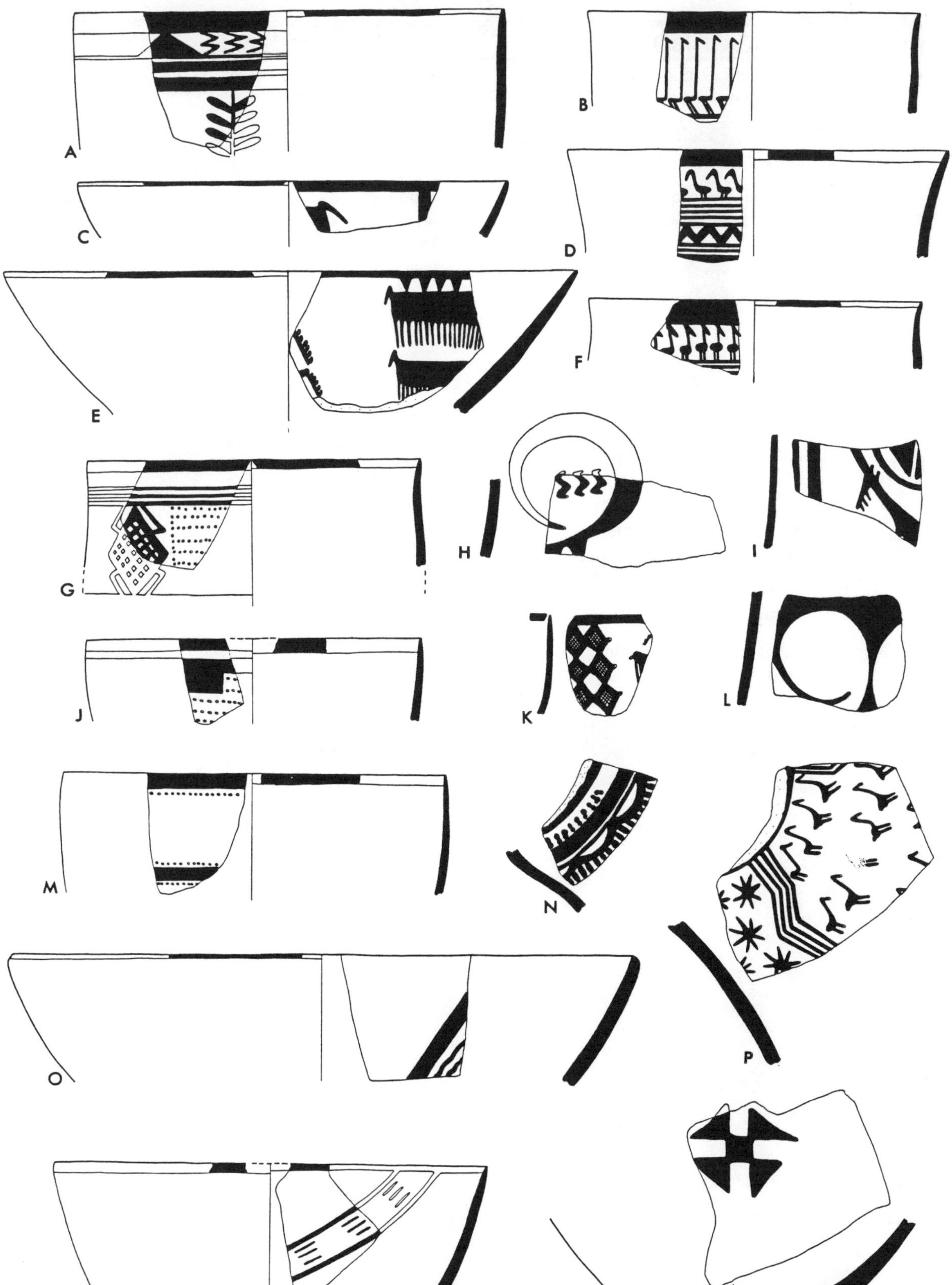
A
B
C
D
E
F
G
H
I
J
K
L
M
N
O
P
Q
R

Figure 58	SITE G86-II		*Scale*: 2/5
	DESCRIPTION	REFERENCES	PERIOD
A	Buff, scattered grits inclusion reddish brown paint.	Qabr-e Sheikhein, Weiss 1976, Fig. 24:163.	MS 3
B	Buff, no visible inclusion, buff slipped, brown paint.	Chogha Mish MS, Delougaz & Kantor, nd.	MS 3
C	Buff, no visible inclusion, sunken greenish brown paint.	Bandebal II, L 14, Dollfus 1983, Fig. 81:16; Giyan Vb, Contenau & Ghirshman 1935, Pl. 45:17. (This motif seems to have developed from the earlier ES motif, cf. Jafarabad Dollfus 1975, Figs. 17:7, 25:3.)	MS 3-LS 1
D	Buff, no visible inclusion, buff slipped, thick shiny brown paint.	Bandebal II, L 16, Dollfus 1983, Fig. 74:5.	LS 1
E	Buff, no visible inclusion, brown paint.	Qabr-e Sheikhein, Weiss 1976, Fig. 22:133; Bakun A, Langsdorff & McCown 1942, Pl. 70:15.	LS 1
F	Reddish buff, scattered grits inclusion, cream slip, dark paint.		MS-LS
G	Buff, grits inclusion, brown paint.	Qabr-e Sheikhein, Weiss 1976, Fig. 22:139.	MS 3
H	Buff, scattered grits inclusion slipped, dark brown paint.	Bakun B, Egami & Masuda 1962, Fig. 15:13; Bandebal II, L 16, Dollfus 1983, Pl. 18:1; Tall-e Sang-e Siah, Fars, Stein 1936, Pl. 23:69.	LS 1

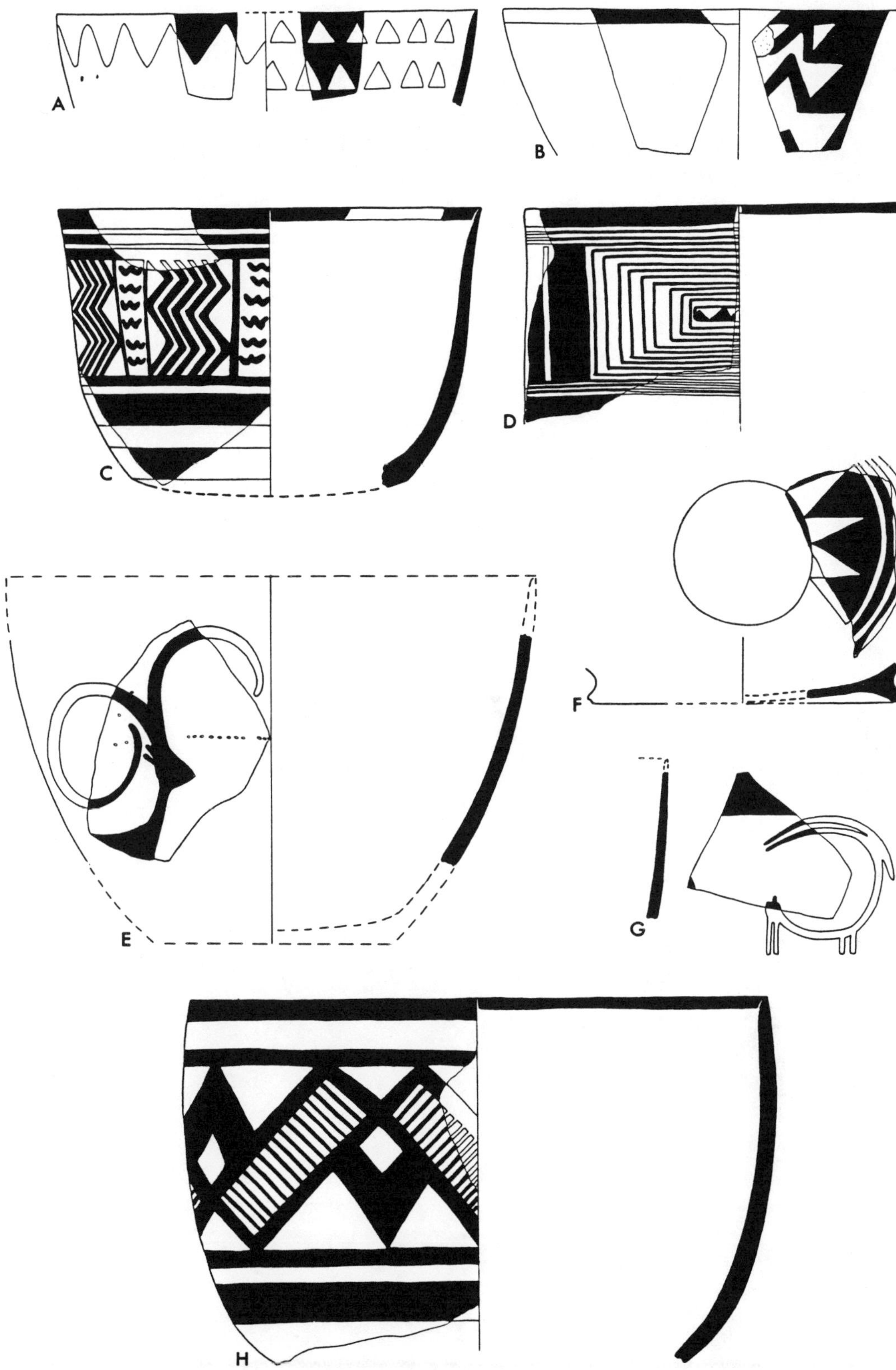
A
B
C
D
E
F
G
H

Figure 59 SITE G86-II *Scale*: 2/5

	DESCRIPTION	REFERENCES	PERIOD
A	Buff, no visible inclusion, greenish brown paint.	Chogha Mish LS, Delougaz & Kantor, nd.	LS
B	Buff, dense grits inclusion, brown paint, probably burnished exterior.	Jawi II, L 10, Dollfus 1983, Fig. 33:13; Chogha Mish MS, Delougaz & Kantor, nd.	MS 3
C	Lid frag. Buff, red & dark grits inclusion, gritty face, greenish dark paint.	Bandebal II, L 14, Dollfus 1983, Fig. 82:9; Chogha Mish MS, Delougaz & Kantor, nd.	MS 3
D	Buff, no visible inclusion, slipped, greenish dark paint.	Chogha Mish MS, Delougaz & Kantor, nd; Bandebal II, L 20, Dollfus 1983, Fig. 60:13; Jafarabad 3n, Dollfus 1975, Fig. 50:9; Gap, Egami & Sono 1962, Fig. 20:2.	MS 3
E	Buff, grits inclusion, brown paint.	Chogha Mish MS, Delougaz & Kantor, nd.	MS 3
F	Buff, scattered grits inclusion, thick brown paint.	Gap, Egami & Sono 1962, Fig. 21:5; Sumner, unpublished survey site 5K2; Tall-e Saku, Fars, Stein 1936, Pl. 24:14.	LS 1
G	Pale brick buff, grits inclusion, gritty face, reddish brown paint.	Chogha Mish MS, Delougaz & Kantor, nd.	MS 3
H	Buff, grits inclusion, brown paint.	Jafarabad 5a, Dollfus 1975, Fig. 27:9.	AS 3 ES
I	Buff, grits & chaff inclusion, brown paint.	Jawi I, L 15, Dollfus 1983, Fig. 14:5; Haji Mohammad, Ziegler, 1961, Pl. 11:a,i.	MS 1

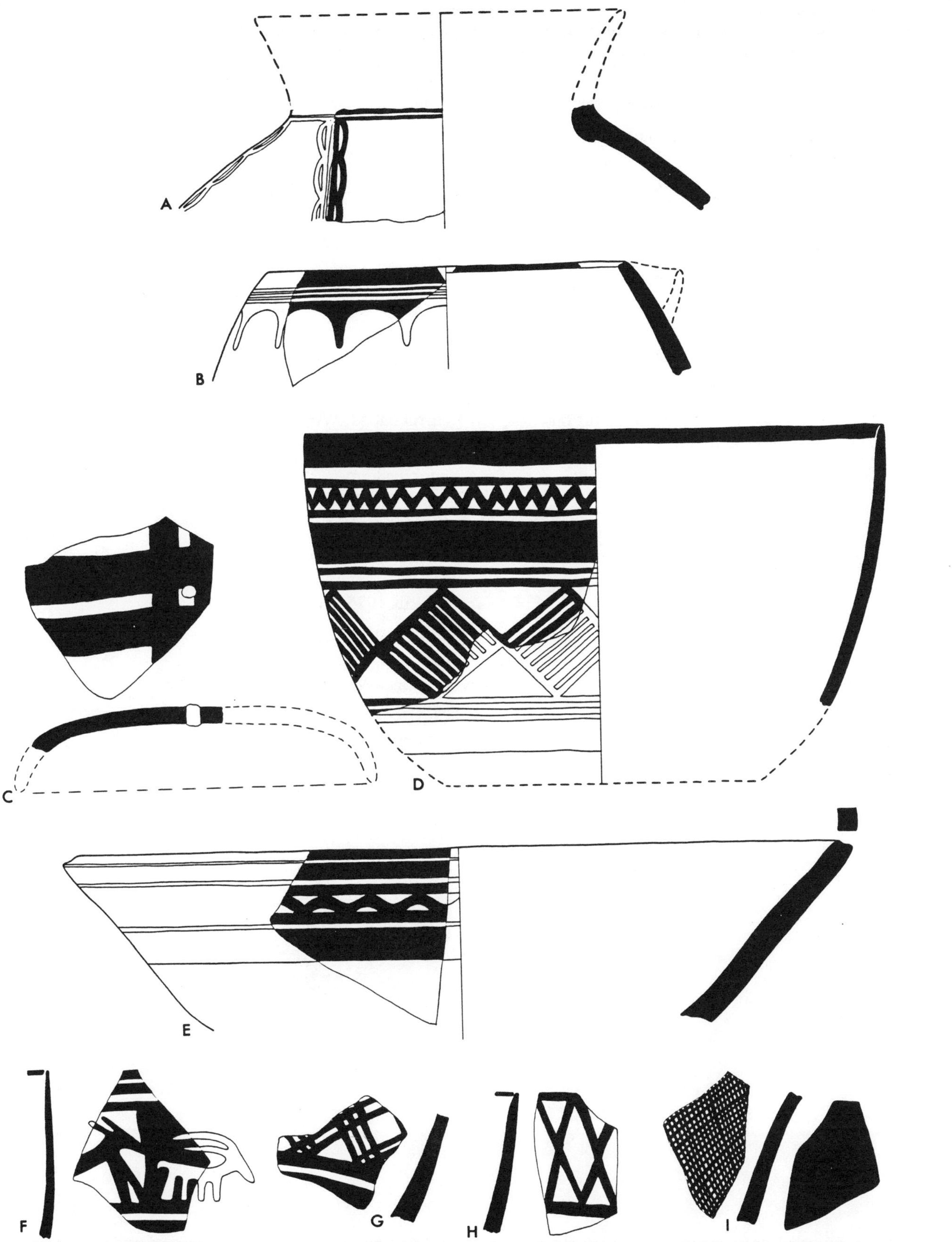
A
B
C
D
E
F
G
H
I

	DESCRIPTION	REFERENCES	PERIOD
A	Yellowish buff, no visible inclusion, slipped, thick, shiny brown paint.	Chogha Mish MS, Delougaz & Kantor, nd.	MS 3
B	Cream buff, no visible inclusion, brown paint.		LS
C	Greenish buff, no visible inclusion, black paint.	Tall-e Rigi, Fars, Stein 1936, Pl. 21:31.	LS 1?
D	Greenish buff, no visible inclusion, thick brown paint, some air pockets.	Qabr-e Sheikhein, Weiss 1976, Fig. 13:20.	LS 1
E	Buff, no visible inclusion, brown paint.	Chogha Mish MS, Delougaz & Kantor, nd.	MS 3
F	Cream buff, no visible inclusion, yellowish green paint, some air pockets.	Gap, Egami & Sono 1962, Fig. 20:1,7.	LS 1?
G	Yellowish buff, no visible inclusion, greenish brown paint.	Farrukhabad, Wright 1981, Fig. 18:a-c.	MS 3-LS 1
H	Buff, grits inclusion, brown paint.	Jafarabad 3m-n, Dollfus 1975, Fig. 50:8; Bakun B, Egami & Masuda 1962, Fig. 14:14.	MS 3
I	Buff, grits inclusion, brown paint.	Farrukhabad, Wright 1981, Fig. 16:a; Jafarabad 3m-n, Dollfus 1975, Fig. 50:9.	MS 3
J	Buff, red & dark grits inclusion dark brown paint.	Farrukhabad, Wright 1981, Fig. 16:a; Chogha Mish MS, Delougaz & Kantor, nd.	MS 3
K	Buff, grits inclusion, dark paint.	Chogha Mish MS, Delougaz & Kantor, nd.	MS 1

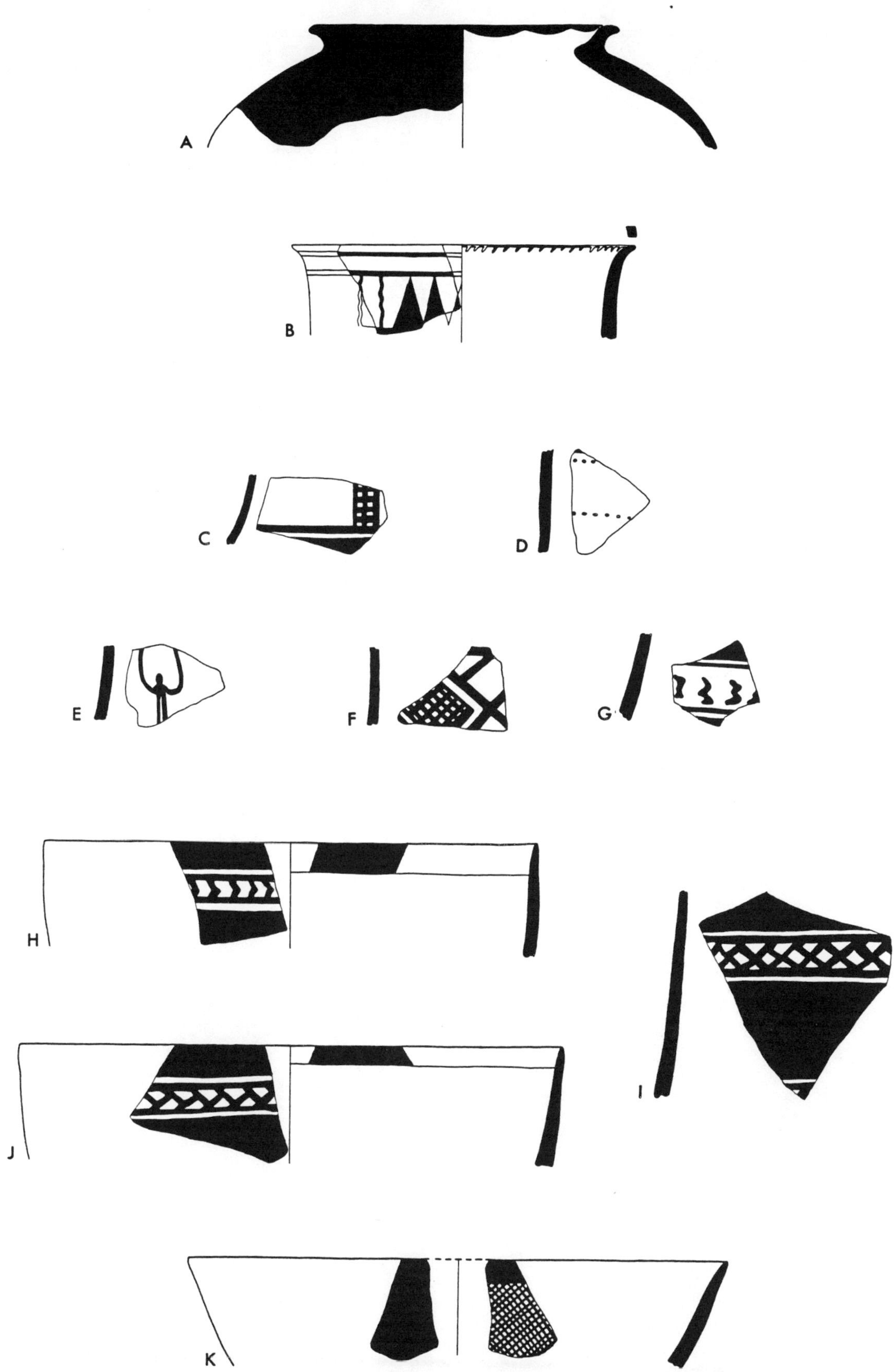
A
B
C
D
E
F
G
H
I
J
K

	DESCRIPTION	REFERENCES	PERIOD
A	Buff, grits inclusion, prob. slipped.	Susa acropole 2, L 5, Canal 1978, Fig. 26:1.	PL
B	Buff, grits inclusion.	Susa acropole 2, L 2, Canal 1978, Fig. 26:2.	PL
C	Buff, grit inclusion, prob. slipped.	Susa acropole 1, L 18, Le Brun 1978, Fig. 32:9.	PL
D	Buff, scattered grits inclusion, brown paint, some air pockets.	Giyan Vc, Contenau & Ghirshman 1935, Pl. 50:25.	LS
E	Buff, grits inclusion, gritty face, greenish brown paint.	Musiyan, Gautier & Lampre 1905, Fig. 165.	MS 3-LS 1
F	Buff, no visible inclusion, greenish brown paint.	Bandebal II, levels 23, 16, Dollfus 1983, Figs. 56:4-5, 71:17.	MS 3-LS 1
G	Buff, no visible inclusion, greenish brown paint.	Susa, Le Breton 1947, Fig. 47:21.	LS
H	Grayish buff, scattered grits inclusion, greenish brown paint.	Susa, Steve & Gasche 1971, Pl. 35:6.	LS 2
I	Buff, no visible inclusion, greenish brown paint.	Bandebal, Le Breton 1947, Fig. 38:9.	LS 1
J	Buff, no visible inclusion, slipped, greenish brown paint.	Qabr-e Sheikhein, Weiss 1976, Fig. 13:20.	LS 1
K	Buff, no visible inclusion, slipped, brown paint.	Similar: Gap, Egami & Sono 1962, Fig. 13:L.	MS 3-LS 1
L	Greenish buff, no visible inclusion, slipped, dark greenish brown paint.		LS
M	Buff, no visible inclusion, slipped, brown paint.	Jafarabad 3m-n/Jawi II, Dollfus 1978, Fig. 16:10; Bandebal II, L 20, Dollfus 1983, Fig. 59:5.	MS 3

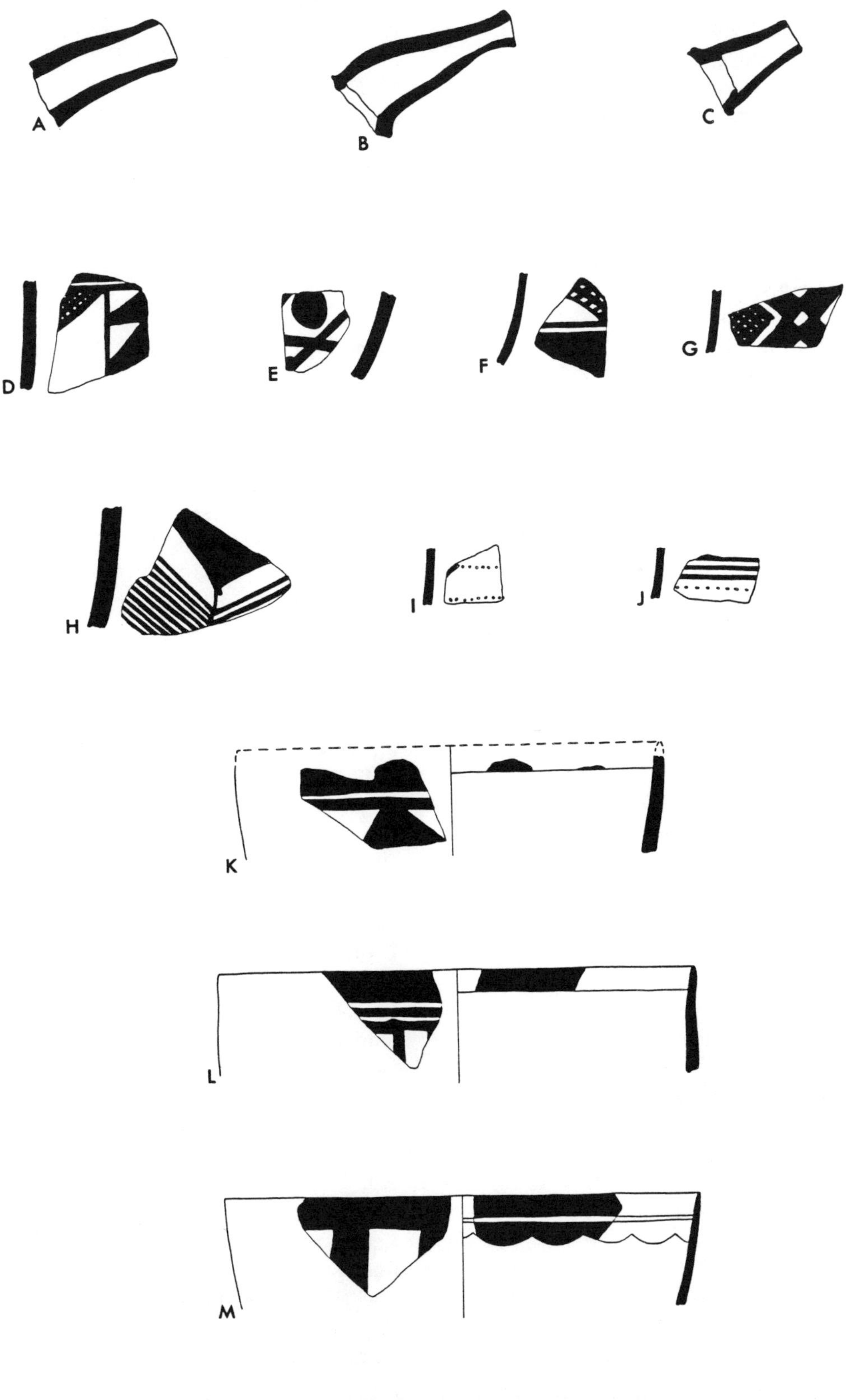
A
B
C
D
E
F
G
H
I
J
K
L
M

Figure 62 SITE G97* *Scale*: 2/5

	DESCRIPTION	REFERENCES	PERIOD
A	Cream buff, no visible inclu sion, sunken green brown paint.	Susa, Steve & Gasche 1971, Pl. 34:20.	LS
B	Buff, no visible inclusion, shiny brown paint.	Susa, Steve & Gasche 1971, Pl. 35:13.	MS 3-LS
C	Buff, no visible inclusion, buff slipped, brown paint.	Susa, Steve & Gasche 1971, Pl. 35:21,26-27; Chogha Mish LS, Delougaz & Kantor, nd; cf. G.	LS 2
D	Buff, no visible inclusion, slipped, brown paint.	Jawi, Le Breton 1947, Fig.30:10; Musiyan, Gautier & Lampre 1905, Fig. 240.	MS 3
E	Buff, no visible inclusion, slipped, brown paint.		MS 3
F	Buff, no visible inclusion, cream slip, brown paint.	Chogha Mish LS, Delougaz & Kantor, nd; Susa, de Morgan 1900, Pl. 17:21.	LS 2
G	Buff, no visible inclusion, slipped, brown paint.	See C.	LS 2
H	Buff, no visible inclusion, slipped, brown paint. Standing human (prob. female) motif.	Chogha Mish MS, Delougaz & Kantor, nd; Jawi, L 11, Dollfus 1983, Fig. 31:18.	MS 3
I	Spout. Buff, scattered grits inclusion,maroon paint.	Bandebal II, L 19, Dollfus 1983, Fig. 61:2; Jafarabad 3m, Dollfus 1975, Fig. 52:12.	MS 3
J	Buff, no visible inclusion, slipped, brown paint.	Chogha Mish MS, Delougaz & Kantor, nd; Qabr-e Sheikhein, Weiss 1976, Fig. 29:227.	MS 3
K	Grayish green, no visible inclusion, green paint.	Bakun A, Langsdorff & McCown 1942, Pl. 70:6; Susa, Pottier 1922, Pl. 1:1.	LS 1
L	Buff, no visible inclusion, slipped, brown paint.	Qabr-e Sheikhein, Weiss 1976, Fig. 14:27; Fars, Site 5N0, Sumner unpub. survey.	LS 1
M	Grayish buff, scattered grits inclusion, greenish brown paint.	Qabr-e Sheikhein, Weiss 1976, Fig. 14:27.	LS 1
N	Buff, no visible inclusion, slipped, brown paint.	Similar: Gap, Egami & Sono 1962, Fig. 21:11.	MS 3-LS 1
O	Buff, no visible inclusion, slipped, dark brown paint.	Similar: Tall-e Sakku (Fars) Stein 1936, Pl. 24:13.	MS 3-LS 1
P	Buff, no visible inclusion, slipped, brown paint.		MS 3
Q	Buff, no visible inclusion, brown paint.		MS 3-LS 1
R	Buff, no visible inclusion, brown paint.	Chogha Mish MS, Delougaz & Kantor, nd; Chogha Mish MS, Kantor, 1976, Fig. 8.	MS 3
S	Buff, scattered grits inclusion, greenish brown paint.	Jawi II, L 12, Dollfus 1983, Fig. 26:8; Chogha Mish MS, Delougaz & Kantor, nd.	MS 3

A
B
C
D
E
F
G
H
I
J
K
L
M
N
O
P
Q
R
S

Figure 63	SITE G97 A*		*Scale*: 2/5
	DESCRIPTION	REFERENCES	PERIOD
A	Cream buff, dark grits inclusion, shiny brown paint.	Chogha Mish LS, Delougaz & Kantor, nd.	LS 2
B	Buff, grits inclusion, brown paint.	Chogha Mish MS, Delougaz & Kantor, nd.	MS 3
C	Mosaic wall-cone. Green, no visible inclusion, over-fired (waster).		PL
D	Buff, no visible inclusion, brown paint.	Chogha Mish LS, Delougaz & Kantor, nd.	LS 2
E	Buff, no visible inclusion, brown paint.		LS
F	Mosaic wall-cone. Buff, no visible inclusion.		PL
G	Buff, no visible inclusion, greenish brown paint.	Gap, Egami & Sono 1962, Fig. 16:9; Qabr-e Sheikhein, Weiss 1976, Fig. 17:70; Ram Hormuz, Site 18, unpub. McCown survey.	LS 1
H	Greenish buff, no visible inclusion, dark greenish brown paint.		LS 1?
I	Buff, no visible inclusion, thick brown paint.		LS 1?
J	Green buff, no visible inclusion, prob. slipped, thick shiny brown paint.		LS 1?
K	Buff, grits inclusion, dark brown paint (flaky).	Bakun A, Langsdorff & McCown 1942, Pl. 28:9-12, 29:1,4,6.	LS 1
L	Greenish buff, red & dark grits inclusion, yellowish brown paint.	Bakun A, Langsdorff & McCown 1942, Pls. 28:9-12, 29:1,4, & 6.	LS 1
M	Buff, no visible inclusion, cream slip, shiny dark brown paint.		LS 1?

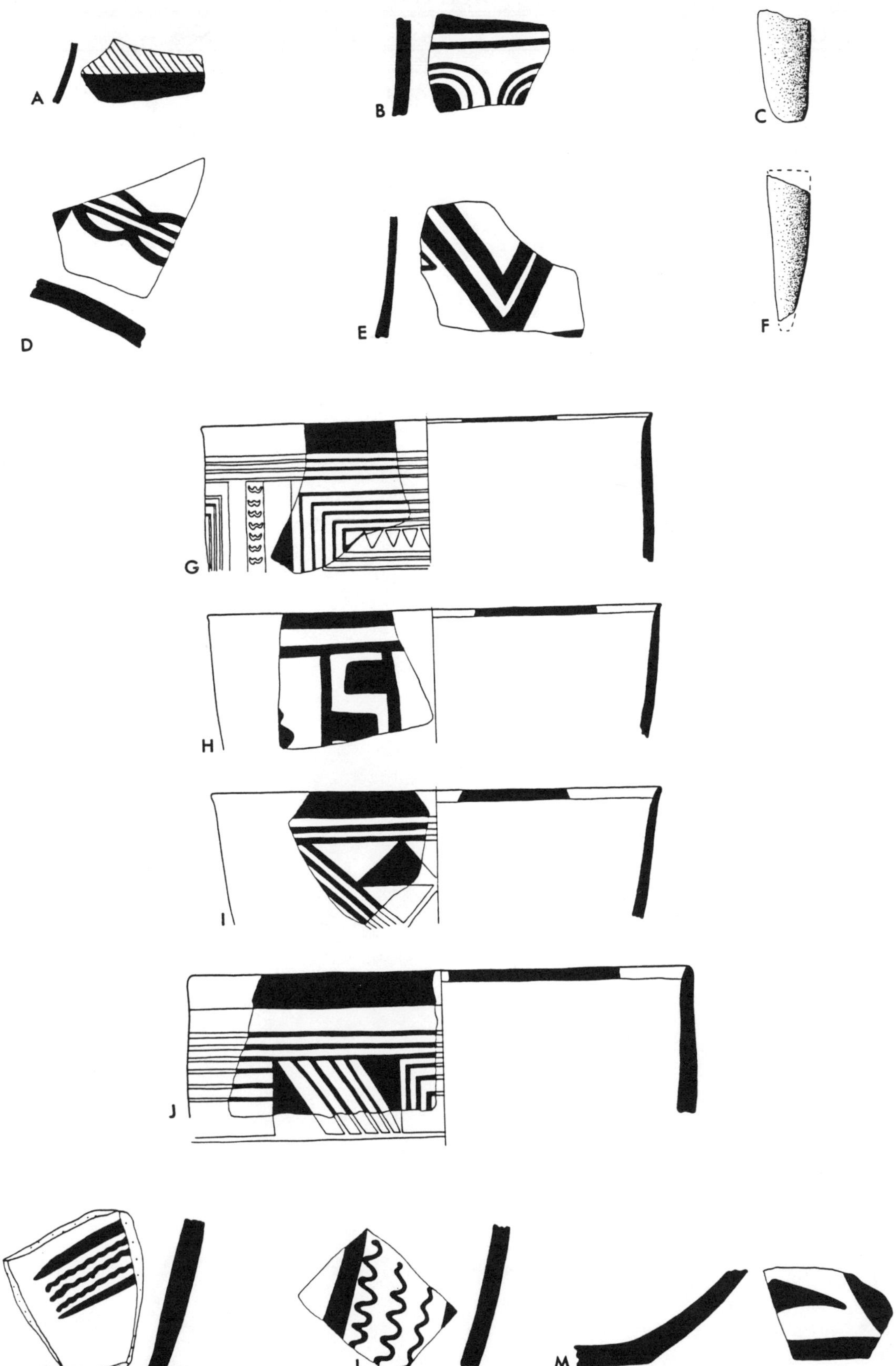
A
B
C
D
E
F
G
H
I
J
K
L
M

Figure 64	SITE G97 A	*Scale*: 2/5

	DESCRIPTION	REFERENCES	PERIOD
A	Buff, no visible inclusion, cream slip, dark brown paint.	Chogha Mish MS, Delougaz & Kantor, nd.	MS 3-LS 1
B	Buff, no visible inclusion, dark brown paint.	Chogha Mish MS, Delougaz & Kantor, nd; Gap, Egami & Sono 1962, Fig. 24: 2, 4.	MS 3
C	Buff, no visible inclusion, cream slip, dark brown paint.	Similar: Qabr-e Sheikhein, Weiss 1976, Fig. 19:102; Bandebal II, L 14, Dollfus 1983, Fig. 81:12.	LS 1
D	Green buff, scattered red & dark grits inclusion, thick, green paint, scraped ext., over-fired (prob. a waster).	Chogha Mish MS, Delougaz & Kantor, nd.	MS 3
E	Greenish buff, no visible inclusion, brown paint.	Chogha Mish MS, Delougaz & Kantor, nd.	MS 3
F	Green buff, scattered grits inclusion, sunken dark paint, over-fired.		MS 1
G	Buff, no visible inclusion, dark brown paint.	Chogha Mish MS, Delougaz & Kantor, nd; ES transition to MS.	ES-MS 1

A
B
C
D
E
F
G

Figure 65 SITE G97 A *Scale*: 2/5

	DESCRIPTION	REFERENCES	PERIOD
A	Buff, no visible inclusion, dark brown paint.	Qabr-e Sheikhein, Weiss 1976, Fig. 20:111.	LS 1
B	Greenish buff, no visible inclusion, greenish brown paint.	Style: Bakun A, Langsdorff & McCown, 1942, Pl. 24:7.	LS 1?
C	Greenish buff, red & dark grits inclusion, slipped, sunken dark greenish paint, scraped bellow rim, dragging grits along.	Bakun A, Langsdorff & McCown 1942, Pl. 28:9-12.	LS 1
D	Greenish buff, grits inclusion, dark greenish brown paint.		MS 3
E	Buff, scattered straw & grits inclusion, brown paint.	Chogha Mish MS, Delougaz & Kantor, nd.	MS 3
F	Buff, grits & chaff inclusion, dark brown paint.	Chogha Mish ES, Delougaz & Kantor, nd; Jafarabad 5a, Dollfus 1975, Fig. 19:2-3.	ES
G	Buff, grits inclusion, dark brown paint.	Chogha Mish MS, Delougaz & Kantor, nd; Jawi I, L 15, Dollfus 1983, Fig. 13:8.	MS 1

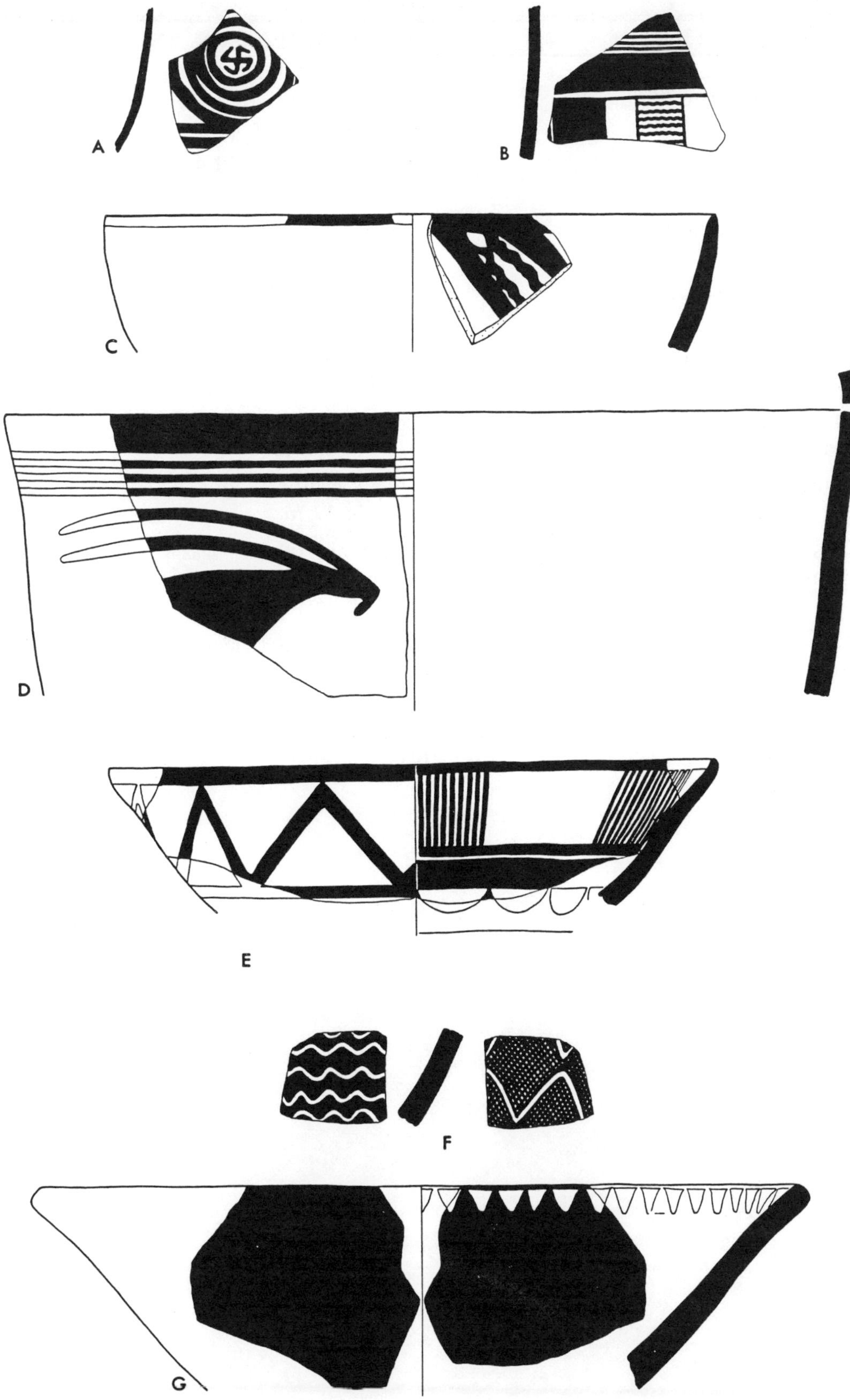
A
B
C
D
E
F
G

Figure 66	SITE G115	*Scale*: 2/5

	DESCRIPTION	REFERENCES	PERIOD
A	Buff, no visible inclusion, brown paint, burnished exterior.	Jafarabad 3d-1, Dollfus 1978, Fig. 19:9; Chogha Mish LS, Delougaz & Kantor, nd.	LS 2
B	Buff, no visible inclusion, slipped, brown paint.	Susa, Pottier 1922, Pl. 1:4.	LS 2
C	Buff, red & dark grits inclusion, brown paint.		LS 1?
D	Buff, no visible inclusion, brown paint.	Chogha Mish MS, Delougaz & Kantor, nd.	MS 3?
E	Buff, no visible inclusion, brown paint.	Qabr-e Sheikhein, Weiss 1976, Fig. 15:35.	LS 1
F	Buff, no visible inclusion, brown paint.	Qabr-e Sheikhein, Weiss 1976, Fig. 18:94.	LS 1
G	Buff, no visible inclusion, dark brown paint.	Qabr-e Sheikhein, Weiss 1976, Fig. 17:76.	LS 1
H	Buff, scattered grits inclusion, dark brown paint.	Chogha Mish LS, Delougaz & Kantor, nd; Jafarabad, Le Breton 1947, Fig. 15:10.	LS 2
I	Buff, grits inclusion, brown paint.	Chogha Mish LS, Delougaz & Kantor, nd.	LS 2
J	Buff, grits inclusion, dark brown paint.	Chogha Mish MS, Delougaz & Kantor, nd; Jawi II, L 11, Dollfus 1983, Fig. 30:1.	MS 3

A
B
C
D
E
F
G
H
I
J

	DESCRIPTION	REFERENCES	PERIOD
A	Buff, no visible inclusion, brown paint.	Susa, Steve & Gasche 1971, Pl. 35:13.	LS 2
B	Buff, no visible inclusion, brown paint.		LS?
C	Red, grits inclusion, buff, slipped.	Uruk, Noldke 1932, Fig. 19D:b.	PL
D	Green buff, no visible inclusion, greenish brown paint.		LS 1?
E	Buff, no visible inclusion, greenish brown paint.	Buhalan, de Mecquenem 1943 Fig. 110:8.	LS 1?
F	Buff, scattered grits inclusion, dark brown paint.	Chogha Mish LS, Delougaz & Kantor, nd; Qabr-e Sheikhein, Weiss 1976, Fig. 27:237.	LS
G	Buff, no visible inclusion, reddish, brown paint.		LS 1
H	Cream buff, no visible inclusion, prob. slipped, brown paint.	Bandebal II, L 12, Dollfus 1983, Fig. 87:2.	MS 3-LS 1
I	Buff, no visible inclusion, cream slip, brown paint.	Bakun B, Egami & Masuda 1962, Fig. 15:13.	LS 1
J	Buff, no visible inclusion, cream slipped, brown paint.		MS 3-LS 1
K	Buff, no visible inclusion, brown paint.		LS 1
L	Buff, no visible inclusion, brown paint.	Jafarabad 3m, Dollfus 1975, Fig. 49:6; Qabr-e Sheikhein, Weiss 1976, Fig. 22:140.	MS 3-LS 1
M	Buff, no visible inclusion, slipped, brown paint.	Qabr-e Sheikhein, Weiss 1975, Fig. 15:57.	LS 1
N	Buff, red & dark grits inclusion, dark brown paint.		LS 1?
O	Buff, no visible inclusion, greenish brown paint.	Chogha Mish MS, Delougaz & Kantor, nd.; Jafarabad 3m-n, Dollfus 1975, Fig. 50:7,9.	MS 3
P	Buff, grits & chaff inclusion, black paint.		ES ?

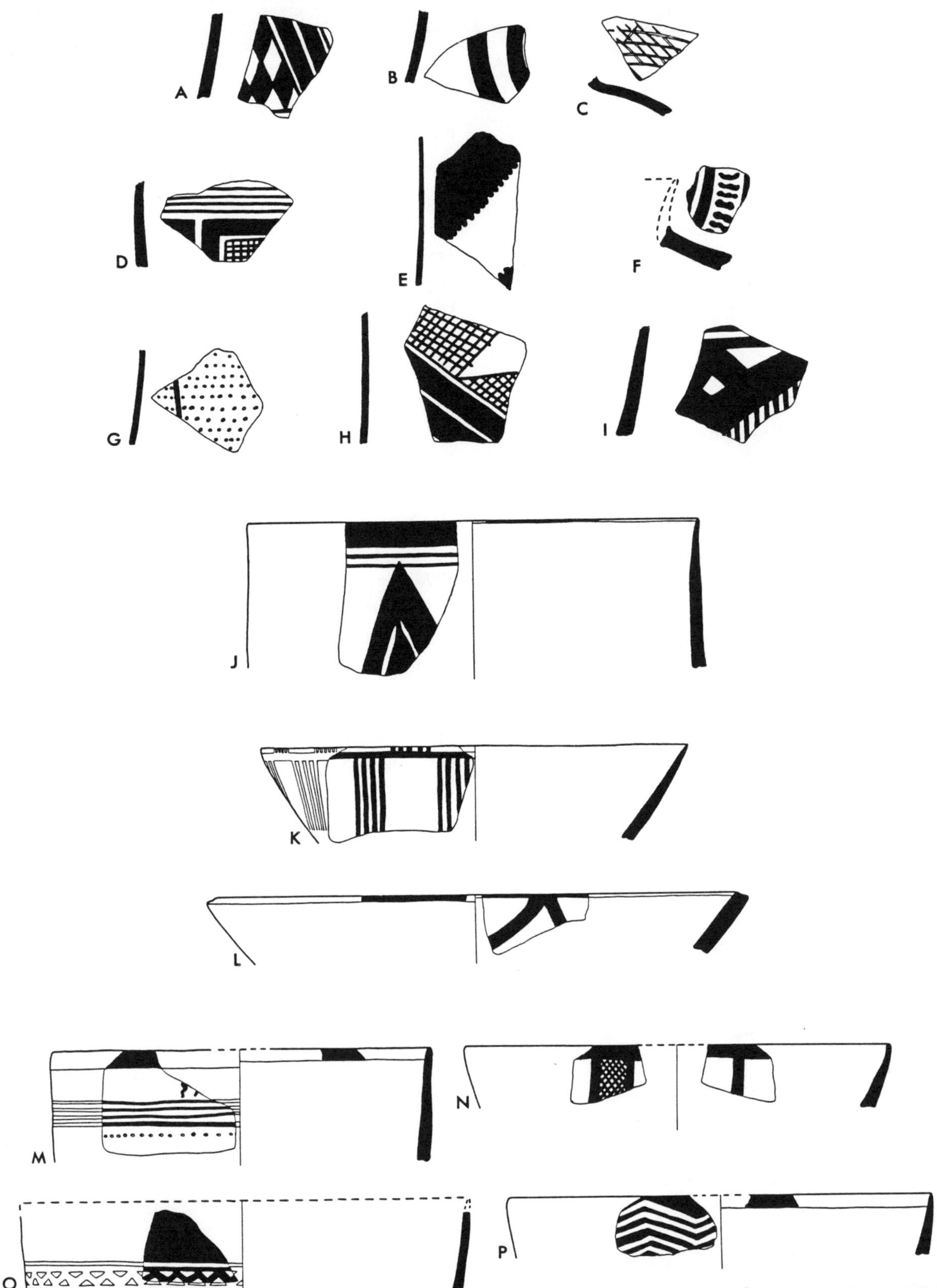
A
B
C
D
E
F
G
H
I
J
K
L
M
N
O
P

Figure 68 SITE G145 A-J; SITE G157 K-S *Scale*: 2/5

	DESCRIPTION	REFERENCES	PERIOD
A	Buff, no visible inclusion, slipped, brown paint.		LS 2
B	Buff, no visible inclusion, slipped, brown paint.	Susa, de Mecquenem 1943, Pl. 4:3.	LS 2
C	Buff, no visible inclusion, slipped, brown paint.	Susa, Pottier 1922, Pl. 2:19	LS 2
D	Buff, no visible inclusion, slipped, brown paint.	Jafarabad 3m-n, Dollfus 1978, Fig. 16:16; Bandebal II, Dollfus 1978, Fig. 17:12.	MS 3
E	Buff, no visible inclusion, slipped, brown paint.	Susa, de Mecquenem 1943, Pl. 4:5.	LS 2
F	Buff, no visible inclusion, slipped, brown paint.	Bandebal II, L 16, Dollfus 1983, Fig. 78:2.	MS 3
G	Miniature bed frag. or lid? Buff, no visible inclusion, dark brown paint.		MS ?
H	Buff, grits inclusion, greenish brown paint.		LS
I	Buff, scattered grits inclusion, dark brown paint.	Jafarabad 3d-1, Dollfus 1978, Fig. 19:4; Bandebal, de Mecquenem 1943, Fig. 12:37.	LS 2
J	Buff, scattered grits, irregular rim, brown paint.	Chogha Mish MS, Delougaz & Kantor, nd.	MS 3
K	Buff, no visible inclusion, slipped, brown paint.		LS 2
L	Buff, no visible inclusion, slipped, brown paint.	Fars, Site 545, Sumner, unpublished survey.	LS 1?
M	Buff, no visible inclusion, cream slipped, dark brown paint.		LS 2
N	Buff, no visible inclusion, brown paint.	Farrukhabad, Wright 1981, Fig. 18:a-c. LS 1	MS 3-
O	Buff, no visible inclusion, dark brown paint.		LS
P	Buff, no visible inclusion, dark brown paint.	Chogha Mish MS, Delougaz & Kantor, nd; Farrukhabad, Wright 1981, Fig. 24:a.	MS 3- LS
Q	Cream buff, no visible inclusion, brown paint, burnished exterior.	Susa, de Morgan 1900, Pl. 17:9.	LS 2
R	Buff, no visible inclusion, slipped, brown paint.		LS
S	Buff, no visible inclusion, red paint, burnished exterior.	Jafarabad 3d-1, Dollfus 1978, Fig. 19:16.	LS 2

A
B
C
D
E
F
G
H
I
J
K
L
M
N
O
P
Q
R
S

Figure 69	SITE G161*		*Scale*: 2/5
	DESCRIPTION	**REFERENCES**	**PERIOD**
A	Buff, no visible inclusion, slipped, brown paint.	Susa, de Mecquenem 1943, Pl. 4:3-5.	LS 2
B	Buff, scattered grits inclusion, brown paint.	Bandebal II, L 16, Dollfus 1983, Fig. 70:1; Jafarabad 3m, Dollfus 1975, Fig. 49:9.	LS 1
C	Buff, no visible inclusion, buff slipped, brown paint.	Bakun A, Alizadeh 1988a, Fig. 6:B.	LS 1
D	Buff, medium grits inclusion, gritty face, brown paint.		LS 1
E	Buff, no visible inclusion, greenish brown paint.		LS 2
F	Greenish buff, no visible in thick, greenish brown paint.	Bandebal II, L 16, Dollfus 1978, Fig. 17:14; Chogha Mish, Delougaz & Kantor, nd.	MS 3-LS 1
G	Buff, no visible inclusion, brown paint.	Qabr-e Sheikhein, Weiss 1976, Fig. 20:111; Jawi II, Dollfus 1983, Fig. 30:1; Chogha Mish MS, Delougaz & Kantor, nd.	LS 1
H	Buff, no visible inclusion, brown paint.	Bakun B, Egami & Masuda 1962, Fig. 17:3.	MS 3-LS 1
I	Buff, scattered grits inclusion, slipped, reddish brown paint.	Bandebal II, L 16, Dollfus 1983, Fig. 71:11; Qabr-e Sheikhein, Weiss 1976, Fig. 20:107.	MS 3-LS 1

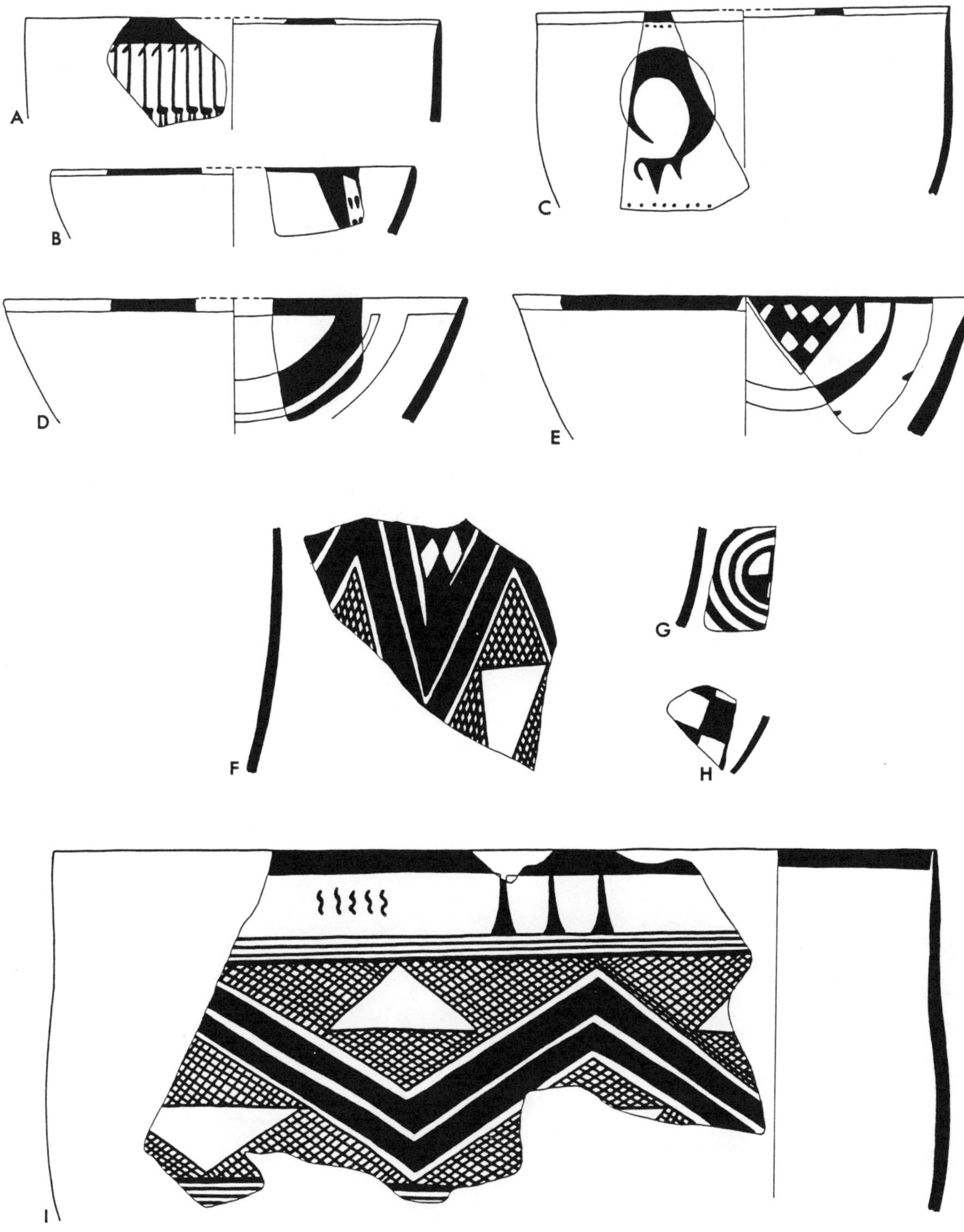
A
B
C
D
E
F
G
H
I

Figure 70	SITE G161*		*Scale*: 2/5
	DESCRIPTION	REFERENCES	PERIOD
A	Buff, scattered grits inclusion, greenish buff paint, over-fired.	Motif: Bandebal II, L 16, Dollfus 1983, Fig. 76:1.	MS 3
B	Buff, no visible inclusion, slipped, brown paint.	Qabr-e Sheikhein, Weiss 1976, Fig. 14:28.	LS 1
C	Buff, no visible inclusion, slipped, brown paint.		LS 1
D	Buff, scattered grits inclusion, dark brown paint. 'Mask' motif.	Chogha Mish MS, Delougaz & Kantor, nd; Khazineh, Gautier & Lampre 1905, Figs. 172-173.	MS 3
E	Buff, grits inclusion, brown paint.	Bandebal II, levels 16-11, Dollfus 1978, Fig. 17:9.	MS 3- LS 1
F	Buff, scattered grits inclusion, dark brown paint.	Jafarabad 3m-n/Jawi II, Dollfus 1978, Fig. 16:10.	MS 3
G	Buff, red & dark grits inclusion, brown paint.		MS 3
H	Buff, scattered grits inclusion, brown paint.		MS 3
I	Buff, grits inclusion, dark brown paint.	Jawi I, L 15, Dollfus 1983, Fig. 14:5; Haji Mohammad, Ziegler 1961, Pl. 11:a,i.	MS 1

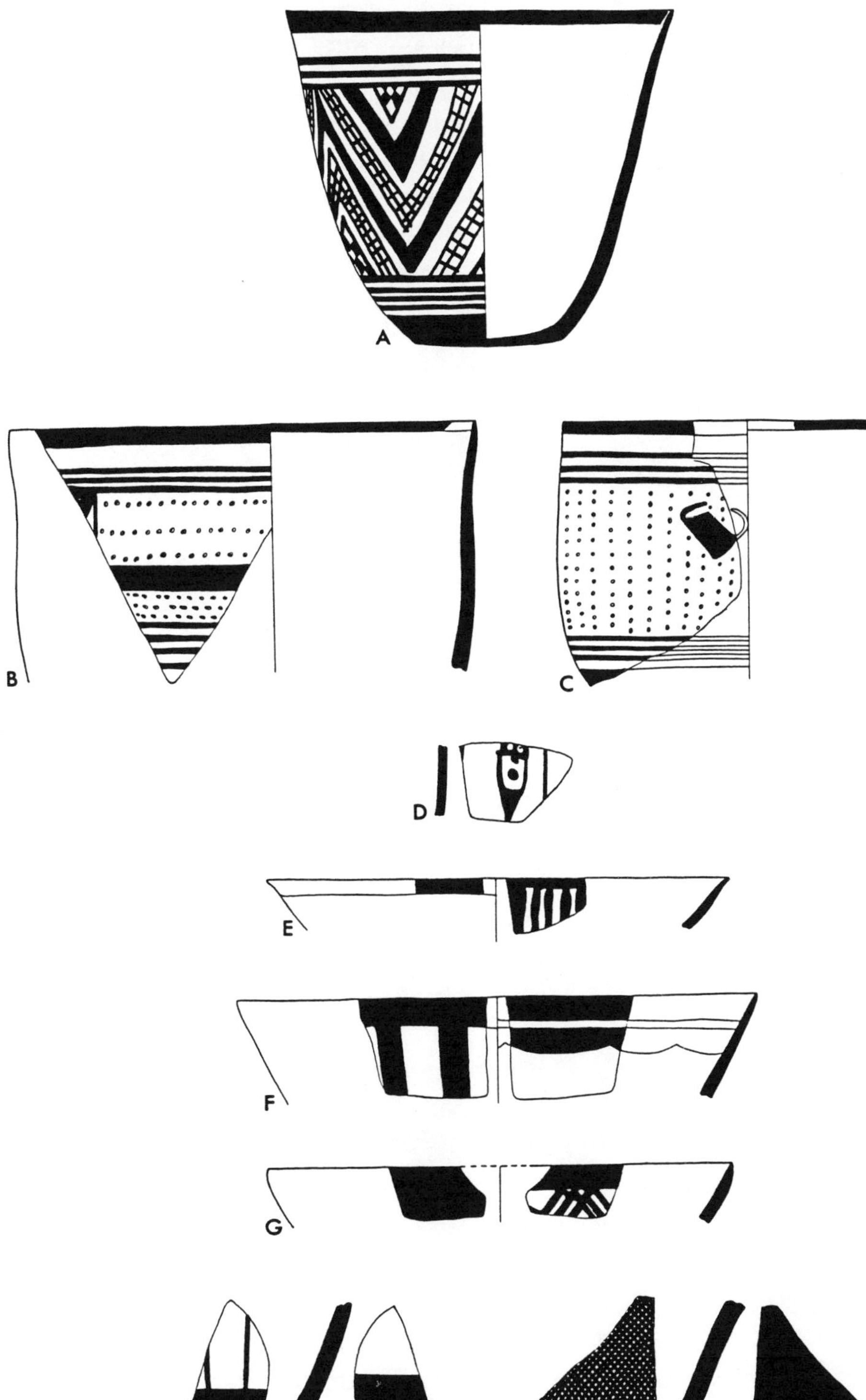
A
B
C
D
E
F
G
H
I

Figure 71	SITE G171		*Scale*: 2/5
	DESCRIPTION	REFERENCES	PERIOD
A	Buff, no visible inclusion, brown paint, burnished ext.	Qabr-e Sheikhein, Weiss 1975, Fig. 27:227; Chogha Mish MS, Delougaz & Kantor, nd.	MS 3
B	Buff, scattered grits inclusion, brown paint, burnished	Chogha Mish LS, Delougaz & Kantor, nd; Jawi, Le Breton 1947, Fig. 15:9,11.	LS
C	Buff, grits inclusion, brown paint.	Jawi II, L 10, Dollfus 1983, Fig. 33:17.	MS 3
D	Buff, no visible inclusion, greenish brown paint.	Chogha Mish LS, Delougaz & Kantor, nd; Jafarabad, Le Breton 1947, Fig. 15:10.	LS 2
E	Buff, grits inclusion, greenish buff.	Chogha Mish MS, Delougaz & Kantor, nd; Jawi I, L 15, Dollfus 1983, Fig. 17: 7-8.	MS 3
F	Buff, grits inclusion, brown paint.	Chogha Mish MS, Delougaz & Kantor, nd; Jawi, Le Breton 1947, Fig. 24:8.	MS 3
G	Buff, no visible inclusion, brown paint.		MS 3
H	Buff, scattered grits inclusion, brown paint.	Chogha Mish MS, Delougaz & Kantor, nd; Jawi I, L 15, Dollfus 1983, Fig. 17:7-8.	MS 3
I	Buff, scattered grits inclusion, maroon paint.		MS 3
J	Buff, grits inclusion, dark brown paint.		MS 3
K	Buff, scattered grits inclusion, dark, brown paint.	Chogha Mish MS, Delougaz & Kantor, nd.	MS 2
L	Buff, grits inclusion, dark brown paint.		MS 2
M	Buff, grits inclusion, dark brown paint.	Chogha Mish MS, Delougaz & Kantor, nd.	MS 2

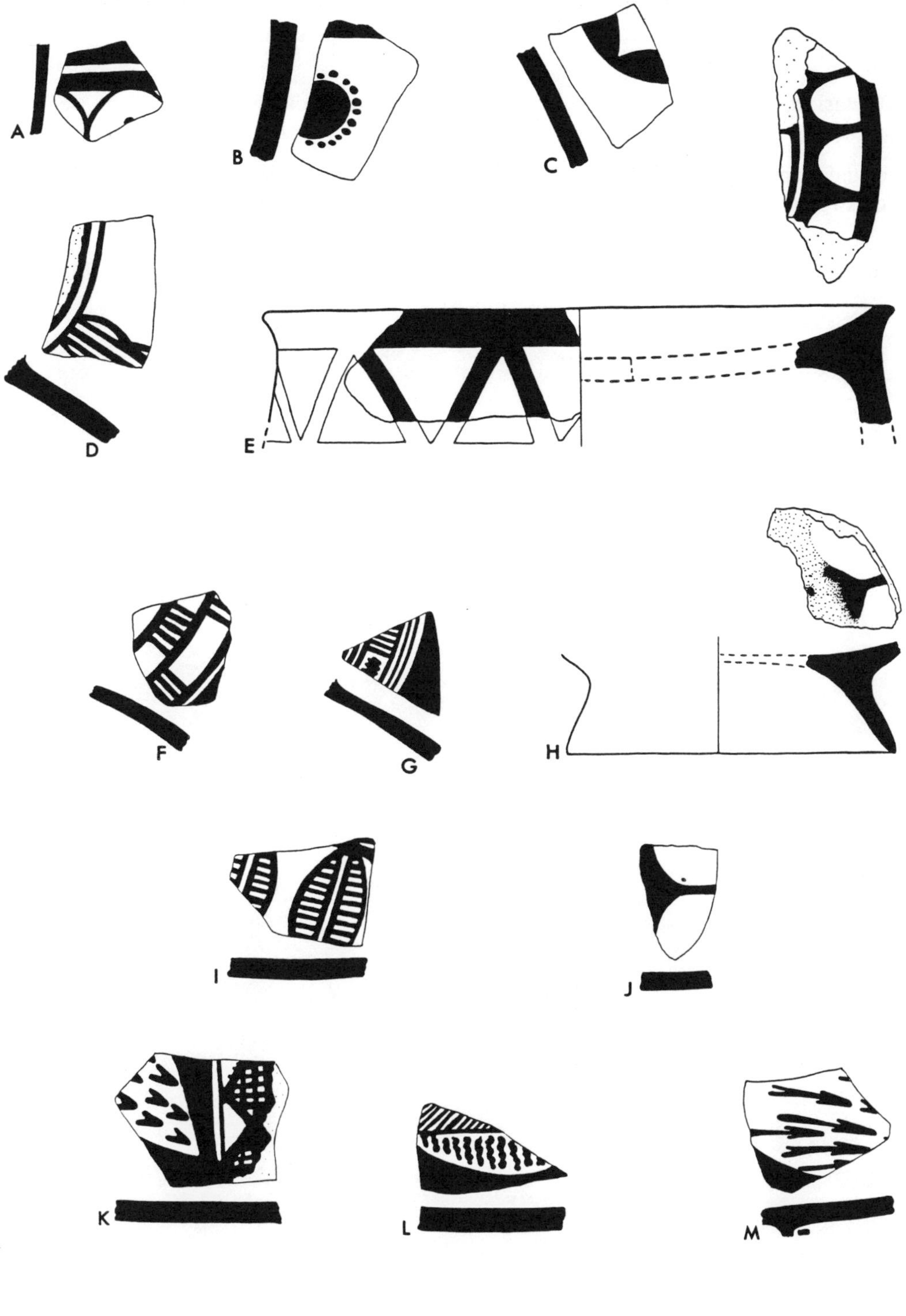
A
B
C
D
E
F
G
H
I
J
K
L
M

Figure 72	SITE G171		*Scale*: 2/5
	DESCRIPTION	REFERENCES	PERIOD
A	Buff, grits inclusion, dark brown paint.	Chogha Mish MS, Delougaz & Kantor, nd.	MS 3
B	Buff, grits inclusion, brown paint.		MS 3
C	Buff, scattered grits inclusion, brown paint.	Chogha Mish MS, Delougaz & Kantor, nd.	MS 3
D	Buff, grits inclusion, brown paint.	Chogha Mish MS, Delougaz & Kantor, nd.	MS 3
E	Buff, scattered dark and calcite grits inclusion, dark brown paint.	Jawi II, L 11, Dollfus 1983, Fig. 30:1; Chogha Mish MS, Delougaz & Kantor, nd.	MS 3
F	Buff, grits inclusion, brown paint.		MS 3

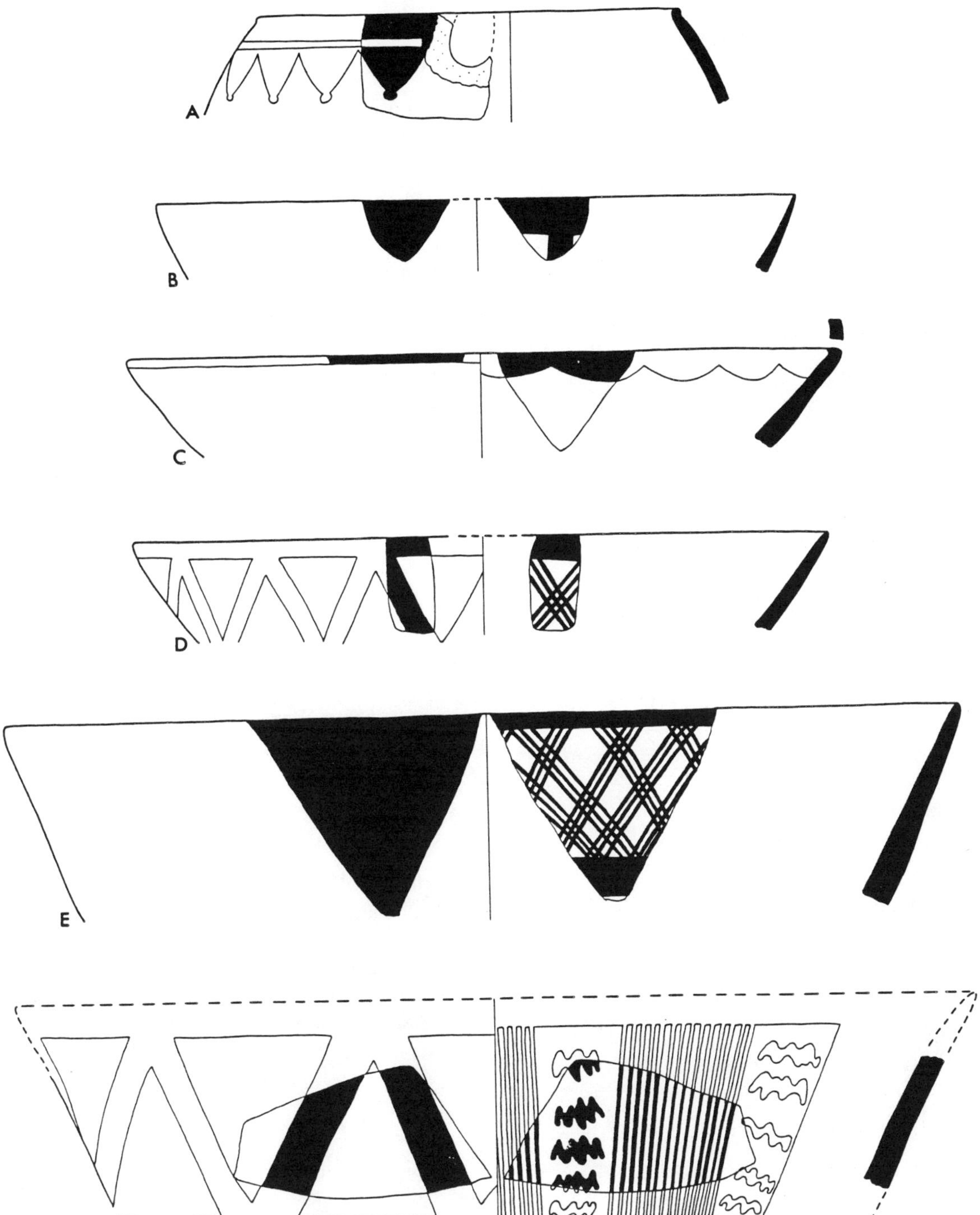
A
B
C
D
E
F

	DESCRIPTION	REFERENCES	PERIOD
A	Greenish buff, no visible inclusion, greenish paint.		LS 2
B	Buff, no visible inclusion, slipped, brown paint.	Susa, de Mecquenem 1943, Pl. 4:3-5.	LS 2
C	Buff, grey core, no visible inclusion, regular striations, dark brown paint.	Susa, de Morgan 1900, Pl. 17:15.	LS 2
D	Buff, no visible inclusion, slipped, brown paint.	Bakun A, Langsdorff & McCown 1942, Pl. 80:17.	LS 1?
E	Buff, no visible inclusion, greenish brown paint.	Chogha Mish LS, Delougaz & Kantor, nd.	LS 2
F	Greenish buff, occasional grits inclusion, slipped, thick, dark brown paint.	Chogha Mish, Delougaz & Kantor, nd.	MS 3-LS
G	Buff, no visible inclusion, slipped, brown paint.	Motif: Qabr-e Sheikhein, Weiss 1976, Fig. 20:111.	MS 3
H	Green buff, no visible inclusion, greenish brown paint, over-fired.		LS 2
I	Buff, no visible inclusion, shiny, brown paint.		LS
J	Buff, no visible inclusion, thick, brown paint.		LS
K	Buff, no visible inclusion, dark brown paint.	Chogha Mish LS, Delougaz & Kantor, nd.	LS 2
L	Buff, no visible inclusion, greenish brown paint.	Qabr-e Sheikhein, Weiss 1976, Fig. 20:111; Gap, Egami & Sono 1962, Fig. 20:12.	LS 1
M	Buff, no visible inclusion, slipped, brown paint.	Bandebal, Le Breton 1947, Fig. 38:15.	LS 1
N	Buff, no visible inclusion, brown paint.	Farrukhabad, Wright 1981 Fig. 17:d. Fars: Tall-e Saku, & Madavan, Stein 1936, Pls. 28: 27, 20:12. Kerman: Tall-e Eblis, Caldwell 1967, Fig. 10; Tappeh Yahya, Beale et al. 1986, Figs. 4.20:X, 4.21:C.	LS 1
O	Buff, no visible inclusion, cream slip, brown paint.		LS 1
P	Buff, grits inclusion, brown paint.		MS 3?
Q	Buff, no visible inclusion, thick dark brown paint.	Jafarabad, Le Breton 1947, Fig. 13:4.	MS 3
R	Buff, grits inclusion, dark brown paint.	Jawi II, L 11, Dollfus 1983, Fig. 30:1; Chogha Mish MS, Delougaz & Kantor, nd.	MS 3
S	Buff, scattered grits inclusion, brown paint.		MS 3

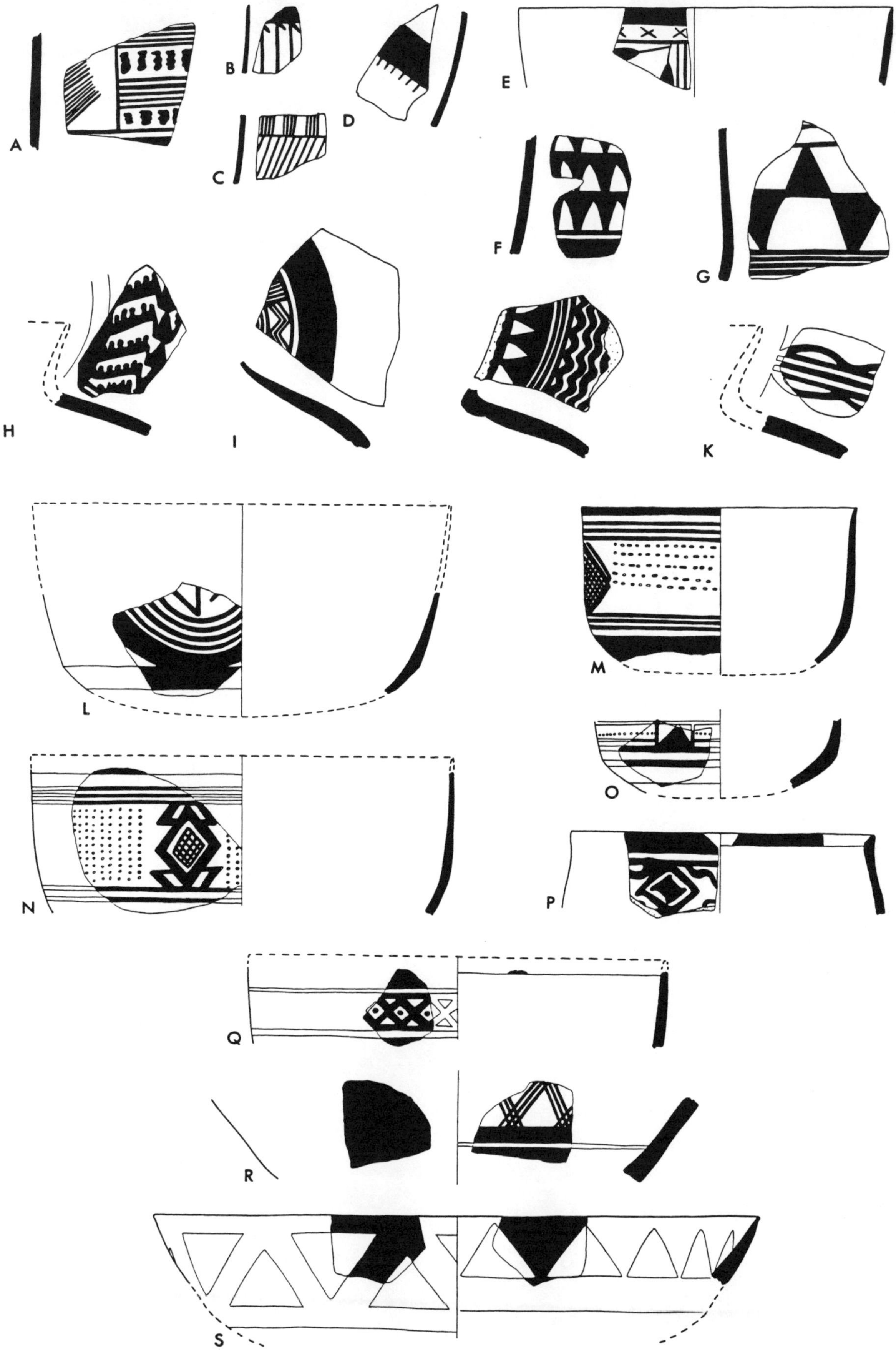
A
B
C
D
E
F
G
H
I
K
L
M
N
O
P
Q
R
S